Karl Mannheim's Sociology as Political Education

Karl Mannheim's Sociology as Political Education

Colin Loader
David Kettler

Transaction Publishers
New Brunswick (U.S.A.) and London (U.K.)

Copyright © 2002 by Transaction Publishers, New Brunswick, New Jersey.

All rights reserved under International and Pan-American Copyright Conventions. No part of this book may be reproduced or transmitted in any form or by any means, electronic or mechanical, including photocopy, recording, or any information storage and retrieval system, without prior permission in writing from the publisher. All inquiries should be addressed to Transaction Publishers, Rutgers—The State University, 35 Berrue Circle, Piscataway, New Jersey 08854-8042.

This book is printed on acid-free paper that meets the American National Standard for Permanence of Paper for Printed Library Materials.

Library of Congress Catalog Number: 2002017990
ISBN: 0-7658-0109-4
Printed in Canada.

Library of Congress Cataloging-in-Publication Data

Loader, Colin, 1941–
    Karl Mannheim's sociology as political education / Colin Loader, David Kettler.
       p. cm.
    Includes bibliographical references and index.
    ISBN 0-7658-0109-4 (alk. paper)
      1 Mannheim, Karl, 1893-1947—Views on sociology. 2. Sociology.
3.Sociology—Study and teaching. 4. Sociology—Political aspects.
5. Sociology—Germany. I. Kettler, David. II. Title.

HM447 .L633 2002
301—dc21

                                                                   2002017990

For
Claire W. Loader
Janet E. Kettler

Contents

Preface ix

1. The Educational Mission of Sociology 1
   Introduction 1
   Mannheim as Educator 3
   The Primacy of Cultivation (*Bildung*) 7
2. Cultivation 19
   Wilhelm von Humboldt: Cultivation 19
   Cultivation and Science 27
   Cultivation and the State 34
3. The Weimar Republic 47
   The Weimar Republic and Cultural Crisis 47
   Sociology and University Reform 50
4. The Legacy of Max Weber 71
   Political Education in the Applied Sociology of Albert Salomon 71
   Competition: Karl Mannheim and Leopold von Wiese 80
5. The Challenge of Fascist Social Thought 109
6. Marxism and Sociology 139
7. Karl Mannheim as Professor: *The Introduction to Sociology* 177

Bibliography 209

Index 225

Preface

This book originated in a conference, organized by Martin Endreß of the University of Konstanz and Ilja Srubar of the University of Erlangen, to discuss Karl Mannheim's first lecture course at the University of Frankfurt in 1930, a transcript of which had recently been discovered in the papers of Mannheim's one-time student and assistant, Hans Gerth. Convinced of the importance of the find by their respective studies of the text and by the rewarding discussions at Erlangen, the authors undertook to collaborate on an English translation of the materials. As they worked on a modest introduction to the translation, however, they were led to follow the leads opened up by their joint encounter with the text beyond the limits of an introduction. The translation has appeared as a companion volume.

The authors have written separately in the past on Karl Mannheim's sociological thought, Kettler as a partner in a long-standing collaboration with Volker Meja of Memorial University of Newfoundland and Nico Stehr of the University of British Columbia, and they derive from different disciplines and traditions of commentary. Karl Mannheim would have been pleased, we think, by this transmutation of past competition into a synthesis. Both authors worked on every part of the volume.

Thanks are due, first, to Martin Endreß and Ilja Srubar, as well as to Gabriela B. Christmann, who edited the original German version of the transcript and supplied it with helpful notes. Generous support with access to supplementary materials and expert advice was provided by Eberhard Demm and Reinhard Laube. Volker Meja was available for consultations throughout, and Joseph Quittner contributed astute editorial comments. The authors are grateful for logistical support to their home institutions, the University of Nevada at Las Vegas and the Bard Center of Bard College. Without Irving Louis Horowitz, such books could not appear.

1

The Educational Mission of Sociology

Introduction

When Karl Mannheim arrived in Frankfurt to assume his professorial duties, he faced circumstances not unlike those facing academics today. In 1930 Germany, as in present-day America, it was a commonplace to speak of higher education in crisis, and to assign political as well as cultural significance to the vexing issues at an impasse. The principal themes were similar too: universities under attack from conservatives who wanted to return to the classics in order to guarantee the proper moral education of students, as well as from innovators who wanted to see excluded segments of society represented in the curriculum; the fragmentation of the academic community, as professors followed specialized research agendas and students sought to advance their vocational objectives; the irresponsibility of academics' public utterances and their unwillingness to accept responsibility for civic education; and the lament that a unifying spirit was somehow missing in the nation, as culture splintered into a myriad of individual avant-garde experiments—a plaint countered by scorn for an establishment vested in its refusal to recognize diversity and change. If the historical crux in recent years has been the interpretation of the Sixties, the earlier dispute turned on the meaning of the German Revolution of 1918. And just as the rise and expansion of cultural studies departments are the locus of present-day conflict, the place of sociology provided the occasion for the most intense conflicts in Weimar. Most important, it is common to these angry debates about crisis in education that the contending parties inveigh not only against each other but also against the many practitioners of higher learning who restrictively define their scientific work as a value-free, autonomous activity remote from all talk of crisis and without regard to its supposed consequences for education in the wider cultural sense.

The conflict, in short, is between proponents of alternate visions for the future direction of the universities, complex institutions that are, in fact, going concerns. Although difficulties in funding and occasional disruptive conflicts are cited as symptoms, the declaration of crisis is as much program as diagnosis. The idea is to disturb complacency. Invariably, however, the talk turns to the politicization of the universities, with the competing diagnosticians of crisis charging one another with injecting destructive political considerations into the work of learning, while the operators of the routinized arrangements fend off both kinds of challenges as "political" interference in an autonomous cultural activity. Under these conditions, even if the immediate issue is something as narrow—and as self-evidently tied to public policy decisions—as "affirmative action" in 2000 or the creation of a Sociological Institute in 1930, no question is left to routine bureaucratic or professional processing. The point of a crisis diagnosis is totalization.

A striking instance of this parallelism is the change in the debates internal to institutionalized disciplines, where questions that the scientific mainstream dismisses as merely pedagogical suddenly appear more important than questions about scientific priorities. The teaching activities of the faculties, as the most direct link between the university and the larger society, come under demanding scrutiny, and claims about the inherent development of science no longer suffice to guide, defend, and legitimate academic practices. Both the German and the American academic traditions celebrated the priority of science as recently won constitutional principles that marked the emancipation of the university from tutelage by external authorities: it was the core of the concept of academic freedom. Yet both traditions also had alternative, latent conceptions of their teaching work available, philosophically related to each other, but politically distinct.[1] In the United States, there was the Emersonian notion of the college as the appropriate scene for the formation of republican individuals (Bledstein 1976: 259–268), and in Germany, the reassertion of the inner connections between university education and the social practice of cultivation (*Bildung*).[2] Stated differently, the idea of a crisis in the university, in

1930 as in 2000, called into question whether a university, oriented to the advancement of science alone, can sustain even those activities without reevaluating and reconstituting its relationship to its community and notably to its youth.[3]

Mannheim as Educator

In a piece of cultural journalism published in 1922 in a liberal newspaper, Karl Mannheim, newly arrived in Heidelberg and freshly disappointed in his hopes of habilitating in philosophy, illustrates a non-conservative argument against allowing conventional scientific considerations to monopolize decisions about university education. More precisely, he argues that a dramatic redirection of the educational function is itself indispensable to rejuvenating sciences that are in danger of sclerosis. The academic disciplines must teach in a way that lets them learn from the youth. Mannheim draws on the language of vitalistic philosophy to state his case, but his critique of imposed specialist schooling is not wholly dependent on that current.

He tells three stories to identify the critical problem, sketches of students who arrive in the university inspired by burning questions generated by their prior commitments to the movements of the times and who are stopped short by a disciplinary course of studies that requires them to forget their questions and to subordinate themselves to the present questions and methods of their respective sciences.

Mannheim reports that his first student comes from an activist political movement, the second, from a religious-mystical community, and the third, from a intimate involvement with art—that all three arrive at the university, in short, with profound experiences and insights. What they are required to do in the faculties of social science, philosophy, and art history, however, ignores or disparages what they bring. Mannheim finds this a cruel waste, but he is, nevertheless, not satisfied with a romantic gesture of solidarity with youth and its supposed vital rootedness in fellowships devoted to ultimate mysteries and missions. He is, in fact, ambivalent about such external, extra-scientific formations. The students' ideas, after all, may be nothing more than faded shadows of obsolete notions, he cautions, and they are, in any case, bound to be vague and unfocused. Besides, youth is destined to mature beyond the attitudes appropriate to these intense involvements. The universities are quite right to initiate the students in the sciences, he concludes, but they must also open the sciences to the urgencies of youth. Work in education should be a source of regeneration for scientific work (Mannheim [1922] 2001).

As the 1920s progressed, the generally hopeful tone of Mannheim's moderate proposal for tapping youthful cultural renewal for the benefit of university studies gave way to more bitter readings of the disparities between the perceived turmoil in culture and the concerns proper to the university, especially among those who saw Mannheim himself as a representative of the forces undermining the order of which the old university and its orderly inquiry had been an integral part. Mannheim's teaching in Frankfurt was deeply marked by these controversies. Heedless of the criticism of his sociology, he sought to exemplify both a diagnosis and a therapy for the crisis in higher education.

When Karl Mannheim became professor of sociology at the Johann-Wolfgang-Goethe University of Frankfurt in 1930, he was the newly famous author of a work which its many bitter critics as well as eager supporters treated as an epitome of the cultural-political controversy. *Ideology and Utopia,* indeed, belongs squarely within the politics of educational crisis. His pedagogical interests, moreover, figured in his public image, as well as in his controversial ideas.[4] Writing in the newspaper that had published Mannheim's article on youth and science eight years earlier, Siegfried Kracauer welcomed his appointment with the following words:

> A marked pedagogical gift especially qualifies Mannheim for the activity of academic teaching. As is known from Heidelberg, he takes a real interest in his students and is a dedicated discussion partner, who always enters passionately into the dialectic of direct exchanges of views. In him, the university gains an instructor who conveys his teachings through teaching. (*Frankfurter Zeitung*, 11 December 1930. Cit. in Hoeges 1994: 78)

In the Weimar context, *Ideology and Utopia* was unmistakably about political education.[5] Mannheim proposed sociology of knowledge as a method for opening practical life to the guidance of sociology. A primary step toward this end was the disclosure that the knowledge on which Mannheim's educated contemporaries relied lacked the authority and sanction they thought it possessed. This deficiency did not render it worthless, in his view, but it made its worth dependent on social circumstances which nonsociological knowledge—ideological knowledge—was incompetent to appraise.[6] Instruction in sociology of knowledge consequently serves as propadeutic to teaching sociology. The educational mission of sociology extends, according to Mannheim, to party schools and other sites[7] where a sociological apprenticeship mediated by sociology of knowledge can be established, while its primary locale remains the university course in sociology.

The intimate connections that interlink sociology of knowledge, sociological education, and the cultivation requisite for civic practice in Mannheim's work have been obscured by the standardized debates over Mannheim's book, especially after it was translated into English and incorporated into the canon of a sociology, notably American, driven, paradoxically, by the sort of teaching enterprise Mannheim sought to challenge; but the records of Mannheim's disrupted tenure as professor in Frankfurt make the importance of his educational project clear. Mannheim's published works during this brief period are few and appear scattered, ranging from a handbook article on sociology of knowledge through a carefully reasoned analysis of the striving for success, a central theme derived from Max Weber, to a lengthy prospectus for sociology as academic subject (Mannheim [1930b] 1952; [1931b] 1936; [1931c] 1953; 1932a; 1932b). Only the handbook article has received careful attention in the literature, since it counts as the prime text for sociology of knowledge taken as a technical academic subject. The others have been neglected. Mannheim's most ambitious project during these years produced a posthumously published volume, *The Sociology of Culture*, but the editorial emendations in the published version in English and the loss of the original German text, regrettably make it unreliable for present purposes precisely where it is most original.[8] The Dutch transcription of a lecture on intellectuals that Mannheim presented to students in Amsterdam in 1932 (Mannheim [1932] 1993; cp. Pels 1993), as well the archival lecture notes of Mannheim's historical sociology courses in 1931 and 1932, have already been used by some commentators to shed light on Mannheim's pedagogical and political aspirations at the time, but only the recent recovery of the notes for Mannheim's introductory sociology course during his inaugural year in Frankfurt makes possible a full appreciation of the extent to which Mannheim's contributions to sociology are channeled through his hope of contributing decisively to the debate about sociology as education.[9]

It is not too much to say that Mannheim's "Introduction to Sociology" course consists largely of a reflection on and justification for the very activity of teaching the course. This surprisingly self-reflexive text is the principal document in the companion volume (Mannheim [1930a] 2001). Supporting texts include three previously uncollected newspaper articles, one of them dating from Mannheim's first years in Germany; a key excerpt from Mannheim's book on the sociological curriculum, never republished or translated; the protocol of a joint seminar held by Mannheim and Alfred Weber; a retrospective exchange of letters between Mannheim and Eduard Heimann, an intimate during the Frankfurt years; as well as excerpts from several other letters and lecture notes. These texts form a primary source for the present study. An understanding of Mannheim's thought enriched by these documents should make it impossible in the future to treat his Frankfurt work simply as a foil for the so-called Frankfurt School (e.g., Jay 1970). Mannheim's creative participation in the Weimar equivalent of the present-day academic "culture wars" shows that neither *Ideology and Utopia* nor his other writings can be interestingly understood as representing nothing but the attempt to neutralize Marxism through a relativistic sociology of knowledge, as his neighbors at the Institute for Social Research maintained. Horkheimer and Adorno did not set the intellectual agenda in 1930, as they do not set it at present.

Mannheim's first teaching assignment, like his last, was in a school of education. In 1919, he taught philosophy of culture in the Institute of Pedagogy at the University of Budapest[10]; in 1942, he was made professor of educational sociology at the Institute of Education at the University of London. Although both appointments have their curious histories and neither one corresponded to his highest aspirations as a sociological theorist, they capture a vital dimension of his intellectual efforts. The contributions that Mannheim makes to sociology by his reflections on the teaching of the discipline bear directly on key issues in social education as well.

The activist and rhetorical components in Mannheim's sociology have been too exclusively assimilated to Marxist conceptions of consciousness raising, themselves traceable, in fact, to Hegelian extrapolations from the nineteenth-century debate about cultivation (*Bildung*). Mannheim certainly offers some textual grounds for such a reading. Yet the perspective on his thought opened by his Frankfurt teaching years allows a concretization of the concepts he abstracts from the Marxist political analyses of his time, specifically their return to the educational contexts in which they are most comfortably at home. The intellectuals Mannheim seeks to bring to consciousness will express themselves not by becoming politicians, let alone revolutionaries, but by becoming teachers in the broadest sense, cultivators of the social mind and instructors of the democratic mass.[11]

The Primacy of Cultivation (*Bildung*)

Seen in the perspective of German intellectual history, the pedagogical issues that Mannheim addressed during his Frankfurt period concerned a new phase in the older conflict between a traditional and elitist system of higher education, on the one side, and, on the other, the intellectual proponents of modernity who had variously called this system into question. What was new was the deep division within each of the historic contending sides. The established humanistic curriculum of the higher schools was now perceived by many anti-modernists as well as modernists as having ever less to do with the knowledge required for effective participation in intellectual or practical life. The advocates of the established institutions were divided between the genuine traditionalists, who upheld a curriculum centered on the old philology, with a canon of Greek, Roman, and German texts treated as "classics," and radical revisionists, who used a romanticized Nietzsche—and the myth of the trenches—as their icon. The modernizers were split, in turn, between those who wanted schooling to be guided by the newer state of the sciences and the newer requirements of the market for educated labor and those who wanted to adapt schooling to the requirements of fostering progressive social change.[12]

Distinctive too was a new urgency attaching to a contentious theme present throughout the more than one-hundred-year history of the characteristic German institutions of higher education. While the question of comprehending the flux of historical change without the loss of standards and ideals was an old one, the problem of "historicism," as it appeared in the early twentieth century, signaled the widely shared conviction—epitomized by the neo-Romantic mood—that the great philosophical systems of the nineteenth century could no longer be counted upon to guarantee order and meaning. In the name of philosophy of history, many historicists acknowledged the flux of history without abandoning the faith that history had meaning.

Karl Mannheim's first German publication in 1920 fit into this context. It was a review of Georg Lukács' *Theory of the Novel* ([1920] 1993) in which Mannheim commended above all Lukács' theory of history for providing norms and structures without denying a dynamism that moved both observer and observed. The periodical in which the review appeared, *Logos*, was founded in 1911 and uniquely brought together an interdisciplinary group of the most prominent writers on philosophy, culture, and society. Symptomatically, each of its bound volumes featured an embossed head of Heraclitus, whose concept of logos was thought somehow to reconcile chaos and unity without idealist transcendence (Kramme 1995: 134–135).[13] The questions were philosophical, of course, but Lukács' central chapter dealt with Goethe's paradigmatic *Bildungsroman, Wilhelm Meister*, decisive also for Hegel's *Phenomenology*, and the key question he found in Goethe emerged from the insufficient and irreconcilable idealist and romantic visions of the formation of spirit over time. Lukács had been Mannheim's most influential, if informal, teacher, and Mannheim's reflections on Lukács over the years were always also reflections on that education. Above all, the recurrent theme was how to live and learn in history.

The Weimar debate about the presumed crisis in education, like the wider debates of which it formed a part, was carried on under the threat of disorienting relativism and chaotic change, but also in the conviction that the outcome of the debate would itself make history. Historically, the rationale for the system of higher education, encompassing collegiate secondary schools for boys as well as the universities in their teaching functions, is traceable to the late eighteenth century. Like the religious designs that it displaced, at least in part, this popular-philosophic account contained strong organic assumptions, namely that the individual could orient himself to unified values because he was embedded in the soil of a national culture comprising a coherent totality that transcended political arrangements but made irresistible claims on political authority in exchange for the widest grants of legitimacy. The central concept of this powerful educational philosophy was cultivation *(Bildung)*. *Der große Brockhaus*, the standard German encyclopedia at the time of Mannheim's arrival in Frankfurt, defined cultivation in this historical sense as follows:

> The fundamental principle of the science of education, it signifies a forming of the soul through the resources of the culture enveloping it. Among other things, cultivation implies a) an *individuality* to be developed, as unique starting point, into a personality endowed with form or enriched with value; b) a measure of *universal-*

ity, a wealth of essential meanings, to be won through the understanding and experiencing of objective cultural goods; c) *totality* or wholeness, meaning inner resolution and firmness of character. (*Brockhaus*, II: 729; quoted in somewhat different form by Ringer 1969: 86)

This summary statement lays out the key concepts that carried the design, and it permits a preliminary overview of the inner difficulties confronting the historic case. Individuality, universality, and totality, in the required senses, were all highly problematic by the end of the nineteenth century.

Karl Mannheim's youthful lecture to the Budapest School for Humanistic Studies in 1917 (Mannheim [1918a] 1970) can well be taken on its own claim to serve as a representative statement for his generation. While he accepts the idea of the soul as the ultimate repository of infinite value, he has no faith at all in the articulation of this soul in an individuality capable of direct development into a personality constrained and empowered by aesthetic, ethical, and cognitive form. All articulations of the soul are caught up in a confusion of clashing, changing forms. The surrounding culture, thus, is rich beyond imagining, but its elaborations do not constitute a universality congruent with the soul. Adapting Georg Simmel's conception of the "tragedy of culture," Mannheim finds the past objectifications of the human spirit—as the self-articulation of the soul is called in this discourse—to be alien and, in effect, hostile to the soul. The wholeness and integration requisite for authentic cultivation, then, cannot be rationally anticipated or explained: it can only erupt in a revolutionary reversal of the current flow. Mannheim and the generational grouping for whom he speaks do not propound an alternative to cultivation through culture, it should be noted, but accept as their own the mission of making the key concepts good, despite their seeming dissolution by time.

During the summer semester of 1919, the last weeks of the Soviet regime in Hungary, Mannheim lectured on sociology of culture in the Institute of Pedagogy, a new subdivision of Budapest University mandated by Georg Lukács, his mentor, who was now commissar for culture in the Soviet regime. The notes for these lectures show clear continuities between the novice teacher, earnestly marking out the only choices he supposes to be open to humanists in a revolution, and the established professor a dozen years later, delineating the place of sociology in the crisis of Weimar. With epigrammatic intensity, the young Mannheim asks his students to consider three "forms of life" and he confesses his own choice. After weighing a life as saint or politician, he opts for the educator. In the peroration of the lecture, Mannheim distances himself from both the saint and the politician:

> The politician does not believe in God; he believes in history. The saint believes in God, but says that his kingdom is not of this world. The educator believes in neither God nor history, but in culture.
> The saint believes that only the direct way—the power of an exemplary life—can heal the world. Evil breaks out. The politician sees evil and suffers from it. Because he believes in history, he fights for humanity through institutions. The educator does not believe in these two ways, but he thinks that there is a means of fighting against mere institutions: cultivation, the inherently transformative effects of culture. He cannot disregard history; and he cannot simply follow the saint, because he does not believe in the power of the exemplary soul to accomplish total transformations....The educator is resigned. He cannot touch people with the immediacy of the saint because he knows that the gesture would be false. He knows that *art*, valuable as it may be, is not a cure, yet he hopes that the music of the soul somehow breaks through by its means. The susceptibility to art is the only thing given unto us all. And if the educator also knows and accepts that he cannot reach the infinite, he does as much as Charon: he guides across the dark water. (Mannheim [1919a] 1985: 230–231; Kettler/Meja 1995: 107–8)

In his Weimar work, Mannheim clearly abandons the attempt, documented in these lectures, to look to a new aesthetic, a concept he expressly traces to Schiller, as the way past the crisis of culture and cultivation, yet he never rescinds his commitment to play educator rather than politician or saint.

The decisive element in Mannheim's subsequent development of these themes was, of course, his conversion to the view that the inner, philosophical difficulties of the ideal of cultivation could not be understood or met without an adequate understanding, at the same time, of its external, social vicissitudes. For present purposes, we put aside Mannheim's own social interpretation of the crisis of individuality, universality, and totality, somewhat narrowly focused on functional logics imputed to class structures and dynamics, in favor of the more institutionalist general consensus of recent historical scholarship.

During most of the nineteenth century, on this view, the educational activities ordered, more or less, in accordance with the cultivational ideal stood in alliance with two other institutionalized practices—university science and the rationalized, non-democratic state. After the failure of 1848 and especially in the era of Bismarck, as the emancipated scientific establishment and the authoritarian state apparatus demanded ever more training for functional specialization, on the one hand, and ideological mobilization, on the other, this alliance required that inherent contradictions among the three be ignored. Along with the converging conservative and national-liberal main currents of which they formed a part, almost all of those concerned with cultivation continued to cling to the belief that the nation formed an organic totality, in the hope that such contradictions could be superseded. The difficulties epitomized by Mannheim's 1917 address were of course already widely discussed in cultural circles. Widespread academic support of Bismarck's anti-Catholic and anti-socialist campaigns, however, and, above all, the wild enthusiasm for the "Ideas of 1914," an epiphany of denial among the educated classes, show the strength of the factors upholding the alliance.

The sociopolitical conditions of the Weimar Republic represented the definitive fragmentation of that assumed totality—what has been referred to as the crisis of classical modernity (Peukert 1993). Notably, this "crisis" intensified questions about the relationship of science (*Wissenschaft*) to both the ideal of cultivation and to the new sociopolitical reality. Again, questions about this relationship were not new, but they did not appear to have reached the critical stage until the demise of the imperial state, which had maintained a "discursive coalition" (Wagner 1990) with the academy. Thus the university representatives as well as the organizational and intellectual spokesmen for the old unified ideal of cultivation were forced to face a set of contradictions which had always been there, but which they were able to ignore as long as there seemed to be some institutional basis for their organic assumptions.

War and revolution drew a firm line. The institutions of science had gained a novel legitimacy by virtue of their direct contributions to the power of the state and the wealth of society, notably during the war, but these gains were a function of a new level of technical specialization, self-enclosure, and opacity to both political and educational agencies. To counter the denigration of their classical cultural subject matter by neo-Romantic publicists and especially by the flamboyant leaders of the youth movement, the guardians of higher education sought validation by propounding aggressive conceptions of heroic vitality, no less remote from the technical demands of science than the orderly enactment of responsibility demanded by public and private officialdom, old and new. The argument is not that these conditions first arose in the Republic, but rather that they reached a level of crisis there.

Crucial to the crisis was the demise of what had been seen as the umbrella organization that provided unity for an otherwise divisive civil society—the nominally impartial, indeed universalistic state apparatus comprising the military, the legal estate, and the bureaucratically organized officialdom under the leadership of the sovereign head. In Weimar, this state was seen to have been replaced by a parliamentary government, which no longer stood above party, class, and interest divisions but rather incorporated them. More accurately, notwithstanding the euphemisms common to the discussions of the time, the state was seen to have been disrupted by the rise of hitherto excluded social actors, widely deemed to be antithetical in their very makeup to the key conceptions of the cultivation ideal—the organized working class, the women's movement, and the cosmopolitan economic actors epitomized in the image of the Eastern Jew. How could these newly influential actors in public life be identified with the "individuality" presupposed by cultivation, how oriented to the "universality" of the national culture, how credited with the soldierly virtues of allegiant, "totalistic" activism. The parliamentary government, however, was seen to treat these interlopers as important supporters and clients, even where they were not actually in command. To academic traditionalists, there now seemed to be no institution able to resist the fragmentation of the organic unity upon which individual values and orientation depended. With the advent of democratic rule, in short, the contradictions between the ideology of idealistic cultivation and the pragmatic-technical interests of both university science and the state apparatus suddenly ceased to be merely an undercurrent of uneasiness among those who spoke for higher education. The fatal threat to cultivation had a name, and it was mass democracy.

Writing in 1924, Max Scheler and his students, notably Paul Honigsheim, developed an analysis of the cultural situation that focused specifically on changes in institutions of culture. Scheler took note of the nineteenth-century expectation that democracy and scientific learning would be mutually reinforcing, but distinguished between the concomitants of individualistic democracy "from the top down" and the emotional mass democracy "from the bottom up." While rule by the liberal elite fostered cultivation for a while, at least in the sense of elementary education and the positive sciences, it could not prevent its own self-transformation into mass democracy, with the extension of the franchise even to women and youth, or the democratization of culture and education, with the consequent disparagement of the ever more specialized higher knowledge in favor of competing "vague metaphysics" that incline the new "ecstatic class and *Volk* movements" in "caesaristic, dictatorial and anti-parliamentary directions" (Scheler 1924: 134). Honigsheim analyzes the institutional articulation of these changes with special attention to the fate of cultural "institutes," notably the university. He finds that the universities during their great epoch, extending throughout the nineteenth century, were characterized by a comparative homogeneity of life patterns among both professors and students, founded upon the converging support provided by the state, the Protestant church, and liberalism, with early socialism serving in many respects as a continuator of liberal interests. Developments internal to each of these institutions undermined their concert and power. The state has been divided up among competing interest groups; the Protestant church has sunk with the unified state; liberalism has been reduced to the interest organizations of commerce and industry; and socialism is now mostly embodied in trade union officialdom. There is no coherent power upholding the university, and its fragmentation turns it into "an accidental assemblage of people who are inwardly foreign to one another." "They do not know each other," Honigsheim writes, "they do not feel that they belong together, they will not stand up for one another or for the whole at the decisive moment, and the effective force will be slight when it comes time to fend off assaults and when a changed public opinion calls their privilege into question" (Honigsheim in Scheler 1924: 432).[14]

While Honigsheim, as a young outsider, envisioned transformative cultural-political maneuvers that built on the new developments, a much more common type of response to this perceived crisis was to reject the political changes, to line up in opposition to the new governmental system in the name of cultivation. Towards the end of the Weimar decennium, this increasingly took the form of frank alignment with enemies of the constitution, but more common was adhesion to the political forces that purported to find grounds for a "dual legality" in the 1919 constitution itself. The legislation enacted by parliament and the regulations imposed by ministers must give way, on this view, to the higher legality of the unrevolutionized state, speaking through the president under his emergency and residual powers and through the courts.[15] Writing under the admittedly extreme circumstances of 1932, Eduard Spranger asserted that the present is always to be understood as an "emergency situation" because there is no natural law to comprehend it, because the valid law that appears applicable may be appealed to a higher authority, and because "there is no moral law that does not first require translation by living choice from its merely legislative form to a conviction infused with the soul (*beseelten Gesinnung*)" (1932: 200). Spranger recognizes that he is introducing a weighty and a highly relevant legal concept when he speaks of "emergency situation." As he was writing, the German parliament had been reduced for two years to the position of helpless endorser of state actions taken under presidential decrees issued under the constitutional provisions for "emergency situations." The emergency situation of 1930, he opined, had refuted the democratic experiment of 1919, and reinstated the orientation to the imperfectly realized but immortal state that the Weimar constitution had attempted to overlay, a state congruent with cultivation. Other commentators did not need the "emergency situation" to deny the validity of the constitutional new founding. Although the Hegelian philosophy had lost favor, its vision of the monarchical and bureaucratic state as the objective actualization of the spirit towards which all cultivation aspires continued to move the self-consciousness of the academic estate.

Yet questions about cultivation were not merely philosophical. Public educational policy and funding were essential features of life in the institutions of higher education. The parliamentary regime, its ministers, and officials could not be simply conjured into unreality, at least until they could be displaced by new authorities. Proponents of the old cultivation ideal had to rethink its elements in the face of practical governmental designs, backed by instruments of power that could have their effect, to a point, whatever the opinions in the academy about their legitimacy.

Public policy, moreover, directly set itself against the charge that the new political order meant the end of cultivation. Some republican officials, especially those based in the Prussian Cultural Ministry, sought to revitalize the traditional ideal in light of the new sociopolitical configuration. A central figure here was Carl H. Becker, who viewed sociology as the critical discipline in this new phase of cultivation. Sociology, he thought, could provide the common civil understanding that would enable individuals to recognize themselves through their dealings with others as peers and partners, without the discredited elitism and romanticism of the older conception. A sociological culture, moreover, would foster respect for diversity, as it encouraged individuals to take distance from themselves without fear of losing themselves. The individual subject of cultivation would reappear as a social being capable of being molded into a citizen; the universalistic assets of culture would be recognized as elements of social cooperation; and the activism integral to cultivation would reveal itself as civic virtue.[16] Becker's ideas, not to speak of his academic appointments and program innovations, attracted much criticism, from conservatives such as the historian Georg von Below, as well as from moderate traditionalists such as Eduard Spranger and Ernst Robert Curtius—and even from certain influential sociologists, such as Leopold von Wiese. What these critics had in common was their refusal to accept sociology as a discipline capable of providing a wider sociopolitical orientation for the individual and their insistence that the sociology envisioned by Becker was, rather, an agent for relativism and reductionism, inherently hostile to the cultivation of the human spirit and thus, in their view, also to the development of higher learning. In his writing and lecturing, especially after 1925, Mannheim, like Becker, attempted to revitalize the ideal of cultivation through the infusion of modern elements through sociology. Although Mannheim did not directly address Becker's writings, he clearly shared his views.[17] Each in his way, it should be noted, accepted the diagnosis of crisis, but they thought of it as a crisis of opportunity. The emerging orientation of the socially aware individual in a changing sociopolitical world is at the heart of what Mannheim called the "sociological attitude." This view of sociology can be seen in Mannheim's description, from the vantage point of exile, of the discipline during its Weimar period:

> German sociology is the product of one of the greatest social dissolutions and reorganizations, accompanied by the highest form of self-consciousness and of self-criticism....In this context, then, sociology is seen to be not only the product of this process of dissolution but also a rational attempt to assist in the reorganization of human society, to help in the reorganization and readaptation of the individual himself. (Mannheim [1934] 1953: 210)[18]

In short, Mannheim saw sociology as a crucial element in a new discursive coalition that would be able to orient people in modern industrial democracies. To understand this "mission" we must begin with an examination of the old discursive coalition that was dissolved in the aftermath of the lost Great War.

Notes

1. Max Weber tried to use the competitive advantage in character development provided by the American collegiate tradition to goad his university colleagues into reawakening to a conception of "academic freedom" (*Lehrfreiheit*) that he characterized in language derived from the corresponding German tradition of cultivation. Weber 1973: 593–4; Hennis 1994: 133–6. See below.
2. The jurist, Rudolf Smend, distinguishes between the "regulative norms of the school and the university," with cultivation (*Bildung*) on the one side, and the free development of the sciences on the other (Smend 1928: 60). His treatment, principally addressed to the interpretation of Article 142 of the Constitution (laying down the freedom of science and instruction), indicates the complexity of the issues in Germany. On the one hand, Smend attaches importance to the distinction, not least because he recognizes the legitimate state interest in cultivation in the schools and builds the case for academic freedom on the integral pre-conditions of university research and teaching. On the other hand, however, he understands the research and teaching guaranteed against state regulation not in terms of positivist models of scientific work but in terms of the idealist conception of the scientific vocation epitomized in the writings of Fichte, and this conception derives in turn from the earlier literature on cultivation and advocates aims of human self-elevation rather than knowledge as such. The idea of the university as a site of cultivation, accordingly, is fraught with ambiguity, especially with regard to the role of public authorities.
3. The similarities between the German and American situations must not be overstated. The differences between the social functions of universities in the two national settings can be epitomized in sharp contrast in the numbers of students enrolled in universities in Germany and the United States in 1930: 99,300 in twenty-two institutions as compared with 1,100,000 in 1,409 institutions (Ringer 1969: 52).
4. This becomes especially clear in the dispute between Mannheim and Ernst Robert Curtius. See below.
5. In the English version of 1936, Mannheim and his translators cut out the opening references to the impasse among political parties caused not only by their conflicting ideologies but also by their mutually crippling insights into the merely ideological character of political knowledge, although they retained the discussion of education for politics which culminates the chapter on politics as science. See Kettler/Meja 1995. For a contemporary's placement of Mannheim in the context of the discussion of "politics as science" and political education, see Salomon 1931: 108. See below.
6. Derrida's "deconstruction" reaches a surprisingly similar conclusion: ideas that have been deconstructed are not dissolved; they are reconstituted by being placed, so to speak, in quotation marks. The similarity is noted not in order to claim the label "post-modern" for Mannheim, but to call the utility of the label into question. There is no grand disruption in twentieth-century thought.
7. Mannheim retained his slightly surprising hopes for party schools as an imperfect but nevertheless positive resource for cultivation to realism throughout the crisis of the Weimar Republic. His reasoning rested on the ultimately benign effects of democratic competition. See Mannheim [1933] 1956: 199, 237. Mannheim's tolerance of the party system, as well as his moderate confidence in the outcome of ideological competition, distinguishes him fundamentally, despite his many mis-

givings, from writers on the left and right whose critiques of modern institutions and ways of thought he otherwise finds attractive. See below.
8. The volume, intended as a sociology of spirit (*Geist*) in the sense of the project Mannheim announced in his 1930 lectures ([1930a] 2001), contains three essays. The last of the three deals with the democratization of culture and is most clearly supported by other contemporary Mannheim texts. Its immediate relevance and its apparent composition in 1933 make it too important to overlook, despite uncertain rendering of key concepts and odd editorial excisions. The other two essays will be left aside, because they are less precisely dated and potentially more damaged by editorial intervention.
9. See Kettler/Meja 1995: 107–146; Loader 1976; Loader 1985. We shall draw freely on the findings of this earlier research. The present study differs from the earlier treatments, first, by virtue of the availability of Mannheim's 1930 lecture, and, second, by virtue of the recontextualization of Mannheim's educational mission in the longer-term contest about science and cultivation in Germany.
10. In a CV found in his personnel files in Heidelberg, Mannheim notes that he earned a teaching certificate on graduation from the university and that he actually began teaching in a secondary school before the revolution at the end of the war.
11. The contrast between Mannheim's educational emphasis and Marxism was not quite so clear in his experience. Mannheim's first academic appointment was made by George Lukács, during the summer of the Hungarian Soviet Republic, 1919. As deputy of culture, Lukács had converted most of the university into a pedagogical institute, to train teachers for service to the masses, and Mannheim was appointed to teach cultural philosophy. See below.
12. Spranger (1923) illustrates the perception of conflict. He classifies clashing reform designs according to the familiar trinity of liberty, equality and fraternity. The liberal motif encompasses all proposals centered on individuality, including quite traditional ones; equality covers the democratic designs of the moderate left; and fraternity is reserved for the communitarian visions best represented for Spranger by the culturally revolutionary religious themes of the youth movement (*Jugendbewegung*). Spranger looks for a loose synthesis of sorts, although he rejects the "mechanistic" democratic designs, on behalf of ultimate cultural values that he insists must inform the choice. On Spranger, see below.
13. Most of the volume was devoted to scholarly critiques of Oswald Spengler's *Decline of the West*. The problem for the commentators was to acknowledge Spengler's enormous success, while demonstrating what they considered to be his radical indifference to scientific accuracy. He was taken as a symptom of the need to bring order to a world understood as history. For Mannheim and for others of his generation, Ernst Troeltsch stood out as the most lucid and honest contender with the problem of historicism. Along with Max Weber and Max Scheler, Mannheim viewed him as the most representative thinker of the age when preparing his inaugural address after his habilitation in 1924.
14. Mannheim celebrates Scheler as one of the three major figures in German intellectual life, and he cites Honigsheim's contributions to the Scheler volume as an important authority in his "Competition" paper. Scheler's characteristic hope that the present crisis in thought will be succeeded by a new age of metaphysics occurs as a theme in Mannheim's earliest writings, although Mannheim soon distanced himself from Scheler's phenomenological leap of faith. See Frisby 1983. Honigsheim's designs are more political and very close indeed to one side of Mannheim's own way. Honigsheim puts his trust in an alliance between some of the newly prominent fellowships, with their own type of inner cultivation and

informal magic, and the organization of the working class, notwithstanding the restrictive rationalization of the latter. This is reminiscent of the sense in which Mannheim and others in the Tillich circle thought of themselves as belonging to the socialist "party" on their own terms. See below

15. The juxtaposition of the "emergency situation" and a thesis of "dual legitimacy," according to which parliamentary legality is superseded by the agencies of the legitimate state, derives from the generally influential writings of the jurist, Carl Schmitt. See below. Schmitt 1932; cp. Kirchheimer [1932] 1967; Kirchheimer [1933] 1976. Legal state theory enjoyed an unusual influence during the Weimar years, as cultural and social theory were confronted with a situation defined by struggle over a constitutional settlement. McCormick 1997; Caldwell 1997; Dyzenhaus 1997; Scheuerman 1997. The terms of legal theory, in turn, expanded beyond the technical issues that had been uppermost in the previous period. Two leading Social Democratic legal theorists, Gustav Radbruch and Hermann Heller, for example, also played prominent roles in the debates about cultural policy within the socialist movement, with Heller especially important in the socialist sequel to the youth movement and the popular education movements. Borinski 1984.

16. Becker, like Mannheim, was no less an opponent than Scheler of the phenomena comprehended under the heading "mass democracy," but he argued for a strategic cultural policy to counteract the effects Scheler and the others saw inherent in the democratized constitution. See below.

17. Becker was not only an intimate and political friend of Mannheim's great academic patron, Emil Lederer, but also a strong supporter of Mannheim's call to Frankfurt, against the opposition of many in the faculty (Kettler/Meja 1995: 144).

18. In a posthumously published article reportedly composed in 1933, Mannheim writes: "Scheler . . . expected [the] dominance of blind impulses to be the final stage of democratic development. It may, however, be something different—a stage in a painful learning process. . . . Educating the mass in reality-oriented ways of thinking, that is, a real democratization of the mind, is the paramount task at the stage of fully developed democracy" (Mannheim [1933] 1956: 199).

2

Cultivation

Wilhelm von Humboldt: Cultivation

The discursive coalition of state, science, and cultivation originated in the late eighteenth century, when German thinkers articulated its key ideas as a counter to the "mechanistic" ideas that they considered central to the Enlightenment.[1] Although the articulation of this world view, including the relationship of cultivation to historicism, varied from one thinker to another, ranging from Goethe's and Schiller's literary expressions of cultivation to the early historicism of Herder (Bruford 1975), we will focus on the ideas of Wilhelm von Humboldt, who is generally credited with raising these various notions of cultivation to the status of a coherent academic ideal (Weil 1967: 85) as well as being an important early formulator of German historicism (Iggers 1968: 57–61). The opposition to the ostensibly mechanistic design of Enlightenment natural law doctrines is a prime constitutive theme of conservative thought, as Karl Mannheim showed in his habilitation thesis ([1925b] 1986), but the seminal importance of Humboldt in the formulation of the cultivation model indicates that this academic ideal is by no means simply a conservative project.

Wilhelm von Humboldt is recognized as a founding genius of German liberalism. While his clearest statement of liberal political ideas, a book of his youth, was not published until years after his death and his lifetime work was politically more ambiguous, his identity as a canonical liberal was fixed when John Stuart Mill drew on *The Limits of State Action,* five years after its appearance for the epigraph of *On*

Liberty.² J. W. Burrow points out that Humboldt's liberalism is full of "tension and paradox," and that it has little in common with the model codified by C. B. Macpherson as "possessive individualism." While Humboldt recognizes that men are a danger to one another and that they need protection, as well, against imposed uniformities, Burrow argues, he "recognizes that men are necessary to each other, that they are constantly modifying each other by example, and enriching their sense of the possibility of living" (Humboldt 1969: xlii-xliii). The relations of interdependence and mutual enrichment are given a home in what amounts to an autonomous sphere of culture (Mannheim [1922–24] 1982: 37–46). For Humboldt, this sphere thrives when the state is limited to "civilizational" tasks, but the conceptions of culture and cultivation are not necessarily overturned when this liberal political thesis is opposed, first of all by conservatives, by a view of the "state as educator."³ The distinctive character of German liberalism, the feature that has been variously characterized by such mistrustful concepts as "positive freedom" (Berlin 1969) and "the German idea of freedom" (Krieger 1957), is best understood by reference to the unique valorization of the culture process. In political effect, this means that the lines between liberalism and conservatism have been fluid and the boundaries open. More important, perhaps, it has also meant that liberals after 1848 had ample justifications available for focusing their attention almost exclusively on the cultural sphere as such, that is, on the institutions of cultivation. The conflicts and compromises constituting the discursive coalition often involved territorial arrangements, with the liberals given greater voice in their specially valued spheres, the law as well as science and the universities.⁴ And the terms of the discourse were profoundly contested within the coalition and in the institutions where it held sway.

As minister of education, Humboldt was a leader in the reform of schools and universities, under the auspices of the Prussian state-building exercise in the Napoleonic Wars, under Hardenberg and Stein (Krieger 1957: 138–173). His ministry, like the others, used strong public authority to displace anti-liberal practices in many spheres, to impose and administer a regime consonant with substantive liberal principles. Although the appearance of a paradoxical and illiberal "revolution from above" is especially striking in the case of Prussia, the example of Poor Law Reform in Britain, let alone the revolutionary measures in France, shows that the use of state power to overcome "irrational" vested local interests was not unique to German liberalism. The central events of the educational reforms, which reverberated through the other German states as well, included the establishment of the humanistic *Gymnasium*, the founding of the University of Berlin as a new model, and the creation of a meritocratic link between schools and universities in the standardized *Abitur* examination. Before these innovations, secondary schools were staffed by patronage, and German universities, with a few exceptions such as Göttingen and Halle, were small stagnant corporations, often bitterly divided among competing privileged groups, dispiritedly purveying scholastic traditionalism without conviction, or offering narrow practical training for offices in church and state. The philosophical faculties were in an especially sorry state (McClelland 1980: 27–33). The new reforms of the "Humboldt Era" were based on the neo-humanist ideal of cultivation, to which was joined a more rigorous concept of disciplined study or science. Accomplished by Humboldt and other state functionaries, the reforms enhanced the authority of educational institutions and guaranteed them adequate funding, and they ended the universities' status as independent but closed, privileged corporations. Despite the reformers' wish to continue the tradition of academic freedom within the universities, they denied that this tradition had been more than a myth in the unreformed institutions that professed it, and they gave recognition to the state as a moral force without which those institutions would have remained in stagnation (McClelland 1980: 122, 141, 148–149). The role of state ministries in academic appointments was an especially striking manifestation of the tensions in this sphere.[5] The conjuncture, if not the full reconciliation, of the three elements of cultivation, science and the state exhibited by his public acts can also be seen in Humboldt's mature writings.

Central to this conjuncture in Humboldt's formulations was the notion of "individuality," that "everything human is individual" (Spranger 1960: 46). This individuality assumed different forms including the individual person, the nation, the state, and the epoch. Each form was seen as a "basic unity" (*Grundeinheit*) that was unique and not accessible to causal analyses identified with the Enlightenment (Troeltsch 1922: 38). This did not mean that they had no meaningful relationship to one another but rather that that relationship was organic. Humboldt believed that for individualities to interact with one another a Leibnizian harmony must exist among them (Spranger 1960:

45, 65). Each developed according to its own unique potential but in harmony with the others.[6] An underlying "idea," a formative shaping force, made possible this organic meaningful totality (Troeltsch 1922: 252–253).[7] Humboldt wrote,

> The idea can entrust itself only to a force that is spiritually individual, but the fact, first, that the seed which the idea implants in the force develops in its own way, and, second, that, no matter how circumstances and individuals may differ, it is on its own that the plant that issues from the seed reaches its bloom and maturity and then wilts and disappears,—these facts show that it is the independent nature of the idea that carries this course to completion in the realm of phenomena.... Every human individuality is an idea that has taken root in the phenomenal sphere, and this idea shines forth so brilliantly from some individualities that it seems merely to have assumed the form of an individual in order to reveal itself thereby.... It is no different with the individuality of nations.... Quite apart from the direction that nations and individuals impart to the species by their deeds, they leave behind themselves forms of spiritual individuality that are more enduring and effective than facts and events. (Humboldt 1956: 107–108; translation adapted from Humboldt 1967: 69)

Here one sees the same principles listed in the Weimar encyclopedia article on cultivation—the inner unity of individuals, the organic symmetry between the individual and other individualities, especially the nation, and the larger ethical meaning, represented by the idea, that was embodied in all of these units.

The vocabulary of the cultivation discourse, influenced by romanticism as well as by the conceptual subtleties of Humboldt's contemporary, Hegel, explicates Humboldt's basic thought with the help of an analytical distinction between two dimensions of subjectivity, soul and spirit. The ultimate individuality of the person was often represented as the soul (*Seele*). Although this term does not have a single unambiguous meaning (*Brockhaus*, XVII: 214–216), the thinkers we are concerned with saw the soul as the internal human life force that develops "on its own" rather than from external circumstances.[8] It is also assumed to possess a certain inner unity, or essence (*Wesen*), that precedes acts of feeling, thinking, and willing.[9] The interaction of this primordial personal unity with outside forces takes place in the realm of spirit (*Geist*), where it is conceptualized and from where it may also be externalized and objectified (*Brockhaus*, VII: 98–99). This potential for objectification (one can speak of subjective spirit) distinguishes spirit from soul by virtue of its quality as a communicative medium. Larger individualities are usually represented as being characterized by spirit, for example, national spirit or spirit of the times (*Volksgeist*,

Zeitgeist). When a thinker used soul in this connection (e.g., *Volksseele*), it was usually to de-emphasize individualism and rationality within the inarticulate, holistic, and unanalyzable larger individuality. This anti-individualist turn of the common conceptual vocabulary illustrates the contested character of the key terms, the continuing tensions between liberal and conservative approaches. In his earliest writings, Mannheim echoed the radical paradox formulated by Simmel and others, that the very articulation of the soul in spirit begins a process of estranging the soul from itself, that all culture is entangled in the tragedy of isolation from the soul which is its only living source (Mannheim [1918a] 1970). Such melodramatic contradictions were remote from Humboldt, and Mannheim himself soon abandoned the pose. When Mannheim, as well as other thinkers, later used the adjective form "spiritual-psychic" (*geistig-seelisch*), it was to emphasize the processive character of interactions between the innermost personal unity and the communicative dimension. Humboldt does not anticipate this post-Romantic refinement, but concentrates on puzzles posed by a world of individualities in harmony.

Humboldt believed that the organic connections among individualities could not be captured by the purely objective approach of the natural sciences, but rather required a special historical method.[10] He wrote,

> All comprehension of a thing presupposes in the person who comprehends it, as a precondition of the possibility of knowledge, an analogue corresponding to that which later will in fact be comprehended—an original, antecedent harmony between subject and object. Comprehension is not merely a development originating in the subject, nor is it merely a derivation from the object; it is, rather, both simultaneously. For comprehension always consists in the application of a generality already present to a novel particularity. (Humboldt 1956: 103; translation adapted from Humboldt 1967: 65)[11]

A similar correspondence applies in the relationship between the individual in his unique particularity and his individuality as an expression of the idea. For the individual to realize his inner potential, according to Humboldt, he must become attuned to the harmony, he must "strive for the ideal within his individuality" (Spranger 1960: 46). He must, in brief, comprehend himself. Such striving was at the heart of the ideal of cultivation. The emphasis on individuality was accordingly found to be fully consistent with devotion to classical models, the great "forms of spiritual individuality" achieved in certain times and places for all humanity. Cultivation, for Humboldt rested on two essential conditions: freedom to act for oneself and social intercourse, that is, the exchanges between one's individuality and that of others. Both conditions presupposed some larger organic unity that gave meaning to this interaction between the acting individual and his analogue at the level of ideas, as well as among individuals in communion. For Humboldt and his contemporaries, the larger unity could be defined in cultural or political terms—the individual as cultured person or citizen, the conjunction of individuals as culture or state. Humboldt emphasized the former, but acknowledged the latter as well.[12]

In the concrete reality of Humboldt's activities, the authoritarian but enlightened Prussian state clearly could not be dismissed, for it provided the agency through which moribund educational institutions could be replaced with the cultural environment necessary for individual cultivation to occur. But the state sought to regulate the life of the individual and could not, therefore, itself provide the freedom and harmony necessary for the individual to form himself organically in keeping with the ideal of cultivation, according to Humboldt. It had to be somehow diverted from too direct an impact on cultural activity (Spranger 1960: 55; Sorkin 1983: 58–60). The university was to have provided an alternative, as the immediate setting for culture. While the process of cultivation within the university should not be directly under the control of the state, cultivation nevertheless had an important political goal directly relevant to self-comprehension—to create "moral men and good citizens" (Sorkin 1983: 61–64). In addition, there was nothing in Humboldt's larger objectives to deny the importance of replacing the "by the book" training of officials and officers of the "Frederician 'machine state'" that had, after all, been defeated in 1806. The new forms of learning would also produce more flexible and therefore capable servants of the state (McClelland 1980: 125). Thus cultivation provided a political training based on the spiritual autonomy of the individual. In short, to shift from Humboldt's philosophical reflection to his programmatic design, the state was to initiate the process of university reform, to continue to support and underwrite that process, and to be the beneficiary of the end product, the good citizen and the capable official; but the direct experience, the relationship of teacher to student and student to student had to occur free of the state's sphere of control. In assessing Humboldt's design, it is important to avoid anachronism about the Prussian state. The Stein reforms, it must be recalled, originated in the immediate aftermath of

Prussia's defeat by Napoleon, when corporations seemed on firmer ground than public authorities and when designs for state reorganization in its external as in its internal relations took the form of complex admixtures of independence, coadjudication, and trusteeships.[13] What Humboldt attempted made better sense in the expanded organizational vocabulary of the time than in the more rationalized language of later, more clearly hierarchical, state formations. His formula for university autonomy was nevertheless full of problems, especially as the state became more uniformly rationalized, and the lines of demarcation were not as easily maintained as Humboldt hoped.

The relationship between the reformed university's newly emancipated sciences and the ideal of cultivation was no less problematic in practice. Humboldt formulated the ideal as follows:

> The concept of the higher scientific institutions as the pinnacle where everything that is done directly for the moral cultivation of the nation coalesces, is grounded on these institutions being intended to work on science in the deepest and widest sense and to supply matter that is not intentionally but intrinsically prepared for the use of spiritual and ethical cultivation. The essence of these institutions, thus, consists inwardly in linking objective science with subjective cultivation and, viewed from the outside, linking school instruction after its completion with the beginnings of self-directed study—or, rather, to effect the transition from the one to the other. (Humboldt 1956: 82)

For Humboldt, the university was a place where individual knowledge was realized in organic connection (*Zusammenhang*) with the totality of knowledge. He wrote, "It is necessary, in essence, that between leaving school and entering into life the young man dedicate a number of years exclusively to scientific reflection at a place that unites many within itself, both teachers and learners" (quoted in Spranger 1960: 143). The university, as the most comprehensive scientific institution, was the only one that could ultimately serve cultivation, comprehending and unifying the work of science. Accordingly, Humboldt distrusted the narrow, specialized training for utilitarian career skills prevalent in educational institutions before the reform period (Spranger 1960: 142–143, 145).

With science (*Wissenschaft*) recognized as also a means to the highest ends of cultivation, the academic freedom of the university was to substitute an internal motivation to study, that of curiosity and interest in the subject, for the external one of furthering one's career. Accordingly the subjective value of science, the degree to which it developed these inner qualities, was no less important than its objective value, its contribution to increasing the store of knowledge. The university teacher was not simply someone who trained and disciplined the student in a particular body of information. Instead, he also served the student as a model of someone who used learning to develop his inner potential (McClelland 1980: 118, 124, 135).

Thus when Wilhelm von Humboldt spoke of the university as a place where both

> teachers and students could "devote themselves to science" (*der Wissenschaft leben*), he meant something radically different from the later positivist or empirical construction of those words. *Wissenschaft* and further discoveries emanating from it were the instrument, not the goal, of the scholar. The full development of the personality and of a supple, wide-ranging habit of clear, original thinking was the goal. . . . Expert training was not to be abolished; but it was to be underpinned by a sounder foundation of general, theoretical education and habits of independent thought aroused and shaped by *Wissenschaft* in the universities. In no sense was *Wissenschaft* regarded as an alienated product of human endeavor. (McClelland 1980: 125)

It will not do, however, to ignore a certain ambivalence in Humboldt arising out of the historical association of cultivation with the schools and science with the university and the independent mature life of the mind. The conventional meaning of *Bildung* associates it closely with pedagogy, and the extended sense begins as a metaphor, albeit an ancient one. Because Humboldt was a reformer of the academic preparatory school as well as of the university, he was not prepared to discard the special relationship between cultivation and schooling. That is why he projects an immanent harmony rather than identity or hierarchy between the school and the university, between the work of cultivation and science. Science need not be sacrificed to cultivation, in Humboldt's view, but they are not one. As the sciences become more specialized and methodologically self-conscious over the course of the nineteenth century—and as it becomes rarer to return the head of a secondary school like Hegel to a professorial position—the tension increases and the application of the metaphorical sense of cultivation to the sciences is equated with dilettantism.[14] The question of the cultivational mission of the university becomes more difficult after Humboldt, but the discourse he founds long contains the difficulties and frames the relationship between the social forms of academic science and what Mannheim called, to some extent retrospectively, the "cultivated culture" and its distinctive "cultivated stratum" of intellectuals (Mannheim [1922–24] 1982: 265–271).[15]

Cultivation and Science

In a surprising work of his old age, Kant mapped the design of the German university at the end of the eighteenth century and claimed a distinctive place for the philosophical faculty, institutionally defined as lower than the faculties empowered to certify their graduates for public functions, theology, law, and medicine (Kant 1992). The "higher" faculties, he contends, quite properly act under governmental directives to expound and inculcate the teachings mandated by public authority, and the functionaries they produce are in turn required to adhere to these norms. The philosophical faculty, on the other hand, comprehending all of the sciences other than the three public specializations, is dedicated to the rational pursuit of truth. It has no other public function. The selection and professional conduct of the professors in the higher faculties are properly under direct state regulation, as are the criteria for the certification of their graduates, while the lower faculty is essentially self-perpetuating and self-governing. Duty-bound to respect the public order, including the work of the upper faculties in implementing the designs of the authorities, the philosophical faculty properly speaks only to its students and to others in the community of the learned. When it speaks within these academic walls, however, it must submit all doctrine, including the doctrine taught by the higher faculties, to ruthless critical inquiry. That is at the heart of the legitimate quarrel of the faculties. The higher faculties do not owe these critical colleagues any answers, since they act by authority, and authority, according to Kant, makes itself ridiculous by playing the philosopher. The authorities determine at discretion how they can best benefit from the findings of the philosophers, but they cannot be threatened by them, and they interfere with academic freedom at the risk of losing a vital resource for improving their rule and strengthening their power.

Humboldt and the other university reformers in the next generation raised the prestige of the philosophy faculty (McClelland 1980: 132–133), as Kant wished, and they adhered, in principle, to the academic freedom he upheld, but they did not accept Kant's idiosyncratic characterization of the higher faculties or, as has been shown, his ascetic conception of the philosophical faculty's duty to search for truth.[16] Kant's Enlightenment zeal for "*sapere aude*" is mitigated by the humanist interest in the self-comprehension and self-perfection supposed to come with the activities of learning, and the contributions that the sciences make to such cultivation are prized beyond the truths they may uncover. This is a public function, but not a political one, in keeping with the new emphasis on the cultural sphere.

There is no challenge by the reformers to the individuality of various scientific disciplines—even if they would be reluctant to speak approvingly, with Kant, of the "factory-like" division of labor in scholarship—but the effect of studying these disciplines is presumed to be unified in the enhancement of the shared culture, a Humanist rhetorical effect thought to be inherent in the methodical study of scientific subjects. With the rejection of "mechanism" comes a rejection of the Newtonian methodological monism professed by D'Alembert in the *Encyclopedie,* and a rejection as well of the Baconian separation between methodical and rhetorical studies implicitly revived by the eighteenth-century Scottish moral philosophers in vogue in many German universities. In this sense, the sciences—and the university that brings them together— are thought to manifest a unity in their diversity. The university serves culture, and culture expresses human excellence.[17]

However, the unity of the university philosophical science disciplines as a common contributor to cultivation became ever more problematical as the nineteenth century progressed. Somewhat schematically, we note three currents whose sequential and overlapping effects did much to shape the state of the problem when the discursive coalition lost its prime institutional supports after the Revolution of 1918: Romanticism, Positivism, and Historicism. Our emphasis is not on the philosophical doctrines variously identified with these world views, but with their specific consequences for the place of cultivation in the universities, as manifested in the practices of actors typically identified with one or the other.[18] All three tendencies called into question the harmonious correspondences envisioned by Humboldt, although the conflicts, in principle, did not preclude continued coalitions among scientists and educators or the persistence of an integrative public ideology embedded in the practices and symbolisms of the institutions. Idealism sustained university legitimacy long after other world views displaced it in the self-interpretation of the scholarly disciplines. The extra work to be done by the ideological discourse of coalition in the face of these intramural tensions, however, affected its tone and symbolisms ever more in the course of the nineteenth century, as with the increased voice given to nationalist versions of the cultivation rationales.[19] Yet on the whole crises were contained and local until the crisis of the Weimar years.

Romanticism as a world view is at home in literary and friendship circles rather than universities, and it assigns its kind of cultivation to participation in such groups, the practice of the arts, and the active engagement with their productions. Romanticism in the universities is indifferent to the comity of the disciplines and recruits candidates for extramural involvement, when it does not colonize whole departments or convert classrooms into Romantic circles. Romanticism, in short, vitally affects the conception of cultivation, tending to divorce it from the university, but it does not systematically influence the work of academic disciplines.[20] Positivism, on the other hand, at least in the loose sense of that term appropriate to its use in German discussions, where there is no measurable connection with the movement originated by Comte, pertains directly to the spirit of scientific work. It separates the specialized work of methodical sciences from questions about broader justifications, not to speak of the cultivating mission of university studies, and it encourages each science to specialize in subject matter and method. Kant's conception of the philosophical sciences as oriented exclusively to truth is honored, but the concept of truth is objectified and methodized, so that the relationship to philosophical rationales like those developed by Kant, with their cosmopolitan implications, becomes moot. Positivism may be characterized as a tendency towards self-referentiality in the sciences.

Diametrically opposed in principles and styles of conduct, Romanticism and Positivism may operate in peaceful complementarity as long as the institutional framework remains intact by virtue of extra-institutional supports and of an ideological fabric wide enough to rationalize their respective spheres of operations. To the extent that this covering ideology of cultivation turned on coordination between the universities and the humanistic classicism of the school curriculum, however, as with Humboldt and the loose idealism of his successors, Romanticism and Positivism had a corrosive effect. Nietzsche's assault on idealist philology, culture, and cultivation, for example, clearly drew ideas and energies from both Romanticism and Positivism before assailing both. He stood in a similar ambiguous relationship to a tendency he was among the first to classify, the historicization of concepts in all modes of knowledge, so that the most general categories of causal explanation in physics are no less perceived as artifacts of a certain time and place than the Kantian norms of the moral world within. Historicism had its own educational mission, in the broad sense, but it relativized both the standards and the methods of the older cultivation, and it was more effectively subversive than either Romanticism or Positivism because it arose within the discipline whose estimation in the cultivation design, especially in the schools, was no lower than philosophy and philology. In historicism, history the teacher of prudence became history the ironic spectator. Nietzsche's epochal heightening of all three tendencies and his heroic claim to have a teacher and a teaching to overturn them all epitomizes the incipient crisis of the discursive coalition, although its extraordinary resiliency is signaled by the extent to which the reception of Nietzsche paradoxically becomes the hallmark of many attempts to renew the tradition.[21]

The deals that constitute coalitions, however, are more tolerant of inconsistencies than of paradoxes. The more characteristic effort to order the work of universities in the postwar period involved a classification of the sciences that implied a distancing from the older aspirations and claims. This can be illustrated by an examination of the entry on "knowledge" in the above-mentioned Weimar-era encyclopedia. The weak academic consensus stated here in popular form is the product of academic philosophers, many of whom continue to honor the aspirations of idealism on symbolic occasions, but concentrate in their professional work on specialized technical issues. The discourse of cultivation is marginalized and largely relegated to the purveyors of world views. In their studies, moreover, the philosophers not only render speculations on non-cognitive consequences of science otiose but also relativize the status of philosophers in the sciences. The ancient hierarchical claim of philosophy, essential to the cultivation rationale, is abandoned. Science, the encyclopedia notes ecumenically, is any "organized body of knowledge, systematically constructed and self-consistent." The sciences are then classified according to three overlapping sets of criteria: (a) the types of problems addressed, whether philosophical, specialized, or applied; (b) the class of objects studied, whether noumenal or phenomenal, ideal or real; and (c) the methodology peculiar to the science, whether explanatory or descriptive, exact or inexact (*Brockhaus*, XX: 400–401). While the first level of classification might be thought to reflect the older hierarchical distinctions, the interplay with the second and third dimensions reduces philosophy to the status of a specialized science, with no normative authority over the others.

Behind the bland encyclopedia scheme lies a dualism widely conceded among academic philosophers, with a correlation between the main distinctions in objects and methods. Wilhelm Dilthey, who emphasized the objects studied in distinguishing between the human sciences and the natural sciences, and Heinrich Rickert, who distinguished between the cultural sciences and the natural sciences according to their methodology, appealed to the same basic dichotomy. As one among the cultural and ideographic sciences, philosophy claimed no authority over the designs and objectives of the physical sciences, and it had no special say either when new specialist disciplines like psychology and sociology appropriated its subject matter and transmuted its questions. These disciplines threatened to multiply without control as new fields of inquiry opened up or established fields were subdivided. While the individual sciences flourished, so did the diagnoses of critical disorientation. If the discovery of truths to challenge the doctrines established by authority justified the coordinate sciences of Kant's philosophical faculty, and if the great, latent work of individual cultivation conjoined the separate scientific enterprises of Humboldt's university, there was no comparable higher purpose credibly claimed for the universities of the time.[22] The instrumental achievement of some classes of science, notably the physical sciences and the applied sciences in general, further undermined the legitimacy of the enterprise in the eyes of those loyal to the cultivation ideal.

As that suggests, the crisis had a strong methodological component, with exclusivist claims made on behalf of the methods of the physical sciences serving as a special provocation.[23] Even though the human sciences successfully resisted the epistemological challenge of positivism—and its advocacy of the nomothetic methodology of the natural sciences in order to "scientize" these disciplines—they were unable (and in many cases unwilling) to resist a major consequence of this methodology when it was institutionalized, a conception of scientific work as an unending accumulation of specialized knowledge. The practitioners of the sciences classified according to the encyclopedic formula increasingly spent their lives in the closed circle of their specialize institutes and immediate colleagues. In 1912, Eduard Spranger wrote:

> In short, this positivism amounts to specialism. And the enterprise of the university has in consequence been splintered into a profusion of specialized sciences, and the very thing that the constitution of the university is supposed to prevent, the rise of specialized schools, has in many cases already actually begun. (Quoted in Hammerstein 1995: 56)

The ever greater emphasis on a scholarship of accumulated facts and empirical research weakened the traditional role of philosophy and the other human sciences—providing meaningful orientation for the larger public as well as for the constitutionalized university. The frame for Humboldt's *e pluribus unum* was in dissolution. Without any interest in offering a philosophical rationale, the disciplines severed their ties from metaphysical presuppositions and normative claims. The priority of specialist scientific practice over meta-scientific reflection in the trend towards specialization is well illustrated by the early case of Leopold von Ranke, the most important German historian of the nineteenth century. Commentators treat his histories as a continuation of Hegel's speculative philosophy of history and the state and place him, accordingly, firmly within the German Idealist tradition in the philosophy of history, and far from positivism. With a different emphasis, Georg Iggers (1968) identifies him as a continuator of Humboldt's individualistic historicism (cp. Meinecke 1936). Such readings, however, result from emphasizing presuppositions and implications that Ranke himself addressed only in passing. A structure of knowledge is better characterized by the terms of reference it sets for itself, including its decisions about questions not to pursue, than it is by the elaboration of answers to such imputed questions (Cumming 1969). The common law, for example, works because it hives off questions about justice or moral psychology. Explication of its premises, as projected from the standpoint of jurisprudence, often reveals an incoherence that makes its intellectual power quite incomprehensible. The relationship between Ranke's work and philosophical commentary is similar. Ranke pioneered the seminar as a form of instruction and the use of archival sources, and this practice gave the discipline an empirical rigor it had earlier lacked.[24] To write a dissertation or habilitation for Ranke was to conduct a rigorous specialist study.

Ranke's empirical approach became typical of history and the other human sciences in the latter half of the century. The generation after 1840, in effect, rejected the Idealist systems of Humboldt's generation in favor of empirical research, but without necessarily arguing against their premises (Russell 1899: 101–102). With the merging of minimally reflected Positivism and Historicism in the practice of the human sciences, detailed historical studies laced with exhaustive footnotes replaced the earlier speculative ventures. Across the human sciences rational (i.e., empirical) history replaced the historical reason of the earlier generation (Scholtz 1991: 46). Such sciences were clearly less able to provide the kind of synthesis of meanings that many felt they should be offering to society at large (Scholtz 1991: 51, 54). That orientation, it appeared, could only be supplied by a philosophical approach that enjoyed genuine authority.

As long as the discursive coalition held up, as we have noted, these developments were more or less absorbed, but the ambiguity eventually came to crisis (Scholtz 1991: 10). The great reputation of German professors in the nineteenth century came from two different developmental lines: the "scientization" of disciplines leading to specialization and empirical methods, and academics' role in the cultivated bourgeoisie (*Bildungsbürgertum*) as the spokesmen for the cultural community. The second line of development gave them a certain amount of prestige among the cultivated bourgeoisie in Germany but not within the international scientific community. International reputations were made in the realm of rigorous science, not cultivation (Bruch 1988: 105–106). This discrepancy between science and cultivation affected the humanistic ideal of cultivation. An object-oriented science, intent on increasing the store of knowledge through collecting and ordering new data, was incompatible with the subject-oriented philosophy of cultivation intent on developing the individual personality to its full potential. As disciplines became more fragmented through specialization, as the absence of any larger whole impressed itself upon those who placed primacy on cultivation, as the historical sciences threatened to descend into pluralism and relativism, there appeared to be no organic ground on which the individual personality could develop.

This academic fragmentation paralleled a similar process in society at large as the growth of modern industry, and with it the rise of socialism, engendered the perception of increasingly irreconcilable social divisions. The harking back to a supposedly unified perspective was how many in the cultivated bourgeoisie depicted their fashionable feeling of "crisis."[25] The declining efficacy of the thin and implicit idealist consensus now appeared to require the installation of a world view (*Weltanschauung*), a term paradoxically derived from Dilthey's historical studies of cultural diversity and change and so likely to suggest relativism rather than consensus. The journalistic voices of the cultivated public nevertheless contended that because of the differentiation of relatively autonomous cultural spheres, social development was without direction (Bruch/Graf/Hübinger 1989: 18, 20). While some believed that the resolution of this crisis could be accomplished by cultural means, others believed that the larger organic unity presupposed by the tradition of cultivation could be restored only through political ideas and the agency of the state.

Cultivation and the State

The promotion of state authority had never been wholly absent from the cultivation ideal. There was a measure of ambiguity in Humboldt himself, as we have noted, and the widespread reception of an idealist blend derived from Fichte and Hegel in the second half of the nineteenth century, notably with the emergence of Bismarck, fostered the prominence of statist prophets on academic pulpits, of whom the greatest was the Prussian historian, Treitschke. At the turn of the century, the representative type of professorial politics shifted in the direction of social idealism (and social pacification) in the face of the "social question," but the "glorification of the state," as Max Weber notes, was never more ardent than in the pronouncements of Gustav Schmoller and his allies.[26] Two structural factors underpinned this intimate connection between state and university. First, there was the exclusive reliance of the university system on an ever more purposive and authoritarian state bureaucracy, with ever less understanding for the autonomy that ostensibly kept university professors from being subject to the same discipline as other public employees. And, second, there was the elitism of the universities, their recruitment from elites and service to them, a dimension that had ever more conservative implications, as the older elitist liberalism was crowded by egalitarian trends both socialist and democratic. Karl Mannheim ([1929b] 1936) classified the resultant variant of conservatism, which does not appear in his habilitation thesis ([1925b] 1986), as bureaucratic conservatism, the ideology of the state bureaucrat and jurist. The trajectory of this aspect of professorial thought, at least in the perception of its "public," from consensual idealism to inspirational world view to an ideology among others, tracks the growing crisis of the discursive coalition.

The era of Bismarck saw the eruptive rise of Positivism and Historicism in the universities, and with them, the decline of distinctively academic idealism and the rise of specialization, as we have indicated. The enthusiastic atmosphere of collaboration in a great state-building project, however, further heated by noted academic prophets, obscured the rising incoherence in the educational effort, at least among the professorate and its immediate public in the state apparatus and higher social strata. Student disillusion and dissidence grew towards the end of the century, as did the prominence of the extramural prophets of the Romantic revival, but the effective leadership was ever more in the hands of state officials outside the universities, especially in Prussia. From a trusteeship of institutions that had to be autonomous to be valid, which is how Humboldt and his successors saw the state's responsibility, state agencies in the Bismarck era thought of themselves as designing and implementing a public higher education and research policy, a *Universitätspolitik*, as the powerful dual term has it in German—both policy and politics. The ministries prioritized objectives in research, practical consultancies, training needs, propaganda, and international status, among other things, and they allocated funds, appointed faculty, awarded public recognition, and gave advice bordering on instruction. Writing in the decade before World War I, Max Weber excoriated the system of the prominent Prussian Universities Minister Althoff, mourning the loss of "academic freedom" and the rise of the "professor of affairs" (*Geschäftsprofessor*) (Weber 1973), but Meinecke, commenting on Weber three years after the Revolution of 1918, objected that Weber "forgot that his own heroic national feelings, his eruptive understanding for a great nation's duties in matters of power and honor, originated in the world of his youth, the 'Bismarckism' on which he now turned his back" (Meinecke 1922: 282). The professors were not passive victims of the newly energized and expansionist state machinery. They adapted and participated, when they could. There were reasons of conviction, in the enthusiasm of unification, but also reasons arising out of patronage and other opportunities, as well as involvement in a newly potent policy process.[27] State officials were university graduates, of course, and not rarely persons who had taken at least the first steps of an academic career as well; and a recognized prime task of the university, especially outside the physical sciences, was the production of officials. University and officialdom, in short, were joined together by the active elitism of the regime.

The ideal of cultivation had an elitist meaning even when it was first formulated by Humboldt (Weil 1967: 148, 170). Although the social standing of the student outside of the university was supposedly irrelevant, the Humboldt era reformers assumed that the student would bring a thorough grounding in the philosophical sciences with him to the university. This grounding would be acquired in the classical *Gymnasium*, whose students almost all came from the wealthier or higher status sectors of society. The expenses of university schooling and the further postponement of remunerative employment that it entailed reinforced the social screening mechanism of the costly preparatory schooling (McClelland 1980: 119). The distinctive feature of the Humboldt ideal was that it disregarded the fundamental social difference between the aristocracy and the bourgeoisie in favor of qualitative intellectual criteria of selection. To speak of elitism in this context, then, is to highlight the distinction between elite and class dominance, despite the practical coincidence between the two across wide stretches of social history.[28]

The relationship between the ideal of cultivation and expanded ruling elites was reciprocal. Not only was the elite the source of those who subscribed to the ideal, but also the operations of the institutionalized ideal helped to define the elite. Cultivation became a measure of social standing, especially for those without aristocratic background. Procedurally, it referred to those with a university education. The most common corollary of this standard of cultivation was government service, which represented in the minds of the cultivated a meritocracy acting for the good of the entire nation (Vondung 1976: 25; Rosenberg 1966: 182–187). Even those who were not employed by the state commonly adopted the authoritative air of the state functionary, if only through their display of the reserve officer status that accompanied university graduation. The social concomitant of the conjunction between professors and officials, which arose as a function of the character of the university as state institution, was the commonality of cultivation within the elite.

The elite concept, however, does not comprehend all social dimensions of cultivation. An ambiguous element in the relationship between the state apparatus as such and the cultivated social sector as a whole is captured in the concept of the public. As Habermas has shown, Kant's demand that philosophers be allowed to pursue truth without regard for its critical effects on authoritative doctrine, as long as they limit themselves to a public of the learned carried a radical cosmopolitan stinger. With Enlightenment and the tendency of individuals to see themselves as members of a cosmopolitan republic, Kant maintained, ever more individuals, in effect, assumed the character of the learned in this privileged sense and became entitled to reason about the doctrines laid down by authority (Habermas 1989: 1102–117). Kant's idea of a public centered on the activities of the philosophical faculty and speaking for wider circles of the society of the propertied and educated captured a phenomenon that carried forward into the world after Humboldt, even if Kant's radical notion of a sharp divide between the arbitrary volitions of the state authorities and the reasoned critical judgments of the public was modified without being wholly rejected in the new Prussia (cp. Hegel 1991: 352–359).

Klaus Vondung has identified a "socially active core" within the larger cultivated sector that not only was cultivated itself but also presided over the cultivation of others in a threefold way: the public interpretation of reality and norms, education at all levels, and the articulation of opinion. This core assumed that it spoke for the larger cultivated public, which in turn was identified with the nation (*Volk*). Its concept of the nation was organic, postulating a spiritual unity that stood above any material divisions (Weil 1967: 172–173). At the center of this socially active core was the professorate, especially those in the human sciences (Vondung 1976: 27). In the years around 1848, the Kantian conception enjoyed a renewed flowering, but even during the years of closest identification between the state and the academy a measure of independence was postulated for this professorially led public. Without it, academic support of the state would have had little legitimating effect. As it was, professors had to compete in public for their commanding position against the ambitions of the romantic or bohemian intelligentsia. The resulting persistence of some tension between the professor as voice of the public and the professor as state official combines with more or less strong residues of the more familiar tradition of professorial autonomy—or academic freedom—in matters of cultivation and science to constitute the compromised but separate social actor with whom the state negotiated the settlements manifested in the "discursive coalition" (Wagner 1990: 55–56).

We are revising this concept because we think that the dynamics of the coalition cannot be sufficiently understood if it is seen as an interaction between political and scientific institutional discourses alone, especially if the scientists are understood as simply identifying their interests with whoever happened to be in control of the state apparatus (Simon 1988: I; 45–48; Wagner 1990: 194). Professors could not assume that their "publics" could be simply molded by them, and professors took sides in intrastate conflicts. There was no parity of power between the parties, and the academics were compromised by their many links of interdependence with the state and with the elite structure, but there were nevertheless material differences to be constantly renegotiated.[29]

As in any dynamic bargaining relation, changes in the power resources and interests of the parties may produce a "drift" in the arrangement, even where there is no convulsive overturn. By the end of the nineteenth century and during the first decade of the twentieth, the tendencies towards fragmentation of sciences and loss of common faith in the mission of cultivation increased the professors' need of the state, as did the concomitant weakening of their command of the cultivated public. Concurrently, the state gained in strength. While many academics continued to believe that influence flowed mostly from themselves to the state, the terms of the coalition drifted ever closer to making them simply providers of technical services and publicists for governmental policy (Bruch 1980). Beyond that, in the hard eyes of the state's officials, the role of professors in the human sciences became that of an instrument by which the state addressed the socially elite, self-consciously cultivated sectors of a public that was assumed to be ultimately organic and presumed to be open to appeals made on that basis. Their work as purveyors of sanctioned world views became abstracted from the primary productive activities of the university.

The changing political setting also affected the discursive coalition by undermining the plausibility of the organic unity of the nation that the state machinery and university both professed to represent. The rise of the Socialist Party, the counter-organization of other parties, and the concomitant increase in the importance of both parliament and other social forums revealed a society divided into conflicting interest groups. As seen from the standpoint of the coalition between university and officials, party politicians stood for conflicting positions, not the interest of the whole, and they resolved differences not through combining in some unified will but simply through the kind of compromise that smacked of economic bargaining. Academics who subscribed to this interpretation felt they had to defend the state against the conflicting and chaotic social interests of parties.[30] In the hope of resisting such a transformation, they commonly opposed democratization through stronger parliamentary institutions, but they paradoxically found themselves cast ever more in the position of partisan ideologists for one or another mode of conservatism, as the public arena became redefined as a field of ideological struggle.

In summary, the mainstream of German academia held a set of organic assumptions that were increasingly challenged by the development of modern industrial society. They assumed that the German nation formed a spiritual unity whose will was expressed through the agency of the state acting in conjunction with the intellectual efforts of the university. The human sciences were charged with interpreting that organic totality and providing orientation for the nation (or at least for the cultivated public that "represented" the nation). Professors, as civil servants, self-proclaimed arbiters of values and meaning, educators of civil servants and the cultivated public, and shapers of public opinion, were challenged by the growing fragmentation of science, society, and the public, which undermined their self-respect and authority, both historically grounded on the humanistic ideal of cultivation. Representatives of the academic mainstream put up a brave front in the face of ideological challenges, cultural pessimism outside the university, and the demands of the younger generation of academics themselves for a rethinking of the relationship of science, cultivation, and the state. Yet despite this effort, the universities were haunted by the disaffection of their students, arising out of dissatisfactions that no adjustment in relations with the state seemed capable of addressing.

Speaking to this last point in 1913, Georg Simmel, the social theorist who was Mannheim's model in so many respects, brought the question back to cultivation, in its purest form:

> Anyone who has been active for decades in the academic sphere and who enjoys the trust of the youth knows how often it is precisely the inwardly most alive and idealistic young men who turn away in disappointment, after a few semesters, from what the university offers them in the way of general cultivation, the satisfaction of their innermost needs. For what they want, quite apart from the most outstanding instruction of a specialized and exact kind, is something more general or, if you

like, something more personal. This can be made available in the treatment of history, art, or philology, to be sure, but it can be offered most purely and completely by philosophy, despite its scientific shortcomings. Call this, if you like, a mere by-product of science—or philosophy as science, but, if it is no longer offered to young people, the best among them will turn to other sources that promise to satisfy these deepest needs: to mysticism or to what they call "life," to social democracy or to literature in general, to a misunderstood Nietzsche or to a materialism tinged with scepticism. Let us not deceive ourselves. The German universities have largely surrendered the inner leadership of the youth to forces of this kind. (Quoted in Lichtblau 1996: 408)

Simmel, it should be noted, was consistently passed over for a major professorship.[31] The inner resources of the academic community did not suffice to meet the situation.

Notes

1. We recognize that this portrayal of the Enlightenment as mechanistic and scientistic is a one-sided caricature (See Reill 1994). Nevertheless, it was a straw man used by many German thinkers in their construction of the human sciences. Ernst Cassirer, a recognized cultural philosopher, whose historical writings on scientific knowledge served Mannheim as an important source, published an important book on the Enlightenment (Cassirer 1951) that questioned key generalizations of the stereotyped view, but not until 1932, too late to influence the Weimar discussion.
2. J.W. Burrow's "Editor's Introduction" to Humboldt 1969 provides a succinct characterization of Humboldt's liberalism, and its relation to other types. Mill quotes Humboldt several times in *On Liberty* and discusses his ideas with admiration. Mill 1977: 215, 261–2, 274, 300–301, 304. R.D. Cumming (1969) shows that Mill can well be understood as the founder of the very idea of a liberal canon.
3. Mannheim draws the contrast more strongly in his 1919 lectures on cultural philosophy and places Humboldt clearly on the liberal side (Mannheim [1919a] 1985: 226), while signaling a convergence between conservative and revolutionary conceptions of the state's pedagogical mission, but his subsequent developments of the theme put the emphasis rather on the project of a synthesis between the political conceptions, and the very possibility of such synthesis depends, first, on competition between the ideologies and, second, on the historical emergence of a culture of cultivation (*Bildungskultur*), whose origins coincide with the rise of both liberalism and conservatism as ideologies (Mannheim [1922–24] 1982: 255f.). Mannheim eventually seeks to probe behind the autonomy of various spheres, an undertaking especially clear in his critique of Alfred Weber's "morphology." See below.
4. Honigsheim (Scheler 1924: 428–429) points out the special importance of the universities and academic careers for nonreligious Jews. The prewar period to which he refers is also the high watermark for liberalism among the Jewish "fathers" and cultural rebellion among the new generation. For Mannheim's immediate situation in Budapest, see Gluck 1985: 76–105; Congdon 1991. See also Botstein 199: 73–92. Jewish liberalism played itself out in the cultural sphere to a remarkable extent, and cultural institutions were indebted to disproportionate Jew-

ish support—even when they practiced anti-Semitic exclusions, as the universities did.
5. The introduction of the merit system in appointments to secondary schools, as well as the standardization of curricula and university qualifying examinations, certainly disrupted local practices, but schools had not been comprehended in the old concept of academic freedom in any case. Cp. Smend 1928. Humboldt's early liberal writings had opposed all state control of education, but, in context, the opportunity to overcome illiberal institutions and to establish structures of liberal cultivation proved irresistible. For J. S. Mill's enthusiastic endorsement of the "beneficial interferences of government" in Prussia, specifically in education, see, for example, Mill 1977, I: 22–23. Especially striking is the parallel Mill draws between rule by the "most highly educated men in the kingdom" and "the British government in India." The guidelines for teacher training and selection were based on the innovations of the great Swiss liberal educator, Pestalozzi.
6. Reill (1994) makes a convincing case that Humboldt was strongly influenced by Enlightenment vitalists such as Buffon and Johann Friedrich Blumenbach, who "defined matter as a complex conjunction of related parts.... The whole was considered a 'synergy' in which each conjoined particle was influenced by each other and also by the *habitus* in which it existed. Organism and environment were locked together in a mutual embrace" (350).
7. Reill argues that Humboldt's idea paralleled the vitalist Blumenbach's concept of a drive for formation (*Bildungstrieb*) that directed the development of organic bodies (1994: 363–364, 354).
8. This is in accord with Humboldt's use of this notion in his formulation of the ideal of cultivation (Weil 1967: 118–125).
9. This notion of inner unity makes the translation of the adjectival form as "psychic" problematical, but there is no acceptable alternative other than the obsolete "soulish."
10. Ernst Troeltsch, one of the three figures that shaped German postwar thought, according to Mannheim, would later credit Humboldt with unique sensitivity to the nuances of the problem of relating abstraction to historical detail (Troeltsch 1922: 300), which was a translation into the language of historiographic method of the issue that Humboldt posed in more philosophical terms. Troeltsch's admiration for Humboldt derived from his own efforts to bridge the gap between the methodological and philosophical statements of the problem.
11. Reill also sees a precedent for this in the work of the vitalists, which sought to reveal the unity in the diversity of nature through a type of understanding called intuition (*Anschauung*). "Its operation was based once again upon the image of mediation, of continually moving back and forth from one to the other, letting each nourish and modify the other . . . through a third, hidden and informing agent that was in effect the ground upon which all reality rested" (352–353).
12. Meinecke ([1921] 1970: 34–48) is particularly strong on the division between culture (or nation) and state in early Humboldt, and he provides a useful reminder of the theme of nationalism which we neglect in this study because it is not an issue Mannheim addresses—or recognizes. From the standpoint of the present study, the national component in the cultivation discourse is mostly a dead weight on the scale against Mannheim and the left. This is a prime difference between Mannheim and his ministerial supporter, Carl Becker, whose preoccupation with overcoming particularism to achieve a national system is a major component of his cultural conception, but the difference is intellectual rather than political in its effects.

13. Meinecke's discussion of Humboldt's constitutional politics remains useful despite his slightly grotesque *Machtstaat* contrast model. See Meinecke [1907] 1970: 138–147. On the cushioned relations between state and corporation, notably religious ones, even in the greatest theoretical model of the state of the time, see Hegel 1991: 290–304.
14. Hegel himself dramatically anticipates the eventual disparagement of cultivation in the lengthy section on the self-estranged spirit or *Bildung* (Hegel 1981). His analysis of the cultural aspect of the Enlightenment touches on many of the elements celebrated by Humboldt, but he continues on to depict this phase of the spirit as dissipating itself in the self-will and confusion of the unhappy spirit (Rosen 1974: 183–228). His argument drives him beyond cultivation in Humboldt's sense to ethics, politics, art, religion, and ultimately to philosophy at its most complex, speculative, and demanding. Shklar 1976: 44–45; for a contrasting view, see Gadamer 1975: 10–19. On a concrete level, see Hegel's letters during his *Gymnasium* time on the incompatibilities between teaching logic to *Gymnasium* students—or writing a textbook for such instruction—and his own work at the same time on his *Logic* (Kaufmann 1965: 331–334). During Humboldt's years as Prussian minister, Hegel was in the *Gymnasium* in Bavaria, where reform had come early. He was eventually brought to Humboldt's University of Berlin by Humboldt's reformist successor. Hegel is a looming presence in the cultivation discourse, but often as a stern judge or disapproving outsider. See below, for Mannheim's fascination with Hegel as well as for his invariant habit of softening Hegel's blows. For Mannheim's unfinished business with Hegel, see Kettler/Meja 1995: 53–57. At the University in Budapest, it should be said, Mannheim wrote his graduation paper in German literature on "Wilhelm v. Humboldt as Critic" (UF); and "critic" was a prized concept in his youthful exchanges with Lukács, expressly distinct from the role of philosopher. When he was nineteen, Mannheim wrote Lukács that he would begin with the former and would consequently address himself to Dostoevsky. (Gábor 1957: 96–7)
15. For the distinction between science oriented to specialists and intellectuals, see especially Nettl 1970.
16. Kant has a minor treatise on education where he discusses the culture and cultivation (*Bildung*) of human endowments (Kant 1964: 729). In contrast to Humboldt, he treats the process as a physical enhancement of physical qualities markedly inferior in dignity to moral development or the search for truth. Cp. Goldman 1992: 27–28.
17. Despite this new emphasis, the certification-granting professional faculties of law, medicine and theology continued to be the ones attracting the most students (McClelland 1980: 119).
18. A classification of diverse approaches to these complex issues not according to philosophical schools or educational theories or concrete historical configurations of events but by three categories of world views is itself a characteristic historicist move.
19. Heinrich von Treitschke is a powerful example of this trend. See Mosse 1964: 199–202. Goldman (1992: 35–36) notes that this development entails an abstraction of the concept of personality from the humanistic context that had given it meaning for Humboldt.
20. Goldman (1992: 33) emphasizes the importance of Schleiermacher and Schlegel as Romantic voices on *Bildung*. Goldman goes so far as to say, "Schleiermacher is the most important figure in the tradition of *Bildung* after Humboldt, and perhaps even more influential" (Goldman 1992: 286n36). Goldman's interests are

more psychological than social, so his emphasis is different from ours.
21. The vogue of Langbehn's *Rembrandt als Erzieher* (1890) illustrates the phenomenon. See Mosse 1964: 40–43. Fritz Stern (1961) examines both Langbehn and Nietzsche's contemporary Paul Lagarde as harsh critics of academic science and culture. More generally, the Nietzschian legitimation of vitalist *Lebensphilosophie* underlies our generalization. See Aschheim 1992.
22. One of Mannheim's earliest publications in Germany, written when he was still intending to habilitate in philosophy under Rickert, was a labored and unresolved review of a book on the classification of the sciences. Mannheim [1922b] 1970; cp. Wolff's astringent comments in Wolff 1993: 11–13. Despite its limitations, the piece indicates the importance attached to the question, and specifically Mannheim's determination that the diversity of the sciences have a genuine grounding and a unified theoretical explanation. The two treatises he wrote in preparation for his habilitation but never published ([1922–24] 1982) represent successive attempts to make a detailed case for cultural sociology, first, as ontologically grounded inquiry, second, as a study with direct consequences for cultivation, and third, as a vital step towards a synthesis that would reintegrate the sciences, in all their variety. See below.
23. One can see this division in the organization of German secondary ("higher") schools during the nineteenth century. In the Humboldt era, the variety of classical schools was streamlined so that all schools entitled to prepare students for the university would be called "*Gymnasien*." At this time the system of final examinations (*Abiturienprüfungen*), which was established in 1788 but remained largely ignored, was revived and enforced. By 1834, candidates for the civil service and the learned professions were required to have received their *Abitur*. By that time, the *Gymnasien* were places where the ideals of Greek culture prevailed in accordance with Humboldt's humanistic philosophy. Students took 86 units of Latin and 42 units of Greek compared to only 16 units of physical science (the same amount given over to drawing and singing) during their *Gymnasium* studies. By 1859 another class of higher school, the *Realschule*, was instituted that placed less emphasis on classical language and more on science. The latter was divided into two levels, which in 1882 became known as the *Realgymnasium* and the *Oberrealschule*. The *Realgymnasium* represented a hybrid of the other two schools and "was designed to afford a liberal education on the basis of modern culture." The *Realschulen* grew rapidly and by the end of the century had gained many of the privileges that had been reserved only for the *Gymnasien*. This growth put the advocates of classical humanistic education on the defensive (Russell 1899: 88–90, 95–96, 100–101, 104–105, 392–393).
24. As a result of these methodological innovations, Ranke's Idealist premises were ignored in the United States and he was viewed there as a positivist (Iggers 1962).
25. The topos of crisis is already so commonplace in the nineteenth century that it is important to caution against taking all of its appearances with equal seriousness. Fritz Stern's slightly censorious characterization of the cultivated bourgeoisie offers a corrective to overvaluing the professions of cultivated revulsion and perplexity in the face of the sordid turn of modern life and its knowledge: "The educated bourgeoisie still indulged in the incantations of culture and personality; but material conditions had changed, and these incantations became more and more spurious and less and less disinterested. Between 1871 and 1918 a new type of idealism prevailed, one that, because of its wider diffusion and subsequent debasement as well as in recognition of its remoteness and specious descent from the earlier Idealism, I would like to call Vulgäridealismus. . . . The unpolitical

German denounced the mass society, democracy, liberalism, modernity, indeed all the so-called importations from the West.... This vulgar idealism widened and sanctified the social divisions within Germany, yet thought itself unpolitical. It had no concern with practical matters and considered itself dogmatically opposed to realism, pragmatism, and above all to materialism. It is ironic that the German bourgeoisie often hid its massive materialism behind this idealism while the Socialists hid their passionate idealism behind a facade of scientific materialism" (Stern 1960: 122–125).

26. Meinecke (1922) proposes generational phases for German professorial politics (*Gelehrtenpolitik*), beginning with the generation of 1848, broadly construed, where oppositional liberal themes play a proportionally greater role, followed by the succession from Treitschke to Schmoller and, finally the conflict-laden and uncertain situation epitomized by Max Weber. For Weber on Schmoller, see Weber 1973; cp. Weber 1949. Schmoller's alliances extended beyond the statist ranks. Max Weber was not alone among the members of the Association for Social Policy (*Verein für Sozialpolitik*) led by Schmoller who had misgivings about the intermixture of state and science in that organization, and the later Society for Social Reform (*Gesellschaft für Sozialreform*), which Schmoller patronized, included radicals who were in opposition to state officialdom, and the organization even invited Social Democrats, who refused to take part.

27. The close connection between professors and state officials should not be confused with the rigid coordination of totalistic regimes, or even with an absence of conflict within the limits of the connection (and thus within the constraints of the fiction that the state machinery itself was not subject to partisan strife). There were sharp differences and power shifts within both groups, and the university professors most intimately linked to the state could find themselves in opposition to present policies—and even victimized by ascendant officials—when their allies in office fell into disfavor. Gustav Schmoller, for example, supported the ex-minister associated with social reform, Hans Hermann Freiherr von Berlepsch, when the latter reacted to his loss of office by founding the politically inclusive Society for Social Reform. Schmoller kept his distance (although he stayed close to his nephew, Ernst Francke who was the editor of the group's periodical, *Soziale Praxis*, and the most active leader) but nevertheless paid some symbolic price at the hands of the new ministry. Other professors active in the organization, not to speak of aspirants to academic posts, were severely penalized (Ratz 1980: 9–47). Except for the degree of tolerance granted to dissenters, the relations between the academy and the agencies of government, at least at the core, were not so different in Germany than they were in other continental nations with well-organized states, or even in England or the United States, especially in periods of state mobilization. At the turn of the century, American reform movements, notably in civil service, budget, civic government, and public administration, were largely comprised of university professors for whom the state role of German professors served as a model (Gunnell 1993: 37–59).

28. Historically diverse processes of elite selection and varieties of elite formations and ideals are a major theme of Mannheim's writings after 1930, with special attention to the rise and decline of the liberal, humanist elite, in relation to the democratization of elites, which he saw as the predominant trend. See especially Mannheim [1933] 1956: 200–239. Mannheim emphasizes the contrast between the "spiritualization" sought by the "modern form of humanism" and "the 'courtly' ideal of the aristocrat and cavalier," but he also calls attention to Humboldt's aristocratic origins (231).

29. It is tempting to trace the marks of the coalitional dynamics in the design of certain key disciplines, notably those closest to state concerns. Wagner (1990) has attempted this with both the Historical School of National Economy, especially in its second generation, under Gustav Schmoller, and legal positivism in public law, identified first with Carl Friedrich von Gerber and later with Paul Laband. As an indication of the coalitional character of both learned discourses, Wagner highlights a feature common to their very different methods, a systematic avoidance of critical distance from the state or its basic institutions, not to speak of criticism. National Economy relegated such possibilities to theory, but Schmoller insisted that theory could neither comprehend actual developments, which had to be understood as history, nor address the central issue of the time, the "social question," a policy problem that Schmoller saw with the eyes of the state, as requiring the integration of the working class into the established spiritual order by alleviating their most pressing material needs. As long as the study of national economy was subordinate to this historical and state-centered orientation, Wagner maintains, there was no need or possibility for a critical sociology. Legal positivism rejected historicism, but came to a similar result. The state was presupposition, not problem. Wagner thinks that the formalist strategy of legal analysis amounted to a systematic science of the state that divorced that institution from the empirical social context and created a purely formal discipline, preempting the place of a political science that investigated the interrelationship between the state and social forces was rejected (Wagner 1990: 191–200). To construe both disciplines as expressions of a simple subordination of science to the state underestimates the unresolved contests in the relationship constitutionalized in the coalition (as well as the variations over time) and loses sight of the corresponding ambiguities in both approaches. On Schmoller and the vagaries of social reform, see note 27, above. The work of legal positivism as a legal practice makes it problematic to bring it in such direct relation to the project of a critical political science as Wagner does, and its liberal constituents are in any case insufficiently recognized in Wagner's reading (cp. Caldwell 1997: 13–39).
30. For classic statements of this position see Paulsen (1899) and Schmoller (1913); for a rebuttal, see Witt (1985).
31. He had four years as full professor at the University of Strasbourg, extending himself to cover wide range of subject matter at the comparatively low level of an understaffed provincial university in wartime, until his death in 1918. Simmel suffered from being a Jew, of course, and he also gained distrust from his reputation as a sociologist, but the popularity of his lectures, notably among middle-class women, counted strongly against him. For a vivid evocation of Simmel as practitioner of cultivation, see the few pages of memoir by his student, Arthur Salz, who was a principal protagonist in the debate about Max Weber's "Science as a Vocation." Wolff 1959: 233–236. Simmel enjoyed the support of Gustav Schmoller as well as Max Weber. Max Weber believed that anti-Semitism was the main reason for Simmel's inability to gain a professorial chair until his last years, despite support of Weber and others (Frisby 1990: 3, 38n14). In a revealing letter in opposition to the appointment of Simmel to a chair in philosophy at Heidelberg the conservative historian, Dietrich Schäfer, wrote, "To wish to establish society as the standardizing organ for human cohabitation in place of the state or the church is, I believe, an ominous error" (Wagner 1990: 142, 152–153). Mannheim's article on youth and the university (Mannheim [1922] 2001), written four years after Simmel's talk, shows Simmel's inspiration. As a student, Mannheim came to Berlin for a semester with Simmel, and he accepted Simmel as a prime

interlocutor in his later sociological work, despite the rather aloof appreciation he wrote as a young man, immediately after Simmel's death (Mannheim [1918b] 1985: 150).

3

The Weimar Republic

The Weimar Republic and Cultural Crisis

The crisis in cultivation perceived by Simmel and others was temporarily suspended with the advent of World War I. When Germany entered the war, many rejoiced that previously divisive elements in the nation had committed themselves to its spiritual unity. Convinced by the "civil peace" between the Social Democratic Party and the government[1] that the war community had overcome class divisions, they echoed the Kaiser's pronouncement: "I no longer recognize parties, I recognize only Germans."[2] Many academics seconded Johann Plenge's description of the new spiritual unity as the "Ideas of 1914," and parallels were drawn to the Wars of Liberation during the Humboldt era. Simmel himself maintained that the war would not only speed the end of the previous epoch but would also bring a new inner unity, a transvaluation of values. Most professors agreed that the war was a defensive struggle by the monarchical German state to preserve the humanistic ideal of culture and cultivation against the aggressive, plutocratic, and parliamentary British civilization (Lichtblau 1996: 393–404).[3] Otto von Gierke spoke for many when he wrote,

> We do not want to sacrifice to the democratic Moloch our historically achieved lofty idea of the state, our harmonic connection of a strong monarchy with the Germanic freedom of the nation [*Volk*], our organization of the governmental and the social in a way that preserves unity in multiplicity. (Quoted in Böhme 1975: 26)

But as the war dragged on, the national "community" proved to be only a veneer over a deeply fragmented class society. Academics were divided about how to address the disintegration of the Ideas of 1914. Moderates sought ways to reconcile the discordant social forces with their own organic aspirations.[4] Conservatives sought ways to repress those same forces and rallied behind the dictatorship of General Ludendorff.[5] Neither side was ultimately successful.

In November 1918, the trauma of the war ended as the authoritarian Empire gave way to the democratic Weimar Republic, whose brief lifespan coincided with Mannheim's German career. The Republic has been described as the paradigmatic site of the "crisis of classical modernity," characterized primarily by the increased fragmentation of both the political and cultural spheres (Peukert 1993). Most of the characteristics ascribed to classical modernity, which include organized capitalism, urbanization, the growth of modern political parties, the welfare state, and modernist culture, originated in the Empire, but all these tendencies accelerated during the Weimar period (Käsler 1984: 204; Bialas 1998). To the difficulties associated with these changes was added the physical and psychic devastation wrought by the war. The shock of the new appeared all the greater because of the collapse of the prime symbols of integration, the emperor and his army.

The term "crisis" was constantly used by academics during this period. Books appeared on the "crisis" of historicism, culture, theology, pedagogy, spirit, science, mathematics, physics, mechanics, and causality, in addition to Oswald Spengler's *Decline of the West* and Paul Ernst's *Collapse of German Idealism* (Bambach 1995: 37–38, 41, 188). Events no longer seemed to cohere, unity was disrupted, reality was discontinuous, the mood was ironic. Fritz Ringer writes, "The crisis existed, if only by virtue of the fact that almost every educated German believed in its reality" (Ringer 1969: 245). It should be said that the motifs of commentaries on the universities, for example, were familiar from the prewar period. So Siegfried Kracauer, an emerging voice of sophisticated postwar cultural journalism, wrote,

> The crisis of the sciences—which is by now a topic of commonplace discussion—is most visible in the empirical sciences such as history and sociology, which are dedicated to the investigation of intellectual/spiritual contexts and to the explanation of meaningful human action.... The consequences of this dilemma have become quite palpable: senseless *amassing of material* on the one hand and unavoidable *relativism* on the other. These alone suffice to explain the "hatred of science"

rampant among the best of today's academic youth. (Kracauer 1995: 213–214; cp. Kracauer on Mannheim as teacher, above)

What was different and uniquely frightening to established academics was the declining saliency of the university question in public discussions about the supposed crisis. Not only the newly prominent political movements of the Left and Right but also important segments of the university's prime middle-class constituency questioned whether the status of professors or their functions in society were important to the state of political consciousness or cultural achievement.

Modernist elements of the new, experimental "Weimar Culture," anathema to the conventional academy but attractive to many cultivated consumers of culture, embraced the fragmentation of the old discourses and institutions, and sought to build upon it (Frisby 1988), but reactionaries, too, turned to popular prophets who were disdained by the university, notably Spengler. Moderates and conservatives, attempting to uphold the positions articulated during the war, refused to relinquish the hope for a unified sphere of meaning mediated by academic practices. There was no consensus, however, on how that would be accomplished. Professors were confronted with an exacerbation of the crises of science and cultivation internal to the university while the crisis of the larger culture called the strategic importance of the university into question. And the political resources used under the Empire to repair deficits in coherence and respect were not to be had on the old terms, if at all.

State apparatus, elite formation, and public now operated so as to create new divisions in the university rather than to create a surface unity, as they had under the Empire. While the Republic is often criticized for its failure to restructure the state and to replace its officials (Rosenberg 1965), this charge, whatever its merits, hardly applies to the domestic ministries of Prussia, where the political leadership of the "Weimar coalition" parties was consistent and reasonably strong. In the management of educational institutions, the forms were relatively unchanged, but the key officials had reform projects that indeed invited collaboration from professors but that implied dramatic shifts in the orientations of the established faculties and a measure of inclusiveness that attacked the premises of the "discursive coalition."[6] The cohesiveness of elites was affected not only by the elevation of leaders from beyond the boundaries of the cultivated classes and the creation of alternative institutionalized channels for their advancement,[7] but also by the shocking disruption of the economic foundations of the old elites, especially after the hyper-inflationary period. Mannheim's decision to use the problem of social mobility as a central theme in his sociology class as well as the theme of cultural democratization in his later writings reflected a widespread anxiety (see Mannheim [1931–32] 2001; Mannheim [1933] 1956). Mannheim is similarly a prime witness to the fragmentation of the public into increasingly closed and mutually antagonistic plural constituencies tied to diverse world views and (party) ideologies. The ideal of a tendentially unified academic cultural perspective informing and inspiring a public sensitized to its leadership by its own academic cultivation appeared so remote as to be utopian, and unattainable, in any case, without the most dramatic changes, notably in political life. An important question became whether a unity could be established in conjunction with the new parliamentary state, with its party formations and interest groups, or whether it would be necessary to revert to something resembling the old monarchical structure. Or put another way: could one democratically extend the ideal of cultivation? And if so, what role were the university and the discipline of sociology to play in this democratization? We shall explore these questions in the two overlapping contexts most immediately germane to Mannheim's work, the politics of university reform, especially as it involved the establishment of sociology, and the internal politics of sociology, especially as it affected the cultivation of democratic citizens.

Sociology and University Reform

A striking feature of educational reform in the Weimar years is that it generated furious resistance despite the fact that the ministers and officials who led the effort were themselves very close to the wartime world view that had united the academy and the schools. The campaign for reform began, in fact, with a wartime salvo against a prewar policy of neutral objectivity in education. In June, 1918, five months before the Republic was established, Konrad Haenisch, the editor of a newspaper subsidized by the government as an organ for socialists active in support of the war, criticized the Prussian cultural minister for saying that his primary task would be to keep the schools completely free of the conflict of daily opinions and political parties, and to focus instead on purely pedagogically technical elements in the strictest sense (Haenisch 1918: 335).[8] Haenisch argued that it was neither possible nor desirable "to keep the school altogether free from the great clash of spirits, from the enormous struggle of world views" (1918: 336). Although schools should not be party schools, it was their duty to orient the student in the cultural-political conflicts of the time. While he did not oppose the humanistic *Gymnasium*, he believed it had to be supplemented to include political and economic subjects (1918: 349; 1919: 21, 25–26). Ultimately the goal of this new pedagogical mission would be "gradually to create a completely new type of German," the citizen of a democratized nation (1918: 343–344, 346).[9]

Relying on the familiar slogans, Haenisch viewed the current pedagogical system as the culmination of the liberal-individualistic nineteenth century, which began with the "Ideas of 1789." This system was concerned primarily with abstract knowledge divorced from a larger world. The person was viewed as an isolated individual, a part of an atomized humanity, and not as a social being, as a part of the larger "national organism." This resulted in underestimating the need for the "cultivation of will and character" (1918: 337). Haenisch contended that the World War had discredited this liberal educational philosophy and prepared the way for a new one based on the "Ideas of 1914," which meant not an overheated nationalism and chauvinism, he maintained, but an ultimately socialist principle of organization. A new educational system would be established that would create a new cosmos from the existing chaos, one based on unified principles out of which the different kinds of schools would develop (1918: 338, 348). Political praxis and theoretical schooling would not be separated but brought together in a pedagogy that would yield, in the rhetoric of the war years, the "most iron performance of duty, most sober factual sense and most soaring idealism" (1918: 345).

In a revealing decision, the Prussian leadership of the Majority Social Democratic Party selected Haenisch for the office of the minister he had earlier criticized, and the ministry soon after began to address the issue of educational reform.[10] Susanne Miller singles out an action by Haenisch to illustrate the devotion to order among the majority Socialists. On November 23, 1918, he asked a leading trade union in Königsberg to intervene with radical students at the university there, whose "council" had seized administrative control, forced the resignation of the rector, and evidently challenged the power of professors to appoint and dismiss faculty. In other universities, he wrote with satisfaction, "the whole apparatus is continuing to function in the old way" (cit. in Miller 1978: 134). The students were to be assured that all would be well, now that two socialists were in charge. Haenisch was decidedly not a revolutionary.

He lent his support, nevertheless, to the leading voice for university reform, a figure of prime importance in university policy for over a decade, Carl H. Becker, who was the under-secretary for higher education in the cultural ministry.[11] Through much of his tenure in this post and, for two terms, as minister, Becker drew a firestorm of criticism from academics charging him with political partisanship, although he was a non-party national and social liberal along the lines of Friedrich Naumann rather than a socialist of any description. In fact, his republicanism was strongly tinged by his hostility to a "democracy of parties" and he harbored hopes for a "parliament of the cultivated," presumably to deal with questions of cultural politics (Becker 1976: 374; Becker 1919b: 6). In a twist on the standard meaning of the German term *"Kulturpolitik,"* he asserted that culture is a modality of politics as well as a subject matter for policy, and he accordingly defined cultural politics as "a conscious deployment of spiritual values in service to the nation or the state in order to strengthen their inner cohesiveness and, externally, to help them in grappling with other nations" (1919b: 2). Becker bitterly complimented the victors in the war for using such politics to brilliant effect and criticized Imperial Germany above all because it had lacked a cultural-political conception or program, and offered only militarism as a common inner bond. Like Haenisch, he saw the new parliamentary state entrusted with overcoming Western individualism and particularism on the basis of the new democratic reality (1919b: 5–6). And like Haenisch, too, he maintained that the current educational system, notably in the universities, was too centered upon the purely intellectual, was too specialized, too much concerned with the isolated individual and, as a result, had lost its sense of the whole (Becker 1919a: ix, 1–2).[12]

Becker wrote that the Republic was experiencing a crisis of culture and cultivation, but that such crises could be means for healing (1930: 46). He believed that the university had to return to the philosophy of cultivation that had characterized it at the end of the eighteenth century. That philosophy sought to create an ideal (*Bild*) that students would try to realize (*nachbilden*) in themselves and others (1930: 79). Accordingly, university teachers had to be able to satisfy both the psychic and spiritual needs of students, something they had not been able to do because of their orientation toward specialization. Universities were too exclusively places of pure research, he complained, attempting to solve narrow intellectual problems and seeking to transmit intellectual contents and methods. In addition, the human sciences under the influence of historicism had sequestered themselves from the larger sociopolitical environment. They no longer played the role in public life that they should have played. Both the disciplines of economics and law had simply accepted the Bismarckian order, offering nothing but rational organization and military pride, and they were content to address specialized problems within that order. Both disciplines avoided any attempt at synthesis, so that "politics as a science" (*Politik als Wissenschaft*), a concept traceable to the mid-nineteenth-century liberal constitutionalist, J.C. Bluntschli, became extinct. The bureaucratic character of the universities became stronger, as they became increasingly stratified, so that any sense of community within had also disappeared. Professors, concerned only with their own specialized research agendas, increased the distance not only between themselves and the realm of public opinion, but also between themselves and their untenured colleagues and their students. They saw their role as simply turning out more researchers, not as producing good citizens (1919a: 3, 5, 10–13, 26, 31). This was a very different task from the development of the total personalities of their students. Without putting character formation in the foreground, without fostering self-responsibility, without forming connections to the nation and the state, they were unable to address the cultural crisis of the time (1930: 47–51, 63–64).

Becker proposed two major reform initiatives that overlapped with one another. The first was a reform in the "sociological structure" of the university in a way that students and untenured faculty would play a larger role. This meant making academia a more democratic place, bringing it more in line with politics and society (1919a: 66, 45). The second initiative involved changing the curriculum in such a way that would allow for more synthesis and thus a greater engagement with the larger sociopolitical environment. Becker advocated a dovetailing of disciplines so that they did not simply stand next to one another vertically, but rather cut across one another horizontally. While assigning the chief task to philosophy, following the convention, he nevertheless gave more practical attention to the role of sociology, which included scientific politics and contemporary history in the broadest sense (1919a: 9). Chairs in sociology were a pressing need in Germany, he maintained, because

> Only by means of a sociological way of thinking can the spiritual habit be created in the intellectual sphere that when transferred to the ethical sphere becomes political conviction. *In this way science becomes for us the path from individualism and particularism to the character necessary for citizenship.* (1919a: 9)[13]

Both of these initiatives took practical form in measures to broaden the social recruitment of universities and in funding and personnel policies to add faculty Becker considered sympathetic to his project. These practical steps provided a gloss on his general sentiments such that the offer to reinstate the "discursive coalition" that might be read into the language alone was not considered by those it might have been thought to persuade. In alliance and interaction with the comparatively small number of professors who responded to his lead, Becker proved to be quite a more stalwartly republican figure than might have been expected from his starting point with Haenisch and the "Ideas of 1914."

Yet it is remarkable how much the rhetoric of this new university reform movement sounded like the language of "cultivation," as it evolved from Humboldt's era. It contained the same vitalistic appeal for the connection of the institution with the sphere of life,[14] the same attack on purely scientific specialization and careerism, the same hope for an organic community within the university, the same demand for addressing the student's personality in order to make him/her a better citizen rather than simply increasing the store of knowledge, the same belief that the university should have strong ties to the rest of the educational establishment, the same looking to the state for the means to carry out this reform while allowing for the continuing autonomy of science, all of which was subsumed under the call for a revitalization of the synthetic ideal of cultivation. The strengthening of the meritocratic element in the general conception and the acceptance of a democratic context made a difference in the ideology, but the major departures were more in the ministry's personnel practices and strategic funding decisions than in Becker's language of justification.

Becker brought academically contested controversial personalities and programs into the Prussian universities. In Berlin, for example, he appointed both Hermann Heller and Carl Schmitt, bitter opponents in legal theory but almost equally admired by the younger generation of intellectuals and equally distrusted by the academic establishment.[15] Becker actively seconded the plans of Kurt Riezler, the chairman of the governing committee at Frankfurt, who brought such figures as Paul Tillich, Max Horkheimer, and Theodore Wiesengrund-Adorno (Kettler/Meja 1995: 109). Riezler was a classicist who stood for a modern renewal of the humanistic ideal of cultivation, but Becker's most notable campaigns promoted a novel departure within that trend, the idea of cultivation as having a vital political dimension and the association of cultivation with the new and disputed discipline of sociology. "The struggle over sociology is really the struggle over the new concept of academic science," Becker wrote, alluding to his attack on narrow specialization (Becker 1925: 41; Düwell 1971: 47). For the position vacated by Franz Oppenheimer—whose own appointment to a position that combined sociology with national economy, although initiated in the last year of the war, had to wait until the Haenisch-Becker era to be consummated (Haselbach 1990)—Becker had initially wanted Emil Lederer, a close confidant and Social Democrat, who was a professor at Heidelberg, where he chose to remain, and then fought through the appointment of Lederer's choice, Karl Mannheim, against the vehement opposition of the faculty. The professors were prepared to accept a Jew and a republican, as indicated by their recruitment of Hans Kelsen, but they wanted to keep out Karl Mannheim and his philosophically tinged sociology (Kettler/Meja 1995: 143–145). Since Mannheim's program for sociology was clear at the time of the appointment, it is safe to assume that Becker wanted precisely what Mannheim had to offer, a sociology with impact on public as well as professional debate, and a sociology oriented to cultivation for republican politics.

Becker's agenda had more critics than defenders. It was decried by many academics as an attack by the SPD on the autonomy of the universities, despite Haenisch's marginal position in the political apparatus and Becker's liberal aloofness from party politics (Wende 1959: 73–74; Stölting 1986: 71, 95). There was no sharper critic than the historian Georg von Below, a strong supporter of the Empire and Ludendorff's wartime dictatorship, who nevertheless voiced his criticism in terms of the same neo-idealism that inspired Haenisch and

Becker (Stölting 1986: 100). An impassioned advocate of the "Ideas of 1914," like Haenisch, he put special emphasis on deeper layers of Romantic and Historicist assumptions. In 1916, vividly recalling Humboldt, he wrote that an organic synthetic approach "envisions the personality as being singularly distinct, [and] the single state, the single nation, the single social association, the single epoch not as a sum of atoms, but as a true individuality." The aim, he concludes, is "understanding in terms of the whole" (von Below 1916: 11). Politically, this invocation of the humanist tradition was directed not only against the atomistic and mechanistic "liberalism" imputed to Germany's enemies abroad, but also against the interest group politics ascribed by conservatives above all to the labor movement, notwithstanding its loyal adherence to the civil peace. Soon after Becker's *Thoughts on University Reform* appeared, then, von Below wrote the first of a series of replies (1919a)[16] in which he focused on two major points: the unsuitability of sociology for the purpose of the synthesis Becker also professed to pursue, and the political motivation of Haenisch and Becker in promoting sociology and democratization within the university.

Von Below argued that sociology was not fit to be a universal science, that the only possible universal science was philosophy (1919a: 1311; 1919b: 553), but the defense of philosophy was not his objective. Instead, he was more concerned with demonstrating how existing disciplines, especially history, were already providing a synthetic approach pioneered by his beloved Romantics, among whom he included Savigny, Adam Müller, and Ranke (1926: 224–226). Their essentially nonrational approach did not separate society, economy, culture, and the state, but treated them as an organic totality complete with its great personalities (1920–1921: 519; 1926: 236–238). Sociology he saw as a product of the French Enlightenment and a pseudo-science that destroyed any organic synthesis by abstractly separating social forms from the unified whole, projecting a dimension of the "social" (*gesellschaftlich*) that undermined the concreteness of the "communal" (*gemeinschaftlich*) actuality. Unlike the fruitful empiricism of the Romantics, the sociological approach yielded a one-sided empiricism (1919a: 1274, 1278; 1920–1921: 514), a "positivist" approach that negated the value of the individual personality by subordinating it to abstract forces, defeating the aims of the philosophy of cultivation (1919a: 1279). Drawing on the defensive vocabulary used to exclude uncomfortable social theorists from the university as Marxists (Stölting

1986: 30), von Below charged that the kind of synthesis that Becker had in mind was that of "dilettantes" rather than true scholars. The chairs of sociology that Becker advocated were, moreover, superfluous, since the properly scholarly study of social relations was already being pursued by von Below and his colleagues, applying methods that gave due regard to the wider organic context (1919a: 1311, 1317–1318; 1919b: 554). Without deviating from his view that sociology was a hindrance to synthesis, von Below seemed willing in 1919 to concede to it a limited status as a narrowly specialized discipline (1919a: 1309–1310, 1321). Shortly thereafter, his position hardened, and he declared that sociology was simply a method applicable for certain purposes by history and other proper studies, unable to stand on its own as a separate discipline (1920–1921: 513; 1926: 231).

If sociology was so manifestly unfit for the role that Becker envisioned, von Below next asked, why did the latter advocate such reforms? The answer was purely political. The existing government was a party government and the creation of these chairs was a way to force socialists and a Social Democratic Party agenda on the university, to violate its autonomy through politicization, as was the attempted enfranchisement of untenured faculty in university governance (1919a: 1296–1300). The university enjoyed much more autonomy under the old Empire than it could under democratic forms of government (1919a: 1322). Given the government's politics, "none of this should be surprising. They are eager in other respects as well to force modern Russian contrivances upon us" (1919b: 550). Sociology, then, was simply a "mask," a means by which party opinions could hide behind abstract discussions. "They are promoting not politics as a science (which Becker claims to find wanting in our past scientific activity) but rather a malformed science or a pseudoscientific politics" (1919a: 1320). Von Below was not above nasty polemical tricks. To undermine the respected Carl Becker, he linked his name with the unabashed radical partisan who had been associated with Haenisch during his first months in office, opening his broadside by meanly associating him with Adolf Hoffmann. Von Below was a blunt reactionary in his hostility to the Republic.

While recent commentators are inclined to dismiss von Below as an example of "sclerosis" of the discipline of history because of his academically traditional and politically reactionary position (Oexle 1988: 303–304), Mannheim drew on him in his study of conservatism and, more important, addressed his key topics with care. Conservatism attracted him as a problem for study not so much because he wanted to expose it but because he felt indebted to it for its corrections of liberalism.[17] What Mannheim drew from Savigny and Müller was not so remote from von Below's anti-"positivist" historicism, and von Below's reformulation of the question about "politics as a science" kept the topic on the agenda for Mannheim too. In his essay, "Is Politics as a Science Possible," which becomes the centerpiece of *Ideology and Utopia,* he takes up, in effect, Becker's cause against von Below, without mentioning either. An especially disconcerting feature of Mannheim's thought, for his contemporaries as for later commentators, is that he seems to "reduce" the ideas of others to the level of political ideology but then refuses to treat this as equivalent to a reduction of their cognitive interest. Accordingly, he was more often chided as a relativist than accused of partisan manipulation, especially by writers dedicated to a more traditional version of Humboldt's humanist cultivation.

Two of these thinkers were Eduard Spranger, a well-known pedagogue and interpreter of Humboldt, and Ernst Robert Curtius, a specialist in Romance literature and critic, who was a colleague of Mannheim at Heidelberg. More moderate than von Below, but distrustful of Weimar parliamentarism, they also rejected sociology as a synthetic discipline. Both men, moreover, criticized not only sociology in general but also Mannheim's *Ideology and Utopia* in particular, taking it as the epitome of what they both called "sociologism."

They brought the discussion of the problematic relationship of cultivation to science and the sociopolitical sphere directly back to the source, since both Spranger and Curtius first of all tried to assess the status of Humboldt's ideal in the late Republic. Both endorsed Humboldt's emphasis on the need for organic harmony between individual freedom and supra-individual webs. While Spranger, in accordance with historicist assumptions, wrote that the national culture was an individuality with a unified objective spirit, Curtius drew on the traditional humanism of the Rhineland instead of German historicism. Both believed the purpose of cultivation to be the development of the individual as a cultural-ethical personality, who had to develop in the soil of objective value contents (Spranger 1928: 2–3, 63; Curtius 1932: 14, 20, 44, 50). Curtius wrote, "We must return to the original foundation and beginning of our tradition and again learn the elements of culture" (Curtius 1932: 63). With that specification as to the cultural source, he agreed with Spranger's contention that education was "the cultural activity that strives to bring about an unfolding of *subjective culture* in developing individuals, by means of an evaluatively guided contact with a given *objective culture* and the activation of a genuine, ethically requisite *cultural ideal* " (Spranger 1928: 3). The larger organic totality relied on the cultivation of the individual for its realization. Spranger described this reciprocal relationship as the "infusion of the [objective] spirit with the [individual] soul and the infusion of the soul with the spirit. Where this succeeds in a productive sense, there is cultivation " (Spranger 1928: 65).

Like von Below, Spranger and Curtius sought to preserve the nineteenth-century character of the university in the face of the new Weimar reform movement (Oelkers 1998: 88). While they rejected the parliamentary democracy of the Republic to differing degrees, they were united in the belief that those democratic forces had to be kept out of the university and that this meant putting the relatively new discipline of sociology in its proper place as a clear subordinate to traditional disciplines such as philosophy and history. All of this was proclaimed in the defense of the classical ideal of cultivation.

While Curtius was more a liberal, Spranger had a national orientation and put more faith in the contribution of the state to cultivation. The dream of a cultural nation separate from the state, he maintained, was unrealistic.[18] At the same time he echoed Humboldt's concerns about a state that was too rigid in its demands. Giving this concern a contemporary conservative twist, he asserted that excessive drilling for service to a supra-individual whole had not disappeared with the passing of the Prussian army and the downgrading of the bureaucracy, but that it continued, in fact, in the party discipline of the Social Democrats (1928: 70). His own formula for the relation between state and individual followed the pattern of his definition of culture: "infusion of the state with the soul and infusion of the soul with the state."

Despite the imprecision of this standard, Spranger had no hesitation in concluding that the existing republican state lacked such mutuality because of its parliamentary structure. The "soulless technique of parliamentary parties," Spranger charged, delivered the state into the hands of economic interest groups (Spranger 1928: 71, 31). Curtius wrote that with the existing parties, none of which had a cultural-political program, there was no room for independent spirituality and that no one seemed to want to serve the national spiritual estate (Curtius 1932: 20, 34–35). Spranger directed this critique especially towards the "proletarian parties." What he characterized as their narrow dogmatism elevated the proletariat to an absolute but left workers without a flexible ideal for life or fully formed ethos and led to their divorce from the deeper culture as a whole. Such party dogmatism, he contended, went hand in hand with the shallow mechanistic "culture" of the times (25, 49–50).[19] Curtius seemed most afraid of the parties of the radical right in which modern irrationalism had reached its peak in the form of primitive anti-Semitism and the racial myth (Curtius 1932: 27, 44; Hoeges 1994: 181–190). In either case, the republic with its parliamentary government did not come into question as a resource for cultivation. Their opinions of the newly established state hovered between distrustful acceptance and fatalistic hostility.

Similarly, neither writer considered sociology as a kind of science that could be a fit partner for a coalition to restore cultivation. For Spranger, the rejection extended to all modern sciences. He wrote that science had come to mean a more positivistic and utilitarian specialization oriented toward the adaptation of practical abilities to the material here and now. He saw sociology as the epitome of this orientation. In addition to its mechanistic methodology, it limited ethical questions to those of social forms. When this concern for the practical removed a will to values (*Wertwille*), he asserted, the result was relativism (Spranger 1928: 14–15, 54, 11).[20] Curtius was less inclined to blame developments within the specialized disciplines as a whole. He focused on the new, as yet insufficiently focused discipline of sociology, identifying it with outside forces that encroached upon the university. By claiming to be the central discipline of the university, it usurped the proper place of philosophy and introduced a political and relativizing tendency into learning. He was not averse to sociology as a scientific study of civil society. German sociology should follow the example of French sociology and recognize that it can only be a specialized discipline. It must first abandon the pretense of mastery over culture. In short, Curtius believed that the destructive approach of sociology in its most prominent guise would weaken the ability of traditional humanism to resist the growing irrationalism in Germany. The end result would be nihilism (Curtius 1932: 80–81, 99, 101–103; 1990: 113–114). Sociology in this sense is profoundly subversive of the university as agent of cultivation.

Both Spranger and Curtius applied their critiques of sociology specifically to Mannheim, describing his work as a prime example of the "sociologism" they scorned. In a short review of *Ideology and Utopia*, Spranger criticized Mannheim's sociology of knowledge as a perspectivistic, that is, relativistic, approach that departed from the ethos of the good and the just (objective inquiry) of ideal science (Spranger 1990). Curtius launched a more intense attack on Mannheim, first in a review of *Ideology and Utopia* and then in a section of the work we have been discussing, *German Spirit in Danger*. His main criticism was that Mannheim did not recognize either the autonomy of spirit or a psychic (*seelisch*) structure separate from social forces. By reducing both spirit and soul to socioeconomic determinants, Mannheim raised the chaotic contemporary mode of experience to the status of a norm. The stability of historical continuity, especially valuable in times of crisis, was to be discarded, as spiritual contents were reduced to being either ideologies or utopias, in favor of the affirmation of continual change, that is, revolution. Mannheim then became the high prophet of relativism and nihilism, who in declaring the centrality of sociology attempted to preside over the destruction of classical humanism and with it the ideal of cultivation (Curtius 1932: 88–103; 1990: 114–118).

Hostile to Becker's protégés and projects and indifferent to his attempt to reinstate the discursive coalition on new terms, Curtius and Spranger looked beyond the politicized Weimar state for a solution to the cultural crisis of Weimar. Spranger spoke a language somewhat reminiscent of that which Mannheim had known in his Hungarian days, especially in his conviction that there had to be a new culture carried by new forces. Spranger noted the idealism of the youth movement, which he described as having "an aristocratic motive on a communal basis" (Ringer 1969: 285). Spranger advocated the cultivation of a cultural leadership by creating "schools for elites" that would be modeled along the lines of the classical *Gymnasium* informed by a neo-humanism. These leaders would occupy commanding heights above the state, law, and economy and put a halt to the stifling of the human soul produced by technology. There would be a new culture. Spranger's conception of that culture, however, lacked the apocalyptical vision of either the youth movement or the revolutionary culturists among whom Mannheim had come of age. The new culture would be based on a larger ideal tied to both the achievements of the past as well as to the meaning provided by religion. Without the certainty that a chain of being existed stretching from God to insensate matter, Spranger asserted, it would be impossible to rise above "the materialism and mechanism of a cultural world emptied of soul" (Spranger 1928: 49-50, 73, 42, 51, 74).

Despite this conservatism, Mannheim thought that he recognized a potential ally in Spranger before the publication of *Ideology and Utopia*. Mannheim's vain hope that his sociology of knowledge would be widely accepted as mediator in the cultural impasse emerges ingenuously in a letter to Spranger, in which he supposes that Spranger would welcome the work. In January 1929, Mannheim visited Spranger to solicit a book for the series of studies on the boundary between sociology and philosophy that he was editing, and in which *Ideology and Utopia* was to be the first volume. Mannheim wrote Spranger a few months later, thanking him for his promise of cooperation, avowing his admiration for Spranger's writings, and expressing the certainty that Spranger would find him a kindred spirit when he read the forthcoming *Ideology and Utopia*. Contrary to the denigration of the spirit in naturalistic sociology, he assures Spranger, his own work is designed to complement the understanding of spiritual development that is provided by the cultural studies Spranger exemplifies. Mannheim closes by invoking their close, even fraternal, affinities, and he throws himself on Spranger's judgment, however stern. Spranger's harsh review presumably soon disillusioned him, although he never replied.

Curtius, on the other hand, elicited Mannheim's only published reply to critics. They were fighting over common ground. Curtius shared Mannheim's conviction that the primary responsibility rested with the intellectuals,[21] but he believed that their proper contribution was precisely the restoration of faith in the Western cultural heritage that Mannheim considered obsolete. Warning that Germany should not make an abrupt break with the past, Curtius looked to religion and the academic tradition. The more democracy brought the masses to the fore, the greater the need for a restored humanistic elite and its secure field of operation in the university would become (Curtius 1932: 20, 42, 46, 56, 73-78, 120-121). He believed that the university, which formed a living community of teachers and students, should be the synthesizing agent for the cultural totality by cultivating an elite. The food for this cultivation was to be humanism reinspired by the Renaissance, a humanism that came from the creative intensity of life and was connected with religious belief. Curtius expressly attacked Mannheim's credentials as educator. As an expression of a world view, he says, Mannheim's brilliant exposition has its rights, but "once it is taught and demands to be heard at German universities as the latest findings of the most recent 'key science,'" the design becomes profoundly objectionable. What is at issue is precisely corruption of the youth. "We hope that youth—German youth—will resist all attempts by scientific authorities," Curtius continues, "to dissuade them from an appreciation of greatness and idealism" (Curtius [1929] 1990: 117). Resentment of this charge fuels much of Mannheim's reply, culminating in an appeal to Galileo's pathetic *"eppur' si muove"* in protest against Curtius' introduction of "an academic vice squad to control the logical methods of thinking that may be taught" (Curtius [1929] 1990: 125 [trans. revised]). The conflict between Curtius and Mannheim had the intimacy not only of their common past friendship with Georg Lukács but also, and above all, of their common attachments to Heidelberg (Hoeges 1994).[22] For both Curtius and Mannheim, Heidelberg meant first of all a decision about Max Weber and his legacy, and they made opposite choices.

In the decade after his death, Weber continued to define the intellectual scene. Marianne Weber resumed his weekly salon in 1921, seconded by his brother, Alfred, and it served once again as a prime stimulus and setting for the intense, "eternal conversation" (Tompert 1969: 42; Weber 1977) about philosophy, culture, and social inquiry that Max Weber had cultivated. Although the Weber Circle was by no means limited to practitioners of social science disciplines, Mannheim, in a survey he wrote shortly after his arrival in Heidelberg, unhesitatingly described it as the sociologically oriented polar opposite to the local branch of the George Circle, distinguished by an antihistorical aestheticism (Mannheim [1921–2] 2001; Hoeges 1994: 25–37; Kettler/Meja 1995: 38–41; Loader 1985: 35–37; also Honigsheim 1926; Breuer 1995; Kolk 1995; Matthiesen 1988: 304–307).[23] Mannheim's choice was no less firm than his analysis of the scene. He identified with the Weber Circle as a center of sociological thinking even before he was compelled to abandon his attempt to secure his habilitation in philosophy with Heinrich Rickert, in favor of work with Alfred Weber.[24] Curtius' early associations, in contrast, were with the George Circle. Although he was declared an "apostate" from the all-absorbing creed of the Master, he remained close to Gundolf and others in that group, and he left no doubt about his distaste for the "world view of the *Geisteswissenschaften*," as represented by Weber. In a letter to a friend, he wrote, "I want to be free to bathe in the Neckar on bright summer nights or to visit with friends, however many congresses or circles may convene in the evening. . . . The world does not exist to be understood historically but to be apprehended with love. The cosmos of the spirit is not a museum for me, but a garden, in which I wander and pick fruit " (cit. in Hoeges 1994: 23). His maiden appearance in the Marianne Weber salon was not a success, he reported, while Mannheim became a favored regular. These social notes from long ago matter in our present context because Mannheim's orientation to the Weber circle, especially when reinforced by participation in Alfred Weber's "sociological evenings," involved him in debates about the relations among sociology, science, and state that were less dramatic but intellectually more demanding than the rhetorical confrontation between Becker and his traditionalist critics. Mannheim affirms his choice of peers and comrades in his reply to Curtius, when he confidently identifies himself with "the new situation in sociology," as it emerges out of the work of Weber, Troeltsch, and Scheler (Mannheim [1929b] 1993: 123).

Notes

1. The SPD demonstrated its commitment to the *"Burgfrieden"* by voting for the first appropriations bill to finance the war, notwithstanding German leadership in the pre-war consensus among Socialist parties against such support.
2. No one expressed this sentiment more clearly than did Thomas Mann in his rambling wartime polemic against the West (and his brother Heinrich), *Reflections of a Nonpolitical Man*. There Mann stated that "the German people will never be able to love political democracy simply because they cannot love politics itself, and that the much decried 'authoritarian state' is and remains the one that is proper and becoming to the German people." And he explicitly connected this nonpolitical attitude to the humanistic ideal of cultivation: "For German higher culture thoroughly resists being politicized. Indeed, the political element is lacking in the German concept of culture [*Bildung*]" (Mann 1983: 16–17, 78). Compare Bruford 1975: 228–229. This view continued into the Republic. In 1923, Mann told a group of students: "The finest characteristic of the typical German, the best-known and also the most flattering to his self-esteem, is his inwardness. . . . The inwardness, the culture [*Bildung*] of a German implies introspectiveness; an individualistic cultural conscience; consideration for the careful tending, the shaping, deepening and perfecting of one's personality or, in religious terms, for the salvation and justification of one's own life. . . . What I mean by all this is that the idea of a republic meets with resistance in Germany chiefly because the ordinary middle-class man here, if he ever thought about culture, never

considered politics to be part of it, and still does not do so today. To ask him to transfer his allegiance from inwardness to the objective, to politics, to what the peoples of Europe call *freedom*, would seem to him to amount to a demand that he should do violence to his own nature, and in fact give up his sense of national identity" (Quoted in Bruford 1975: vii). Stern (1960) labels this attitude "vulgar idealism." For complicating nuances in Mann's position, as they emerge in his relations with his brother, see Thomas Mann/Heinrich Mann (1969: 299-310, 110-118, cp. 126-136).

3. The most famous expression of this position was the "Appeal to the World of Culture," on October 4, 1914, by 93 intellectuals, including many professors. They denied that Germany started the war and declared that the country would fight to the end "as a cultural nation" (In Böhme 1975: 47-49). For a general discussion of this document, see Schwabe (1969: 21-22).

4. A good example of this group was Alfred Weber, who would become Mannheim's sponsor at Heidelberg following the war. Weber believed that Germany should assume a position of spiritual (not military) leadership in Europe as well as develop its own internal "spiritual leadership," which could give direction to the different social groups. He wrote that with democratization would come a development of both individuality and communality, a new relationship between the leaders and their followers. However, he imagined a democracy different than those of Britain and the United States, which he described as rationalized, mechanized and atomized. Weber hoped for a new political national faith that would be articulated by the nation's spiritual leaders, who would not simply dictate to the masses as the old leaders had, but instead capture the consciousness and faith of the masses (1918: 111, 114–115, 120–121). It was in this spirit that Alfred Weber became a founding member of the German Democratic Party (cp. Demm 1999).

5. Many professors supported the Fatherland Party, a propaganda organization in support of Ludendorff and his expansionist war aims. When the Reichstag, behind the leadership of the SPD and the Catholic Center Party, passed a peace resolution rejecting those war aims, the conservatives issued a petition of protest signed by 1100 professors. A counter-petition supporting the peace resolution garnered only about 100 signatures. The two petitions are in Böhme (1975: 184–186; cp. Meinecke 1922).

6. For the conflicts over the designs of Carl Becker, see below. As noted above, our generalizations slight differences among the states. In Baden, for example, the terms of relations between the ministry and the Heidelberg professorate were modulated into a liberal key with less dissonance, and conservative states carried on much as before.

7. Most obvious is the great growth in institutions for popular "higher" education, organized especially by the labor movement, with its apex in the Academy of Labor at the Johann-Wolfgang-Goethe-University in Frankfurt; but the redevelopment of this university itself, taken into state charge only in 1914, as well as the other large urban centers, represented an opening to new elite aspirants, not least the Jewish middle class and independent women (Antrick 1966; van der Will/ Burns 1982; Kettler/Meja 1993).

8. Before the war, Haenisch had been a left-wing party journalist, most prominently as the embattled editor of "one of the most radical Social Democratic papers in Germany" (Schorske 1955: 134; see also 251). His vivid confession of the delight with which he succumbed to his "burning desire to throw [himself] into the powerful current of the national tide" is a frequently quoted set-piece of wartime nationalist conversion rhetoric (Schorske 1955: 290). He was the author of an

influential book which not only defended the SPD decision to vote war credits but also urged a nationalist strategy for the SPD. For Haenisch's argument, see Berlau 1949: 77–91. An important complication is the close link between Haenisch and Parvus, who sought to promote the Russian revolutionary effort through alliance with the German war effort. First published in 1916, Haenisch's *Social Democracy in and after the War* appeared again at the war's end. In a heated introduction to the 1919 edition, published when he was Prussian Minister of Education, Haenisch vituperated against those who wanted Germany to accept the war-guilt imputed to it by the Versailles Treaty. "This termination of the war," he wrote, "this peace of shame . . . which represents the temporary victory of Entente capitalism over German socialism is not yet the last word. . . . In the end, the 'ideas of 1914' . . . will yet carry the victory over the . . . ideas of 1789, which now seemingly are victorious . . . The peace of dishonor of Versailles will ultimately mean nothing more than 'a scrap of paper'." (cit. in Berlau 1949: 305. See also Ryder 1967: 224). The most extreme among the nationalist Social Democrats, August Winnig, counts Haenisch as a wartime ally and reports a surreptitious offer of help from Haenisch, speaking in his office at the Ministry, after Winnig disgraced himself with his party by refusing to oppose the Kapp Putsch (Winnig 1930: 104; Winnig 1935: 304–306). To put Haenisch and Winnig in perspective, it may be useful to recall that Haenisch's counterpart in the Budapest Soviet regime, the Minister of Culture, Georg Lukács, served as commissar at the front in the military campaign that his government was conducting against the Rumanian attempt to execute the Trianon Agreement (Kettler 1971).

9. Haenisch indicated that he was thinking of creating a "free university for the political sciences" in Berlin (1919: 24). For the eventual *Hochschule für Politik*, see below.
10. In keeping with the formula applied throughout the first postwar Prussian government, Haenisch at first shared the office with a minister drawn from the antiwar Independent Socialist Party (USPD), the notoriously undiplomatic partisan, Adolf Hoffmann (Miller 1978: 91). The joint ministry drew furious political fire during the first months because of Hoffmann's aggressive policy against Catholic influence in the schools, a policy that Haenisch did not oppose in government but disowned in press briefings, in part because of opposition to the USPD strategy of creating "revolutionary facts on the ground" before the installation of a new constitutional order (Miller 1978: 215–217).
11. Before accepting office as minister of state, Becker was himself a well-established scholar. Close to Ernst Troeltsch and Max Weber at Heidelberg, he was a specialist in Arabic language and culture, and the founder of the pioneering German journal of Islamic studies. This gave him a base of support and a measure of authority in the universities that Haenisch did not possess. In 1921, Becker succeeded Haenisch as Prussian Cultural Minister; he returned to his position as State Secretary from 1922 to 1925; and then he was again Minister from 1925 to 1930. Because there was no national Minister of Culture and because of Prussia's weight in Germany, the Prussian Cultural Minister was the most important official for educational matters in the country (Becker 1976: 365–366). Particularism was a major danger in Becker's view, and he argued for constitutional measures to foster coordination among the state ministries (Becker 1919b).
12. Becker was unable to produce any structural changes in the higher schools and universities, although he played an important part in creating unified elementary schools. Writing in 1930, as the economic and political crisis made further reforms ever more unlikely, he regretfully concluded that the elementary and higher

schools still represented divergent ideals (Becker 1930: 50–53). Policy towards the schools was constrained not only by regional variations but also by the historic claims of religious communities, especially the Catholic school system. With the Center Party critical to virtually all imaginable coalitions during the Weimar years, at both the national and Prussian level, at least, school reform was impeded. The Weimar Constitution expressly called for a unified system at the primary level but it remained vague about the allocation of powers for reform and said nothing about the organization of the higher schools and universities (Brunet 1922: 329–331). In the event, the higher schools and universities resisted any attempt at reform (Brunet 1922: 227–228; Alexander/Parker 1930: xxi-xxiv, 290–292).

13. Haenisch also advocated the creation of new chairs of sociology (1919: 23).
14. Stölting (1986: 93) writes that Becker was very much in the tradition of neo-idealistic vitalism (Nietzsche, Bergson), understanding socialism as an ethical thing rather than a material one. Lepenies (1988: 273) writes that Becker wanted to bring Friedrich Gundolf, a vitalist and leading member of Stefan George's Circle, to Berlin; but not too much should be read into this project, since it was part of a wider undertaking to bring controversial personalities bent on cultivation to Prussia's universities. See below.
15. Müller/Staff 1984: 81. In an essay on the history of the legal faculty of Berlin published in 1960, Rudolf Smend still bitterly characterized both as "political appointments." Heller, the foremost Socialist constitutional law theorist, came to Berlin after several years as a principal figure in the workers' education movement, aligned with the segment that identified itself with the tradition of the youth movement (Müller/Staff 1984: 89–110). In 1932, Schmitt and Heller were opposing counsel in the lawsuit over the federal takeover of Prussia (Müller/Staff 1984: 287–311), where Schmitt won the Court's approval for the preemptory ouster of the government that had given him recognition. Mannheim encouraged a refugee student at the London School of Economics, who had been an admirer of Heller in the days of labor education, to write a thesis comparing Schmitt and Heller. The dissertation was finished as war broke out, and the manuscript is lost (Müller/Staff 1984: 89). Becker's friendliness to labor's educational projects manifested itself as well in his key role in the negotiations that established the Academy of Labor at the university in Frankfurt over the opposition of the faculty. It is worth noting, however, that he successfully opposed the wishes of the major trade union association in linking the new institute to the autonomous processes of the university (Antrick 1966: 28). Our emphasis on universities should not be taken as an indication that the ministry simply abandoned all hope of reform in the preparatory schools. For a fictionalized account of struggle between a rightist town and a republican schoolmaster dispatched by Berlin to head the local *Gymnasium*, see Frank 1932.
16. Only the most important of which are cited here. When he died in 1927 he was working on a book on the origins of sociology, which he saw developing in a way contrary to German historiography (1916). A segment of this last work appeared posthumously under the editorship of Othmar Spann (1928).
17. In the opening pages of his Habilitation, Mannheim cites Gustav Radbruch's 1922 discussion of party ideologies, a citation that he recalls in a letter to Radbruch in 1930, thanking him for kind words about *Ideology and Utopia* (Mannheim 1996: 43). Radbruch had criticized the Social Democrats for continuing a liberal attitude towards state power, when the political turn had in fact freed them from their dependence on defensive reliance on rights and brought them closer to conserva-

tive appreciation of the ethical mission of the state. For Franz Neumann's use of the same text, see Kettler/Meja 1995: 105.
18. Spranger believed that, in fact, it was the state of laws (*Rechtsstaat*) that provided the individual the freedom to develop his potential. "The transcendental nexus (*überpersönlicher Lebenszusammenhang*) stemming from the divine . . . legitimates the state, and . . . the individual must voluntarily accept and assimilate [this], if he wishes to raise himself to a higher level of spiritual life" (quoted in Ringer 1969: 122). Although the individuality of the nation lived more strongly through the spiritual individual than through any other cultural unit, individual cultivation could not occur without the concurrent development of the national character. This meant developing individual identity with national culture and the state (Spranger 1928: 68–69).
19. Spranger wrote: "True fraternity . . . [is] a total relationship from man to man, which involves the whole nature and not merely the interests of human beings. . . . The sense of these unique sociological forms cannot be experienced by everyone who approaches them only from the conceptual side, least of all by those who think in democratic categories" (quoted in Ringer 1969: 285).
20. Earlier Spranger (1925: 1383) had written that in dealing with cultural phenomena such as public opinion, the press and advertising, which could not be clearly brought into a theory of meaningful cultural content, sociology had gotten the reputation of being an unsolid pseudo-science. This article was cited with approval by von Below (1926: 235–236).
21. In his otherwise unsparing criticism of *Ideology and Utopia*, Curtius surprisingly praises the book for containing, for the first time in German, "an outstanding analysis of the sociological problem of the intelligentsia" (Curtius [1929] 1990: 119). Curtius's own discussions of the intelligentsia are oriented to Maurras, Peguy, and other French writers, notably including Julien Benda (Hoeges 1994). Mannheim makes a special effort to rebut Benda's attack on the "politicization" of the intellectuals. Speaking to Dutch students in 1932, he insists that the only question open to intellectuals is how they will play their political role in a politicized society ([1932] 1993).
22. Although not the most vocal opponent, Curtius was the sole dissenter from the otherwise unanimous decision of the Faculty in 1922 to permit Mannheim to habilitate. He withheld his vote. Alfred Weber, who fought Mannheim's request through the Faculty and Senate, singles out Curtius as an opponent who was motivated both by an "emotional anti-Semitism" and suspicion of Mannheim as foreigner and collaborator with the Hungarian Communists (Demm 1999). Hoeges points out that Curtius lowered himself to the point of making dangerous polemical allusions to Mannheim's status as outsider and Jew in his polemic, and that this misconduct took on special meaning in the context of the publicized "war about Mannheim" arising out of barely disguised racialist objections by Bavaria and Württemberg to his naturalization. Hoeges thinks that the instance was out of character. Alfred Weber clearly did not, although he was associated with Curtius in the German Democratic Party (cp. Hoeges 1994: 87–91). See also Kettler/Meja 1995: 90–91.
23. Matthiesen speaks of the "multipolar structure" of the Heidelberg milieu, "between the pathos-filled ascetic scientificalness on the one hand and the pathos-filled aesthetic life renewal on the other" (1988: 304). In that context, it is striking that Curtius is quoted by Matthiesen as referring to this Heidelberg as "the synthesis of the European spirit." It is fair to say that Mannheim's own choice of the

sociological pole did not entail abandonment of all hopes of life renewal in Heidelberg.
24. Mannheim arrived in Heidelberg as a philosopher after a semester with Heidegger in Freiburg, and he attended seminars with both Rickert and Jaspers, as well as Alfred Weber's lecture course. In a congratulatory message to Alfred Weber on his seventieth birthday in 1938, Mannheim expressed his gratitude to Weber for permitting him latitude to do his own work on the Habilitation, after his frustrating experience under a "bearded philosopher" who wanted him to hew a prescribed line (BK). Alfred Weber's correspondence confirms that Mannheim meant Heinrich Rickert, although Jaspers was also strongly opposed to his habilitation. Alfred Weber wrote to Else Jaffé early in 1922 that the philosophers were "too dumb" to accept Mannheim and that he was happy to have him. Weber had already been using Mannheim as a reader of articles submitted to the *Archiv für Sozialwissenschaft und Sozialpolitik* (Demm 1999; Demm 2000). See below.

4

The Legacy of Max Weber

Political Education in the Applied Sociology of Albert Salomon

Max Weber's most immediate legacy to the wider intellectual community was the decade-long dispute about the relations between science and politics set off by the publication, in the year before his death, of two lectures that he presented to the Free Students' Society at the University of Munich, in a series ambiguously called "Spiritual Work as Calling." The ambiguity arises from the range of meanings attached to the key concepts, with both "spiritual work " (*geistige Arbeit*) and "calling" (*Beruf*) capable of denoting nothing more than occupational census terminology but extending as well to concepts heavily freighted with ethical meaning. In view of the student discontents noted earlier and the express dedication of the sponsoring organization to the "Humboldt-Schleiermacher university ideal of the *civitas academica*" (Buckmiller 1980: 20), it seems obvious that the students expected Weber and the other speakers to address questions about the meaning and value of the work they were formally preparing to be certified for and thus about the point of their education.[1] In any case, the author of *Protestant Ethic and the Spirit of Capitalism* clearly followed his own lead in that earlier work and applied a secularized version of the novel Protestant meaning of "calling"—"its present meaning in the everyday speech of all Protestant peoples"—as "a task set by God. . . . a life-work" that entails duties having a moral character (Weber 1958: 79–80; Weber 1922: 62–69; cp. Brunner et al. 1972–84: I, 488–507). For his original audience and for many of the participants in the subsequent dispute about the works, accordingly, Weber's lectures on the callings of "science" and "politics" are charged with the question of cultivation.[2]

The central message of Weber's lectures is the categorical separation and contrast between the two spheres. Education for science can bear on political life only indirectly, and political didacticism is averse to scientific norms. The quest for meaning, moreover, belongs to yet another sphere, where the choice among warring gods is left to the decision of the individual, guided only by his personal daemon. From the standpoint of the traditional cultivation ideal, Weber's thesis is deeply ambiguous.

On the one hand, his passionate invocation of the ethically freighted concept of calling, as well as his insistent confrontation, in the presence of students, with Tolstoy and the prophets of "experience" and direct action show clearly that questions of moral cultivation through education for intellectual responsibility are hardly matters of indifference to him.[3] On the other hand, he calls into question the Humboldtian premise of organic wholeness and the possibility of cultivating integral self-development, harmoniously unfolding from inner self-recognition. Instruction in the sciences, accordingly, is stringently constrained by the objectivity specific to each science; the personality of the teacher, or the wider personal enrichment of the student, have nothing to do with it. The prime qualities of the political personality, conversely, arise without reference to anything that can be taught. Weber scorns the old idealism in education, especially in the political forms it assumed with Treitschke, Schmoller, and the prophets of the "Ideas of 1914." To these old targets of criticism, he now adds the students who come to the classroom in search of inspiration, and he takes special aim at the hopes for a wide-ranging knowledge capable of orienting conduct in the manner of a comprehensive world view. "Science today," Weber insists, "is . . . not the gift of grace of seers and prophets dispensing sacred values and revelations," but "a 'vocation' organized in *specialist* disciplines" (Weber 1946: 152, trans. modified). The work of science, moreover, is inherently intellectualistic and inevitably contributes to the rationalization and demystification of the world, the transmutation of human life-space into orderly spheres where objects and relations are instruments for the achievement of routinized ends.

As with science, Weber makes politics turn on a characteristic directly antithetical to the ideal of organic wholeness. Politics is a sphere of unreconcilable conflict, and the calling of the politician is conducted through relations of power. The choice of one political objective implies an attack on those that are passed over. The dream of universal pacification is antithetical to politics and dangerous to humankind. If the political vocation is supposed to counteract the devitalizing consequences of the rationalization promoted by science, among other things, it is nevertheless harnessed to that emergent reality and precluded from mobilizing against reason. The energy and security that the politician provides serves to sustain the conditions that make it ever more unlikely that politicians with vocation will arise and flourish.

Weber's pessimistic conclusion and assault against idealism generated grumbles of reservations from the older generation and vehement rejoinders from the young, notably from Erich Kahler, an ardent follower of Stefan George.[4] Mannheim himself invoked the difference of generations in setting himself against Weber's "disillusioned realism" (Mannheim [1925b] 1986). His own answers to the old question, "Is Politics as Science Possible," however—and especially to the educational questions associated with it—are much closer to Weber's intellectual astringency than to Kahler's enthusiastic claims on behalf of a new, all-encompassing philosophical vision. Having laid out a sociological method for achieving a realistic level of discourse by relativizing totalistic ideologies, he proposed a scheme of political education for choice that is illuminated by comparison with the programmatic rationales of the Hochschule für Politik in Berlin, an institution that came into being in 1920, with the support of Becker and others close to Max Weber.[5]

The school had two rationales, in effect, relating respectively to external and internal politics, with the latter especially relevant to the question of designing political cultivation after Weber. For Ernst Jäckh, the head of the College throughout the Weimar years, the crux of the matter was the model of the French École Libre des Sciences Politiques. Citing Droysen and Meinecke, Jäckh portrayed the school as a place to cultivate the "reason of state," offering both research and instruction to fill the place of a general staff for the diplomatic service and other foreign policy officials (Jäckh 1931: vi, 175–178).[6] In this connection, Jäckh reported with pride that the College made a major contribution to the "scientific planning and academic preparation" for the political decisions that shaped the German Locarno initiative for stabilizing the post-Versailles boundaries, having first transmitted the idea from its Austrian originator to German officials (Jäckh 1931: 9ff). The Locarno example was especially important to Jäckh because it illustrated the crucial distinction between the Berlin institution and its Parisian model. Similar in being founded with express reference to Humboldt's foundation of the University of Berlin in 1810 in the aftermath of a massive national defeat and in being intended to foster a unity of spirit and sober understanding among political leaders, the Berlin College is not only different, according to Jäckh, but also diametrically opposed in one critical respect to its French counterpart which he bitterly terms "the victor of Versailles":

> Together with its school, France fell victim to chauvinistic *revanchisme*. It has to be our mission, in contrast, to be the point of crystallization for the reconstruction of Germany in spirit and soul—a new Germany and by this means also a new Europe in a new spirit (by no means the senseless, violent "spirit" of Versailles), so that the dead of the war shall not have been sacrificed in vain.

The mix of German nationalism and European perspective in Jäckh's embellishment of his main substantive theme testifies to the influence of Friedrich Naumann, whose "School for Citizens," originated in the last year of the war, was the immediate precursor of the subsequent foundation. Naumann's specific agenda in this last major project before his death in 1919 was defined by his conviction that the parliamentary party system could not articulate the new mass feelings emerging during the war and that it would be necessary, rather, "to position in the stream of things a stratum of men and women with a strong sense of responsibility" through a novel political education in a new type of educational institution (Heuss [1946] 1994: 124–125). Naumann was not, however, the sole influence in the development of the domestic rationale for the Hochschule. Jäckh acknowledged as well the need for new civic and welfare-political education generated by the Weimar constitution, and the search for a suitable center for such schooling among national and state agencies.

The detailed explanation of the program for domestic political education (*Innenpolitische Bildung*) was laid down not by Jäckh but by Albert Salomon, a Heidelberg comrade of Georg Lukács and Emil Lederer and later a friend of Karl Mannheim.[7] According to Ulf Matthiesen (1988), Salomon was offered a position at the Hochschule as a result of his review-article of Max Weber's posthumous *Works*. A major theme in Salomon's admiring expose is announced in the following passage:

> If one uses the concept of philosopher... in the old, classical sense, to apply to someone for whom it was a necessity of the soul to philosophize, to grasp the meaning of the world and to educate human beings as citizens of their cities.... Weber was a philosopher and a one of the great educators and cultivators of his people. (Salomon 1926: 134)

The Weber he presents is, above all, dedicated to the ethological questions of political character formation that Humboldt's admirer, John Stuart Mill, had also declared to be central to both the scientific and political agendas of the modern age. Yet Salomon sharply distinguishes Weber's spirit from the humanism of the German classics. No "sublimation of a feudal and courtly aristocratic culture" marks Weber's work. Rather, he concludes, a "Bourgeois gallantry and democratic heroism shape a new humanism" (Salomon 1926a). He credits Weber with seeing, as well, that the idealization of an heroic "new man" in the manner of the Stefan George circle is "sociologically impossible" and that "no ideal for living can be actualized today...that is not somehow democratizable" (Salomon 1926b).[8]

Writing to mark the tenth anniversary of the Hochschule in 1930, then, Salomon left no doubt, first, that the political cultivation the school sought to provide was intended to replace the older cultivational design in its effects on both individual development and integrative political orientation, and, second, that the intellectual medium of political cultivation was, above all, political sociology, with its key elements derived from Max Weber, Carl Schmitt, and Karl Mannheim.

Although Salomon's article was not published until after Mannheim's 1930 course, its character as an explanation for a well-known program under way for ten years and Salomon's closeness to Mannheim's closest associates, notably Emil Lederer, mark the ideas as part of the context in which Mannheim developed his own thoughts. Albert Salomon was two years older than Mannheim and his time at Heidelberg coincided with the most active years of both the Weber and George circles, as well as Lukács' vital presence in the Weber Circle as radical voice of a culturist ideology comparable to the George critique of the "Americanist ant-heap" of bourgeois civilization and its utopian celebration of artistic form (Matthiesen 1988: 304–313; Lukács [1911] 1971). His dissertation, not finished until after the war and supervised by Emil Lederer, examined eighteenth-century literary forms of life, including the contextures in which Humboldt generated his design of cultivation, expressly addressing the methodological conundrum of reconciling a sociological explanation derived from Max Weber with a subject matter grounded in the soul and resistant to rationalization (Matthiesen 1988: 313–316; Salomon [1921] 1979). This delayed completion coincides with the writing of Mannheim's methodological treatise on the puzzling nature of a sociology of culture, derived from precisely the same discursive setting and addressing identical issues in very similar ways (Mannheim [1922–24] 1982). Salomon's first major publication, then, was an extensive article on Max Weber, based on an early reading of the posthumous works as well as on the biography published by Marianne Weber. In it, Salomon signaled his departure from the earlier fascination with culturist paradoxes and his dedication to the Weberian ideals of sober intellectual rectitude, although he took distance from the political direction of the figure he called, to the annoyance of Marianne Weber, the "bourgeois Marx " (Matthiesen 1988: 317–318; Salomon 1926a). For Salomon, the political complement to a realistic analysis of modernity, inspired by a suitably secularized adaptation of Jewish prophetic impulse, is a commitment to the proletariat. His program for a "Marxistic sociology," however, rejects all dialectical philosophy of history.[9] Its core is to "lay out the functional connections and causal links between the structures of the 'spirit' and culture, on the one side, and, on the other side, the social life stream, that is. . .the immediate socio-economic happenings" (Salomon 1926a: 508, cit. Matthiesen 1988: 319). Like Mannheim's thought, then, that of Salomon originates in a dual orientation, first, to a crisis in culture traceable to the paradoxical consequences of the soul's creative work, and, second, to a realistic sociology of modern social relations, strongly influenced by Max Weber. Like Mannheim too, he soon veers sharply from romantic or revolutionary approaches that dramatize the former problem at the expense of the latter task.[10] The cultural questions must be moderated so as to encompass them within the realities unfolded by social theory. The sociological interpretation of philosophy, art, and religion, as well as of structures of social interpretation, plays a central role in their social theorizing, and its primary payoff takes the form of education for realistic practical judgment, notably in the domain of politics.

Salomon begins his explanation of the political cultivation aimed at by the domestic program of the Hochschule by situating the older humanistic cultivation in the transitional historical space between the patriarchal and bourgeois epochs. With the complete establishment of the capitalist order, then, this classical ideal of personal fulfillment gives way to constantly escalating standards of maximal performance, epitomized in the unprecedented notion of record shattering. The university adapts to the historically mandated need to train for expertise, depersonalizing its education, with the result that "the active sense of cultivation, in the Goethean sense of forming and shaping human powers into a personal unity, altogether disappears " (Salomon 1931: 96). Salomon admiringly cites the grand pathos with which Max Weber confronts enthusiastic and rebellious youths in 1918 with the demand that they recognize the inescapableness of unconditional commitment to objectified specialized bodies of knowledge as integral to a cultivated vocation, yet he also points out that Weber's injunctions are undermined by the realities that they insist on acknowledging. Specialization and technicization work against commitment as a source of meaning. Weber's "calling" is reduced in fact to an occupational category. This dilemma explains the tendency of modern ideologies to ascribe meaning to forms of action that are without intrinsic meaning to the individuals engaged in them, although this stratagem fails, in Salomon's judgment, to resolve the tension between specialization and fulfillment. Catholicism retains some of the capacities of the corporate past to link a place in the status order with an experienced social ideal, but it is fading, and the life-forms of organized capitalism, its organizations and parties, are experienced as mere functional instruments. Only the trade unions and parties of the working class differ in this. Despite distracting scientistic ideologies, they offer dedicated individuals "an identity of experienced life with objective work for the ideal," and thus a chance "to live its truth and to demonstrate it in their own person" (Salomon 1931: 98). Yet Salomon does not leave the argument at this seeming reversion from Weber's concept of "calling" to a Marxist conception of the proletarian mission, as his one-time mentor, Georg Lukács, clearly did (Lukács [1924] 1971).

Profound personal cultivation, he maintains, pertains more broadly to "political man," as he is the pedagogical objective of the Hochschule für Politik. The program is by no means designed to impart specialized technical knowledge, and it is not limited to leaders. Salomon furthermore agrees with Weber that it is impossible to impart by any education the underlying qualities that direct individuals to participation in the struggle for power, that is, active partisanship, but he insists that, given such qualities, persons can be schooled to responsibility. The presupposed essential qualities themselves have to be awakened and articulated through such education. The fate of German democracy depends on it. Political cultivation in this sense aims, above all, to foster the "intellectual conscientiousness" requisite to judgments that weigh decisions by the full consequences of the actions taken, without which there cannot be the courage, for example, to prefer long-term goods, such as the interest of the state, to immediate objectives, even when the latter accord with the ardent wishes or solemn principles of one's political following. If political education begins with partisanship, it aims to foster a mental and emotional disposition to act beyond party, where party is constricting.

Salomon highlights two courses of political education, corresponding to his own offerings at the Hochschule. Focusing mainly on issues in constitutional politics, he argues first for a sociological approach to organizational forms, situating the constitutive conduct in the designs of society as a whole, in the given historical moment. The transmutation of the constitutional clause on parliamentary non-confidence votes (Brunet 1922: 309) into a practice of sweeping delegation, for example, cannot be understood by formalistic commentary on the basic law, as Salomon credits Carl Schmitt with showing, but becomes clear to a sociological examination of both the norm and the practice. Supplemented by comparative studies of comparable elements in successfully functioning democracies, Salomon maintains, the sociological analysis opens onto a critique of discrepancies between the justificatory objective of institutions and their practical reality, as well as an informed exploration of legal reform. Again, the point is not to use the teaching situation to advocate one or another set of political values, but to condition the quality of political judgments.

The second emphasis of political sociology as political education, accordingly, is "the relationship between political ideas and their effectiveness, their relationship to society as a whole " (Salomon 1931: 106). Salomon again cites Schmitt as a pioneer in showing that the ideas that the different social strata advance serve them in historically appropriate ways either to safeguard or to revolutionize the ruling ideas of the age. Yet he thinks that Schmitt's disjunctive understanding of the dynamic character of ideas at any given time as a stark determination of friend or foe is too simple. The legacy of past ideas in the present allows for anomalous formations, such as National Socialist ideology, which utilize old ideas—pre-capitalist ones, in this case—for revolutionary purposes. The aim is to build a nuanced stylistic history of political consciousness, alert to the fact that sets of ideas not only express the life-forms of the respective strata but also articulate the revelations and myths they aim to promote.

Such a sociological and historical understanding, he contends, invariably raises the question of true and false consciousness of an age. Salomon cautions, however, that this question is beyond the limit of scientific study. It shifts matters from the process of scientific imputation to the political attitude of observers. Salomon acknowledges that history and the social sciences in general are affected by political positions, but he denies that this difficulty licenses a politicization of cultivation. Referring to Mannheim's "Politics as Science" essay and the debate around it, he insists that scientific truth cannot be reached through a summation of political approaches, the solution he evidently imputes to Mannheim, but only by relying on the approach "that offers the greatest opportunity for knowledge because it stands closest to reality" (Salomon 1931: 108).[11]

Political sociology contributes to political cultivation, then, not because it guarantees meanings for political orientation, as Catholicism and the major ideologies purport to do, according to Salomon, but because of its effects on the ways in which individuals hold the partisan political commitments that first open them to political schooling. As noted, the sociological understanding of the life-forms of politics makes for a sophisticated and subtle reading of the layered forces operative in political life, an understanding that, in itself, effectively precludes doctrinaire arbitrariness, and it imparts a dynamic understanding of one's own standpoint and thus of the ramifications of one's actions for the constellation as a whole. The political person knows what he is doing. Salomon contends that this requires a breaking down of the "barricaded enclosures" set up by political parties, an isolation oddly reinforced, in his view, by historical German mental habits of self-satisfied inwardness or utopianism. Political cultivation ultimately hopes to foster a demanding and perpetually unsettled conscience.

Conscience manifests itself in the clash between responsibility and conviction, whose elements, according to Salomon, have never been better portrayed than by Max Weber. It is the uncertainty that comes about when individuals are freed from the rigid concepts of party life, standardized for mass democratic mobilization that opens individuals to the direct look at reality which is the only possible source of a "living and creative language" of politics.

In his study of Max Weber, Salomon contends that for Weber sociology ultimately came down to a method for engaging in historical and contemporary studies. That the posthumous *Economy and Society* did not constitute a system, he argues, was not an accidental effect of his early death, but a necessary consequence of his approach (Salomon 1926a; Salomon 1934–5). But Mannheim, he pointed out, "felt that it was his duty to systematize and integrate Weber's suggestions, ideas, and methodological principles in order to put forth convincingly the claims of sociology. He wanted to demonstrate that sociology has systematic unity and cohesion . . ." (Salomon 1947: 353). In his late writings, Salomon considered this ambition a key to what he considered to be the fatal fault of Mannheim's theory of sociology, its aim to displace philosophy as the basic science, but even earlier, he kept his distance from the struggles for disciplinary legitimacy. At the Hochschule and in his subsequent position in a training school for vocational teachers, he could characterize his work as "practical sociology" and evade the question of sociology's place among the university disciplines. His claims about sociology and political education, accordingly, were context specific. Mannheim was concerned to speak for the discipline and these larger claims compelled him to face quite different challenges.

Competition: Karl Mannheim and Leopold von Wiese

For Mannheim, the problem of political education was inseparable from the institutional constitution of sociology, both as scientific discipline and as academic subject. Despite the variety of scholarly and popular writing invoking the term since the beginning of the century and the debate about it in relation to university policy and curricular design during the 1920s, sociology was poorly delimited. There were no chairs of sociology in German universities at all until the early Republic, when Becker was able to establish a number, beginning with the professorship in Frankfurt that Mannheim would occupy after Franz Oppenheimer's short tenure. By 1933 there were fifteen chairs at eleven different universities and a total of fifty-five full—or part-time teachers of sociology.[12] But these appointments hardly achieved a thorough institutionalization of the discipline. The new chairs were mostly attached to other disciplines, such as national economy, or they were located in institutes that were not integral parts of the universities. In addition, there were serious divisions among sociologists themselves about the boundaries, methods, and objectives of the discipline. No one emerged to define the field as Emile Durkheim had done in France. Sociologists conjured with the name of Max Weber, but he had never called himself a sociologist and had not supported the call for sociology chairs. The three most prominent survivors among the self-styled sociologists, Ferdinand Tönnies, Werner Sombart, and Alfred Weber, were unable to build distinctly sociological institutional bases (Stölting 1986: 105–117; Lepsius 1987: 39–40; Käsler 1983: 237, 266). The sociologist who achieved the greatest degree of institutional success during the Republic was Leopold von Wiese, slightly younger than the others but already active in the decades before the war. From one point of view, Mannheim's efforts in the discipline between 1928 and 1932, although tactically cautious in consideration of the older man's initial advantage, may be understood as a strategic competition with von Wiese.[13]

Von Wiese's position as a formally recognized sociologist was actually indeterminate enough to be representative of the uncertain status of the sociological enterprise as a whole. He came to Cologne in 1914, after several short-term appointments and a time in a training institute for adult education instructors, and he joined the municipal commercial academy as professor of sociology and economic policy science (*wirtschaftliche Staatswissenschaft*). During the last year of the war, in a political move, Konrad Adenauer, the mayor of Cologne, persuaded the local council to establish an institute for the scientific study of the social question. The Institute of Social Sciences was to have been divided into three sections, corresponding to the conceptualizations of that key political issue in the three principal parties that Adenauer wanted to hold in coalition. For his own Catholic Center party, there was a social policy section; for the Social Democrats, a section for social law; and for the Liberals, a section for studies in social economic policy (*Sozialwirtschaft*). In the event, the personnel decisions revised the design and led to a consequential relabeling. While the social law section was not staffed until 1930, the section intended to meet liberal interests was shared by von Wiese, an outspoken liberal in his economic writings, and Max Scheler, close at the time to Catholic social perspectives; and the section was named the sociological section, perhaps because the vague term was thought to encompass this combination. Despite periodic doubts among city administrators about the justification for its continued independent existence, especially since neither von Wiese nor Scheler had any interest in researching the social information that the officials sought, the sociological division was not linked to the municipal University of Cologne when the commercial academy was upgraded a few months after the institute's founding (Alemann 1981). The institute was, in any case, a very modest affair. Each of the "directors" had no more than a single assistant and a share of a secretary. But von Wiese combined his control over the university's Sociological Seminar and his directorship in the institute to transform himself into the leading figure in the institutional life of sociology in Germany, in the name of a program of complete autonomy for the discipline as a specialized field. While his seminar at the university provided him with a core of devoted students, originally attracted to an institution without academic traditions and overwhelmingly oriented to practical training, the institute provided facilities for the administration of the German Sociological Association and for a carefully targeted publication program (von Wiese 1920: 349; Alemann 1981; Liebersohn 1982: 124, 141; Stölting 1986: 168–170). As executive secretary of the Association under the largely ceremonial presidency of Ferdinand Tönnies throughout the Weimar years, he exercised a large measure of control over the biannual meetings, and he felt increasingly confident in using his position to exclude voices hostile to his program for delimiting and legitimating the discipline. Despite continuing overlaps in membership between the Association and the Social Policy Association, moreover, von Wiese worked effectively to exclude policy themes. Full membership was limited to 100, with formal academic rank an important criterion, and the executive exercised exceptional control (König 1987: 351–2). The quarterly journal of the institute, initially alternating between social policy and sociology issues, was divided in 1923, and von Wiese was able to bring out the first German journal dedicated exclusively to sociology, the *Kölner Vierteljahrshefte für Soziologie*. The official organ for the German Sociological Association, the journal regularly contained, in addition to von Wiese's reports on organizational plans and a review of sociological literature, a section of articles under the rubric of von Wiese's "relational" sociology. According to Alemann, von Wiese's extraordinary management of his resources enabled him to serve as "gatekeeper" for the profession (Alemann 1981: 359).

From the time of his arrival in Cologne, von Wiese's program was single-minded and consistent. As he wrote in his memoirs, one of his primary goals at Cologne was "the creation of a clearly demarcated specialized science of sociology and the corresponding instructional subject-field [*Lehrfach*]" (quoted in Alemann 1981: 359). Thus, von Wiese responded to the Becker-von Below controversy about sociology in the universities in 1920 by siding with neither man. His aim was to reject the whole political dimension of the dispute. Von Below was wrong to identify sociology with socialism and to deny that it could be a separate discipline, he maintained, but Becker was also wrong to portray sociology as a universal science for the political education of citizens.[14] Instead, von Wiese portrayed sociology as a specialized science (*Einzelwissenschaft*), a study of the forms of sociation with no larger claim to synthetic orientation (von Wiese 1920: 347–350). He agreed with von Below that content-rich sociological knowledge demanded research in all disciplines of the cultural sciences, as well as some of the natural sciences, but he contended that grounded knowledge of concrete factual interrelationships presupposed a elaboration of a distinctly sociological type of abstraction. No other discipline asked systematic questions about the forms of social relations. The study of forms, moreover, freed sociologists from the wild speculation of the philosophy of history that made sociology appear to be not only undisciplined but also politically suspect (von Wiese 1920: 357, 363–366). As he began to develop his doctrine, von Wiese substituted the term "relations" (*Beziehung*) for Simmel's "form," to avoid some of the misunderstandings concerning the contrast of form and content.[15] The task of the discipline, he wrote, was "to describe, analyze, group, measure and systematize social relations" (Von Wiese 1921: 48–49).

Von Wiese's principal sociological writings, anticipated in his journal articles and elaborated by his students, were a two-part systematic treatise (1924, 1928, 1933), encompassing his doctrines of social relations and social formations, and a critical history of sociology ([1931] 1960), judging past writers unapologetically by the standards of "relational" and "general" sociology, by which he meant his own system.

Unlike Simmel, whose formal sociology was an expressly problematic dimension of a reflexive context defined by philosophical questions, von Wiese denied that sociology as a discipline could go behind its constitutive categories, which are to be generated logically from the fundamental contrast between "together" and "apart." [16] Social happenings were to be distinguished and classified according to a complex conceptual grid, focusing on types of relations as well as patterned formations. Although von Wiese spoke of quantification and utilized mathematical notations, his statements were generally understood as definitional only, as in his general formula for the situational component of social processes (to select a concept that was also important to Mannheim), $S = U \times H$, where U refers to the material environment and H equals the attitude of the participants other than the actor. Despite admiration for his industry (and respect for his power), von Wiese made few converts to his sovereign terminological decrees among his peers, since most of them devised their own systems.[17] Alemann summarizes the consensus of post–1945 German sociologists when he treats von Wiese's system as a laborious and ingenious attempt to devise a "realistic reproduction of social processes in a comprehensive morphology," fatally lacking in testable explanatory propositions about either structure or function (Alemann 1981: 361).[18]

For present purposes, von Wiese's method can best be illustrated by his 1928 paper on "Competition," the presentation to the Sixth Meeting of the German Sociological Association, where his co-presenter was Karl Mannheim. This illustrates not only von Wiese's classificatory project but also the clash between the professions of his rigorous adherence to Max Weber's principles of value-free social science and the logic of rhetorical performance, which leads von Wiese to several revealing political evaluations. He starts by challenging the equation of all competition with its appearance in the capitalist economic system and its consequent rejection by critics of capitalism. Relations doctrine aims for distance from old controversies, a new start. Competition in all its manifestations is to be understood as a distinctive way of performing the function of social ordering, which "consists in consigning individuals or groups to their sphere of operations and to delimiting these operations" (von Wiese 1929b: 15). Oddly, von Wiese specifies competition, not by an analytical model but first by means of a clumsy metaphor and second by contrast with the fixed caste order of Indian *dharma*, which he likens to a cemetery, and the hierarchical feudal status order. Competition is pictured as a complex of ladders, with climbers scaling the heights or falling, and interdependencies among those who rise and those who decline visualized by lines linking them to one another. Competition is next termed "the Yankee system" and epitomized in the concept of an "experimental" ordering, presumably in the sense of trial and error.

During the Empire, von Wiese had subscribed to a cultural individualism whose "demands were inner self-determination, freedom of thought, feeling and will, and a social order furthering this culture of soul and spirit" (quoted in Liebersohn 1982: 133). Unlike many of his colleagues, he saw the Prussian bureaucratic state as hostile to this individualism and called for the restraint of governmental programs that interfered with the individual's freedom. Von Wiese's political preferences were liberal, but, like many continental liberals, especially in the business community with which he had close ties, he was not in favor of parliamentary government or democratic reforms (Liebersohn 1982: 133–135). When the Empire disappeared in 1918, von Wiese directed his suspicions toward the new democratic state: "The power struggle against 'agrarians and Junkers' seems more important to it [democracy] than the representation of personal values and rights against state and society" (quoted in Liebersohn 1982: 140). These views are quite evident in his "Competition" submission.

A drawback to the Yankee system, he contends, is that the attributes selected as decisive for advancement are a function not of genuine "quality" but only of "demand." While competition is not conflict or warfare, he insists, it can nevertheless turn into one or the other. Yet what counts, above all, against competition as an ordering mechanism is not harm to the losers but dangers to persons of quality by competition from below, with the attendant uses of underbidding, clique manipulation, and belittling rumor-mongering resulting in cynicism and the discouragement of the conscientious. Intellectual workers, for example, are in a chaotic competition of this sort, von Wiese maintains. The answer, he contends, is a cartel arrangement, constituted in accordance with a "golden rule" to keep competition within bounds. In his opinion, von Wiese concludes, the gains and losses of competition balance out, but the mechanism should be invoked in moderation. With traditional ordering mechanisms everywhere suppressed by democracy and socialism, competition must be supplemented by recourse to both statute and bureaucracy. Von Wiese closes with a literary fable to illustrate his injunction to avoid completely free competition, which would favor opportunism, or its total elimination, which would be in any case impossible. Even allowing for the rhetorical traditions of public lecturing at the time, it remains striking how far this performance deviates from von Wiese's programmatic scientific asceticism, and yet it is his program rather than his practice of sociology that he has been seen to defend against competition from Mannheim and others who came, as it were, from below.

Dirk Käsler sees von Wiese as representative of a general movement in the human sciences, and especially sociology, toward "scientization" (*Verwissenschaftlichung*) and depolitization. He explains it by the eagerness of socially unestablished sociologists to secure their place within the academic mainstream as quickly as possible (Käsler 1984: 250–263, 442). Perhaps this claim should be taken with some caution. The program of sociology as a specialized and value-free science, essentially coterminous with university-based production, may be understood, at least in part, as precisely the sort of exclusionary cartel "golden rule" that Von Wiese thought necessary to prevent "chaotic" competition in this intellectual field. Within the precincts of the cartel, however, the understandings could be more relaxed and conversations could be conducted as among cultivated gentlemen who understood one another perfectly well. Sociology had received massive support from the new political system in hopes that it could deal with the crisis of meaning in a way that the old human sciences could not. And there is no question that, as Käsler points out, most of these sociologists did not live up to their end of the bargain. In the statutes of the Association, if not consistently in their practice, they moved away from the interpretation of meaning (*Sinndeutung*) and the "social question" to more normative-indifferent, abstract "scientific" theories (*Gesetzlehre*), and they sought to exclude Marxist and cultural-sociological approaches that were concerned with the public interpretation of reality.

Mannheim tested these limits in his co-presentation on competition at the 1928 meetings by calling into question the assumptions upon which the dedication to value-free social science had rested. There are no records surviving to explain how it happened that von Wiese and the others in the directorate of the association gave Mannheim, lacking academic rank and being philosophically suspect, this prized and closely guarded opportunity. Because he had been offering provocative seminars on Georg Lukács' Marxist writings since he was licensed as *Privatdozent* at Heidelberg, his influential academic sponsors, notably Alfred Weber, cannot have been surprised either by his refusal to align simply with the front against Marxism or by his attention precisely to issues arising out of the public interpretation of reality. Two considerations doubtless weighed in his favor, putting aside his reputation for exceptional brilliance and his attractiveness to the younger generation whose allegiance to the authority of the Association had yet to be solidified. First, his publications in 1927 and 1928 differed from his earlier writings in adhering quite religiously to the limits of sociology as a specialized science (Mannheim [1927] 1953; Mannheim [1928] 1952; Kettler/Meja 1986). Second, the Association had made room for the Austro-Marxist, Max Adler, on the program of the first two meetings, perhaps as a gesture to the presumed preferences of the new cultural authorities, notably in Prussia, but his defiant equation of a genuine scientific attitude with "proletarian science" and his baiting of his critics had created a furore; and the selection of Mannheim may have been intended to show that the exclusion of Adler and others like him was an expression of professionalism rather than ideology. In the event, there was controversy enough after Mannheim's talk, including charges that he had violated the norms of the group, but it cannot be said that Mannheim's competitive move caused him harm. He took care, nevertheless, to protest in his closing remarks that the discussion had paid insufficient attention to the narrowly explanatory sociological findings contained in his presentation and to avow his intention "to put new life into the basic option in favor of value freedom" (Adler [1922] 1982: 401).

That "new life," in his view, required a sociological engagement with the competing public interpretations of reality, rather than the limitation of sociology to a specialist subject matter. Mannheim characterizes his treatment of this competition as consistent with von Wiese's "logical and systematic" explication of the concept, but the terms he uses to identify his own efforts in the presumed division of labor are both highly charged. He says that he is simply conducting an exercise in "applied" (*angewandte*) and "historical" sociology. Historical sociology was, in fact, an enterprise that von Wiese equated with cultural sociology and relegated to a sphere outside of sociology properly understood (von Wiese [1931] 1960: 38f), and "applied sociology," was a coinage of the Berlin theologian-turned-sociologist, Karl

Dunkmann, having nothing to do with the familiar meaning of the term, as when speaking of "applied science" in the sense of technology. It was also the title of the journal Dunkmann launched in the same year as Mannheim's talk, only the second periodical in the field, and thus inevitably a lively topic at the meetings in Zurich. "Applied sociology," in Dunkmann's sense was a reflexive sociology, a sociology applied to sociological knowledge (König 1987: 283–290) and prepared to pursue the question "that must have occurred to every sociologist," Dunkmann writes, "if his sociology is anything more to him than a mere investigation of formal relations between individuals" (Dunkmann [1927] 1982: 204). Mannheim certainly does not adopt Dunkmann's openly provocative stance towards von Wiese. His subsequent newspaper report of the event, in fact, celebrates the breakdown of internecine warfare among sociologists at the conference and hails a new era of cooperation among proponents of systematic, empirical, and historical-philosophical approaches, in a passage that von Wiese slyly quotes at length without endorsing in his introduction to the printed proceedings (Mannheim 1928; von Wiese 1929a: vii). Yet neither this cautious courtesy between a resourceful newcomer and the established power nor Mannheim's diplomatic incorporation of surface aspects of von Wiese's definition of competition (as the mildest form of "apartness," subject to deviations towards either harsher ones or togetherness) can disguise the radical differences between them.

Audaciously, Mannheim uses the theme of value-freedom in scientific social knowledge to illustrate, first, that even such basic methodological premises are differently conceived within the three distinct concentrated ideological "worlds" that have emerged through the very operation of competition upon the atomistic competition consequent to the disruption of the earlier church monopoly in the public interpretation of social existence; second, that it is possible to minimize but not to dispense with a political element in negotiating one's way among these alternatives; and third, that competition among them will tend towards a measure of synthesis, a common terrain, but that this will never fully overcome the political tensions. Sociology, as Mannheim presents it, is such a synthetic domain, and its norm of value-freedom is consequently provisional and deeply problematic at the borderlines. If phenomenology of the spirit, as realized by Hegel, was the mission of the generation of the French Revolution, the present generation is destined to work out, instead, a sociology of the spirit; and this project expands organically from its original non-evaluative starting point across the boundaries of normative philosophical inquiries, notably epistemology. Mannheim professes Max Weber's methodological principles for the "factual inquiry" he considers central to sociology as a specialized discipline, and he joins his colleagues in disavowing "sociologism," but he treats this delimited and autonomous disciplinary space as a provisional constitution, upheld only by pragmatic considerations, notably the division of labor.[19]

Sociology's boundaries are permeable not only where they abut on philosophy, it would appear, but also where the discipline emerges from the interpretive insights of literary intellectuals. Thus, in specifying the subject matter for his reflections on competition in the realm of the spirit, Mannheim proposes to limit himself to "thought linked to existence," explaining that this includes historical and political thought, the social and other cultural sciences, as well as the thinking of everyday practice. The concept itself, which might be thought to prejudge many philosophical questions, is brusquely presented as corresponding to a self-evident fact, on the authority of Wilhelm Dilthey. In answering the question why differing thoughts linked to existence might be thought to be in competition, moreover, Mannheim draws on Heidegger to aver that different social actors not only postulate a distinctive "world" for themselves but also seek to have that "world" serve as the "public interpretation of existence." The reception of Dilthey and Heidegger in this context is not technical. The point is, rather, that sociology is the place where questions widely recognized among the cultivated are best addressed. It is itself a competitor among the interpretations, arising out of vital interests in social life and contributing its own set of pervasive meanings. But the interests in question look beyond the clash of the combative social forces of class, and the meanings aspire to synthesis.

The possibility of synthesis arises out of the operations of competition itself. Mannheim illustrates this conception at the instance of value freedom in the context of the concentrated competition of the ideological epoch. Following Carl Schmitt, he contends that the conception of value-freedom arises out of the liberal valorization of discussion and the consequent segregation of all questions not resolvable by rational discussion into a category of the irrational. Conservatives, in contrast, find multiple incommensurable world views rather than a uniform reason. Socialists draw on both competitors, claiming the scientific reason of the liberals for themselves but characterizing the views of their opponents as irrational expressions of their calculable interests. Mannheim does not work through the social and political side of the generation of a synthesis out of this competition, but he insists firmly that there cannot be a totally unpolitical generation of relative objectivity in social analysis. The determination to make the effort must have a political dimension if only because the very question whether there needs to be an analytical grasp of these issues rather than a morphological contemplation of them is bound to the contending standpoints. But the need for such political judgment is not decisionism, in Schmitt's sense. The contest among styles of thinking has a dimension where performance counts. The competing groups adopt each other's most effective achievements, as measured by usefulness for practical orientation. The aspiration to synthesis consequently has a cumulative common store of political knowledge upon which it can draw. Hegel's phenomenology of the spirit prefigures the possibilities open to the sociology of the spirit that is to come, as noted, while sociology of knowledge provides the essential analysis to link and to distinguish the spheres of theory and practice.

Mannheim locates the sociopolitical sources of the drive to synthesis in the intelligentsia, whose mission is central to the argument of his essay on politics as science, first published in *Ideology and Utopia* in 1929 but already delivered in some form as a lecture in February of 1927 (Blomert 1999: 139–40), more than a year before his Zurich talk. The complementarity between the texts becomes clear when they are related to the two Max Weber lectures to which they refer. The "Competition" paper takes "value-freedom" as its illustrative theme, negotiating throughout with Weber's "Science" essay, while "Politics as a Science" focuses on "theory and practice," with ultimate attention to Weber's question about the knowledge requisite to action in accordance with an ethic of responsibility, as posed in his "Politics" essay. In both essays, Mannheim contends that he is close to Weber, professing his spirit of realism and hostility to ideological abuse of scientific authority, but in both essays, too, he suggests that Weber overstates the separation between science and the dynamics of practical life. That this difference in degree amounts to a difference in kind is evident precisely from Mannheim's conception of political knowledge as a synthesis of ideological perspectives, his focus on the political tasks of the intellectual rather than on the distinct vocations of the scientist and politician, and his conception of political education.

For Max Weber, the contributions of science to the activities of the responsible politician are no doubt substantial, but they are not constitutive. Disciplined social knowledge can enhance social technologies and improve calculations of costs and benefits, and responsibility entails command of both kinds of capabilities. The pursuit of such knowledge, however, is a function of inquiry driven by an ascetic dedication to science, for its own sake. The politician comes to make use of it on the strength of following his own quite different daemon. For Mannheim, in contrast, the decisive contribution to political life comes with the intellectuals' pursuit of the self-clarification that leads them to sociology, notably political sociology. The sociologist of knowledge is an intellectual who is enacting a prime political role in the very act of elucidating ideologies. And an education in political sociology is thus simultaneously and inherently a cultivation of political responsibility. The point is not that the sociologist or sociologically educated student becomes a politician, but that the politician is exposed as a narrow if inescapable party operator whose effectiveness in the crisis is very much a function of the qualitative transformation in both public interpretations and public confrontations achievable by sociological education. Weber's heroic leadership personality, affected with charisma, is gone. Responsibility is a quality of a political mode to be implanted through an intergroup style of political life and action.

Like Salomon, then, Mannheim is oriented to a less plebiscitarian conception of democracy than Weber. His conception of political education is nevertheless both more ambitious and more differentiated than that of Salomon. The ambitiousness does not, however, consist of a hope for sociological system, as Salomon thought, but of a stronger link between knowledge and judgment. Salomon, having stressed the educational importance of social critique of ideologies, concludes,

> It is only on the basis [of such informed uncertainty] that it is possible to create the political conscience-searching, the resolute responsibility, and spiritual honesty without which a political life cannot be thought.... The path leads through the most acute self-criticism and searching of conscience, as well as the passionate determination to be faithful to reality. (Salomon 1931: 110)

Mannheim, too, postulates "a form of political education which presupposes a relatively free choice among alternatives," but he contends that sociology can provide the "level of consciousness" uniquely appropriate to politics at the "present stage of intellectual development," a thinking "in terms of structural situations" (Mannheim 1936: 157). It is a conception reminiscent of the humanist image of the statesman with foresight and perspicuity, notably that of Machiavelli. Mannheim writes,

> This ability to reorient oneself anew to an ever newly forming constellation of factors constitutes the essential practical capacity of the type of mind which is constantly seeking orientation for action. To awaken this capacity, to keep it alert, and to make it effective with reference to the material at hand is the specific task of political education. (Mannheim 1936: 157)

While Salomon intended his design specifically for individuals with a prior commitment to politics, Mannheim saw political education as reaching far beyond this group, to extend, first, to the intelligentsia aspiring to cultivation, for whom sociology was the apt form of self-awareness, and second, if only indirectly, to the democratic masses as a whole.[20] For Mannheim, cultivation was inherently open to sociology, and sociology was inherently open to politics, at least in the age of partisan democracy and ideology. There are implicit qualifications to this general view, but these did not become prominent in Mannheim's thought until he was confronted more directly with the thoroughly politicized sociology of the Left and—especially—the Right. Setting those limits is an important theme in his 1930 class lectures and his 1932 address to sociology teachers (Mannheim 1932a, translated in Mannheim 2001).

The activist element in Mannheim's conception of political education extends to the communicative methods he considers appropriate to this instruction. Mannheim recalls the Romantic criticism that the academic lecture is characteristic of the intellectualism culminating in liberalism, and he evokes the educational achievements that workshops like the Bauhaus derive from the traditions of dissenting sects and conventicles. In view of the technical complexity of present-day politics and the relevance of "civilizing" sciences, in Alfred Weber's sense, he does not think that the more systematic transmission of information can be altogether dispensed with, but he calls for a "realistic mediation" between it and more personal modes of teaching (Mannheim 1936: 162). Even the parties have seen the need to move beyond education within the confines of clubs and to found party schools. For Mannheim, however, such schooling is too restrictive. In an uncharacteristically vehement outburst, he rejects the idea that political education adequate to the sphere of action must take the form of partisan indoctrination. Somehow, he insists, there must be a way of educating intellectuals who are relatively free to choose their politics on the basis of a comprehensive orientation that is not closed to criticism (Mannheim 1936: 163). This "new mode of active orientation to life" can be taught. He writes,

> Thus it seems certain that the interrelations in the specifically political sphere can be understood only in the course of discussion, the parties to which represent real forces in social life. There is no doubt, for example, that in order to develop the capacity for active orientation, the teaching procedure must concentrate on events that are immediate and actual, and in which the student has an opportunity to participate. There is no more favorable opportunity for gaining insight into the peculiar structure of the realm of politics than by grappling with one's opponents about the most vital and immediate issues because on such occasions contradictory forces and points of view existing in a given period find expression. (Mannheim 1936: 164)

Blomert points out well that Mannheim's conception differs from Max Weber's most markedly in attempting to incorporate in education precisely that element of "experience" that the elder Weber sought to extirpate, but he is probably mistaken in identifying Mannheim's scheme too closely with Alfred Weber's provision of a student discussion forum in conjunction with the Heidelberg Institute with which Mannheim was associated (cp. Demm 1999: 108–9). Max Weber was not averse himself to such organizations, as witness the fact that his two famous addresses were delivered in just such forums. There is, in any case, no record of a Frankfurt program of guest appearances by public figures that in any way resembles Alfred Weber's scheme at Heidelberg. Mannheim intends a closer integration of pedagogy and the elaboration of political choices. In some important measure, at least, the classroom and its extensions into intellectual life are themselves to be the locus for the competition that generates a growing common store of practical knowledge; education in "politics as a science" is to constitute the "platform" no longer available in parliament or in the public sphere. As Mannheim's conduct in Zürich shows, however, he is not at all prepared to stake everything on this most ambitious practical hope. Like the transition to epistemology and evaluation, the unfolding of the broader political meaning of sociology belongs to the borderland. Except for the transcript of a joint seminar with Alfred Weber, to be discussed below, there are no records of Mannheim's classes in discussion format. Information about any attempts he may have made to implement in the fullest sense his design for a "realistic mediation" between systematic and personal instruction must be indirect.

There are suggestions in Norbert Elias' memoirs (Elias 1994; cp. Sallis-Freudenthal 1977) that Mannheim delegated the close work with students to Elias and other assistants, but there is also evidence of painstaking attention. In the personal archives of Nina Rubinstein, a Mannheim student from 1928 to 1933, there are repeated drafts of her dissertation project, beginning with a seminar presentation, and these are all corrected in Mannheim's hand (Rubinstein 1999). Her recollections were colored by a deep sense of personal regard and closeness. Kurt H. Wolff also speaks of Mannheim's intimacy with the students (Endreß/Srubar 2000).[21]

A remarkable testimonial is contained in the tribute composed by Mannheim's Heidelberg students for his leave-taking in 1930. "'The Clouds' or 'Politics as Science'" caricatures Mannheim's equivocations between progressive and conservative political conceptions, his hope that exposé can pacify conflicts, and his exhortational assurances that intellectuals can rise in society by practicing their vocation. The subtitle of the parody answers Mannheim's title-question in the central essay of *Ideology and Utopia* (1929, 1936): "Is Politics as Science Possible?" The skit mocks up the "platform" that Mannheim desiderates in that essay, the "free space" mentioned in his Frankfurt lectures, where new social formations constitute themselves. At its heart is Socrates suspended (*schwebend*) in a hammock, archetype of the "socially unattached intellectuals" (*freischwebende Intelligenz*) of Mannheim's theory. In a twist on Aristophanes' story, this mentor promises success (*Erfolg*) and upward mobility (*Aufstieg*) through mastery of scientific politics, invoking three more Mannheimian motifs suspect to his admirers. Such mastery presupposes a regenerative insight (*Umbruch*) into the universality of partisanship. A despondent father brings his failed son for instruction, and the novice gains instant elevation above ideology. The story ends in burlesque confusion, set off by the telephone as *deus ex machina*, literally calling Socrates away. Apart from the principals and antiphonal choruses—the deracinated intellectuals and the rooted existences—the cast features a twosome named for the most leftist students in the group, Richard Löwenthal and Boris Goldenberg. Five quatrains rehearse their experiences as "Socrates' products, the heirs of his spiritual force." No one, they declaim, could have been more willing to swallow "politics as science." They honored Socrates and attended his school so he might teach them the dialectics "that gives power over the masses." To strengthen them in debate, they say, Socrates taught them "above all, the newest terminology." They learned about political perspectivism: "Shamed, the layman must keep still, when we teach him how he thinks." Their conclusion teasingly anticipates the ultimate doubt that haunts the memoirs later written by several of the student intellectuals on whom Mannheim had counted most (Elias 1984: 32–36; Speier 1989: 35–49): "Once this wisdom has dissolved science as well as religion," they rhyme in witty German jingles, "dissolution also gently overtakes the master's own design."

The criticism is consistent with the combative seminar culture encouraged by Alfred Weber (Demm 1999: 90–91), and the students' confidence that Mannheim would welcome the jibes along with the affection testifies to Mannheim's early adherence to the principle of openness he later credits to Alfred Weber in a letter on his seventieth birthday (Mannheim 1996; Mannheim 2001). Except for Elias, whose political engagement was marginal and who was remarkable above all for his interest in Zionism, the major contributors were committed Leftists, several of them Mensheviks and others close to the Communist student movement. In their satirical way, they recognized the political core of the education Mannheim attempted to offer.

Mannheim restated his conception of education for politics at the end of his Frankfurt years, on an occasion laden with multiple pathos. Writing to the Communist son of the more liberal of his Budapest mentors, Oscar Jászi, two weeks before Hitler's designation as chancellor, Mannheim describes the political dimension of the education he designed:

> What we can offer you is a rather intensive study group, close contact with the lecturers, but little dogmatic commitment, we do not think of ourselves as a political party but must act as if we had a lot of time and could calmly discuss the pros and cons of every matter. In addition, I think it is very important not merely to continually discuss dialectics but to look at things, carefully to observe individual problems and aspects of social reality rather than merely talking about them. (Mannheim to G. Jászi. January 16, 1933. CUL)

Mannheim's primary pedagogical activities were naturally directed to his lecture classes, especially after his Frankfurt appointment, rather than to his work with the inner circle of his students. Here too, however, he deviated from the formal lecture method that he identified with an overly academic approach to sociology. Mannheim distinguished between a "scholastic" method of presentation and one that is grounded in life. ("A Life-Based Methodology," Mannheim 2001).[22] While the former lays out its materials in accordance with a formal architectonic guided by universal principle, the latter is problem-oriented, connecting issues in the manner that they are encountered. The dual movement of sociological education, Mannheim maintains, is one of self-clarification and clarification of the situation, with the latter possible only on the strength of the former. As a first step, it is essential to eliminate the misinterpretations that are everywhere historically given. Sociology, he asserts, is not for those who have not suffered from such misinterpretations. He cites women, youth, and intellectuals, above all, alluding to the clash between the public interpretations of their situations and their own experiences, and calling on the students to recognize this discrepancy in their own lives. The substance of the courses, then, after these introductions, was largely historical, with the aim of developing a subtly articulated structural diagnosis of the times. In the essay on politics as a science, immediately after laying out the elements of political education, Mannheim had already emphasized the connections among the "new mode of active orientation to life," the search for "sociological structural relations," and a "new form of historiography." "Our present-day orientation to life cannot be complete," he wrote, "until it has appreciated its continuity with the past." Historical sociology and the practical study of the present are integrally connected and essential to sociology as a teaching subject.

Mannheim's convictions on this score led to a major difference with von Wiese in 1932, a disagreement whose public expression was only slightly moderated by their shared interest in having sociology present a united front towards the public educational authorities. The issue arose in the context of an effort to develop a common policy among all university sociology teachers to promote their interests under the conditions of the economic crisis. Von Wiese initiated the plan for a special professional meeting with this objective in early 1932, and Mannheim hastened to offer Frankfurt as the site (von Wiese 1931/2). According to von Wiese, the question of sociology as an academic subject had been explored in a series of meetings and publications since the beginning of the Weimar period, mostly under the auspices of the German Sociological Association and under the leadership of von Wiese himself. The idea of calling a special meeting for the end of February of 1932 arose after it was decided to postpone the regular biannual conference of the association until 1933. For von Wiese, the matter was urgent because the old emphasis on founding more chairs in sociology had been rendered irrelevant, first because of the unavailability of funds and, second, because of the scarcity of students in the programs already established. The latter problem was ascribed, by Mannheim as well as von Wiese, to the new tightening of specialization in cognate disciplines, especially through rigid requirements for mandatory examinations within the specialty. They decried this further transmutation of the university into a compartmentalized vocational institute, but accepted that sociology as a discipline would have to make some suitable adjustment in response, that is, to establish itself as a guild. The two primary items on the agenda in Frankfurt on February 29, 1932, then, were the relationships between sociology and various examination regimes and the qualifications of individuals who were properly entitled to be deemed teachers of sociology, given the continued loose use of that term.[23] In the latter connection, then, there was ultimately a resolution as well on the contents of sociology to be covered in courses and examined.

While von Wiese gave way to Mannheim on the location of the gathering, he tried not to take any chances with the organization of the meeting. Above all, he succeeded in dividing the meeting day into two parts. The first was restricted to the persons eligible to vote and designed to produce binding resolutions, while the second was open to all interested persons and precluded from taking any votes. Von Wiese kept the first session firmly in his own hands.[24] Mannheim's detailed and controversial presentation on the tasks of sociology as an academic subject (Mannheim 1932a; translation in Mannheim 2001) was relegated to the open forum, along with a talk on sociology and its cognate fields by Theodor Geiger. The submission of the resolutions to the various state ministries, universities, faculties, and examining bodies was also left to von Wiese, who incorporated his own article on the meeting (not excluding the section called "personal impressions") as a gloss on the decisive compromise concerning the relationship of systematic sociology to historical sociology, descriptive sociology, and the study of current issues (*Gegenwärtskunde*) in the sociology curriculum.

In his opening remarks, according to his subsequent report in his journal, von Wiese identified this as one of the two "danger-points," the other having to do with the undesirable by-products of introducing mandatory examinations, notably in the threat of attracting students oriented to rote-learning. In his "personal impressions," von Wiese gave Mannheim full points for his analysis of this latter problem and described his own position as being fully in accord with Mannheim's reluctant approval of competing with other specialist guilds on their own terms. There was little such complaisance in von Wiese's defense of the primacy of system in sociology.

The question of historical sociology came down to a straight fight with Hans Freyer,[25] rather than Karl Mannheim. Von Wiese shrugged aside a proposal he ascribes to Mannheim, to operate with a rotation among systematic, historical, and concretely descriptive sociology. That would presuppose a discipline made up of distinct equal parts, "a dissection that is completely impossible from the standpoint of relations doctrine." The most he would concede is that both historical and contemporary materials will be called upon to exemplify the categories of the social. In the end, the compromise on this point used language that distinguished between the foundations and the concretization of the sociological subject matter, with both to be taught.[26] Freyer and von Wiese agreed that the mix of history and system would have to be left to the professor, provided that "the systematic sociologist must take notice of the historical development and the historical sociologist, of the categories of systematic sociology, each in the manner he deems best" (von Wiese 1931/1932: 447). When it came to the "more threatening" question of instruction in current issues, however, von Wiese was altogether unbending. "Under no condition," he wrote, "must our discipline accept contents that are an accommodation to mere preferences, fashionableness or party interests." The fashion for instruction in current issues, in his view, arose from unwarranted concessions to the times. He wrote,

> It is clear that in a time that has so little sense for abstraction and conceptual rigor but is rich in highly contested practical problems there will be an inclination to substitute a free-ranging discussion for a rigorous theoretical system. If only in order to escape the feared reproach of being "remote from life," and to engage the active attention of students who are often quite unwilling to think but passionately moved by the currents of the time, and finally—and most important—in order to contribute one's own mite to the overcoming of the political and cultural emergencies, it is both necessary and desired at many universities to limit sociological theory and to give as much space as possible to current issues. . . and very soon

this tendency extends to taking evaluative positions on the issues of the day. I do not for a moment deny what is correct and necessary in these demands. But precisely because the temptation is so great, the dangers of superficiality, subjectivism, partisanship, and unscientific conduct that are inherent in this tendency must be fought off with all vigor. (von Wiese 1931/2: 448)

Von Wiese insisted that relations doctrine certainly meant to apply to concrete situations, but the leading position of systematic sociology cannot be abandoned. Under no condition can sociology heed any demands of the times, except insofar as these are fully reconcilable with the priority of timeless theory. The extent to which von Wiese's harsh argument, reminiscent of the recurrent charges against Becker's sociological enterprise, is directed against Mannheim becomes clear only through an examination of Mannheim's case for current issues study, contained in his talk at the afternoon session, his most elaborate statement on the links among sociology, political education, and cultivation (Mannheim [1932a] 2001).

Mannheim begins by calling into question the institutionalized achievements of German sociology, notably in its systematized form. The structure of a discipline, he maintains, is strongly dependent on the conditions of its origins and on the way it is systematized for instruction. Social studies in Germany are conditioned by Romanticism. They are strong on spirituality and historicity, but they are quite helpless in the face of the empirically rich subjects that are central, for example, to the constitution of sociology in France, such as the social formation of the individual. The best hope for sociology in Germany, then, is precisely to accommodate the extra-academic actors whose concrete experiences are generating the actual current need for sociology. This section of Mannheim's talk is organized by three criteria, two of which von Wiese obviously means to dismiss. The teaching of sociology, he contends, must be governed by threefold demands of the situation: the demands arising from the state of society, the state of teaching, and the state of research.

Social democratization is the single most important feature of the social situation. Sociological education must penetrate the mass of citizens if the democracy of understanding is not to be displaced by a riotous democracy of feeling. What sociology provides, above all, is the Machiavellian rationality that has historically allowed elites to balance their pursuit of interests against the realities of essential constraints. Interests will continue to conflict, but a sociologically informed public will know when compromise is essential. Mannheim returns to Max Weber's question of values and choice. On the one hand, teaching is not to be limited to one political alternative, given the common core provided by Machiavellian insight. On the other hand, however, the awareness of the ineluctability of a volitional element in political knowledge is not to be taken as a license to celebrate wilfulness and arbitrariness. Sociology of knowledge remains in service of politics as science, and political education is its primary locus of operations. It is also its prime stimulus to self-correction and refinement. The encounter between sociology and concrete contemporary issues—the responsiveness to social need—enhances sociological theory; it does not, as von Wiese contends, diminish it.

From the standpoint of education, then, the approach to sociology by way of the study of current issues, serves cultivation (*Bildung*) without disdaining the modern need for specialization. Cultivation is only contingently tied to the subject matter of the old educational system. The meaning of humanistic cultivation as experience was a distinctive self-expansion of the breadth of personality and the deepening of experiential dimensions, and these may well arise today for new groups from different substructures. Mannheim contends,

> We can see that, without our having contributed much to it, a new type of genuine intelligentsia is arising spontaneously by virtue of the fact that there are ever more persons who are discovering, while wrestling with social problems, the problems of socialization and the social character of being human, and that this insight is leading them to just such a deeper understanding of self and expanded understanding of the world as quite differently situated themes of life did at an earlier time (Mannheim [1932a] 2001: 156).

It is this socially conscious intelligentsia who must be fostered through sociological teaching. This, according to Mannheim, is the unique contribution of sociology to cultivation, in the fullest sense. Like earlier forms of cultivation, sociological study also leads through history, a study that would otherwise be opaque to the current generation, and "the cultural aspect of the sociological problem complex becomes especially prominent if . . . one wishes also to include in the educational enterprise something for the cultivational dimension of modernity." The aspects of sociology that von Wiese finds most problematic, even where he grants them some conditional justification—historical, cultural, and problem-oriented sociology—thus belong together for Mannheim. They generate the rest of the curriculum.

In making this argument, however, Mannheim found himself compelled to draw back lest he be identified with the radical version of this case that was being made by the sociologists of the Right, especially Hans Freyer. From this standpoint, as events proved, he and von Wiese were ultimately joined by a common immersion in the older rationality. Fourteen months after the meeting in Frankfurt, Mannheim was involuntarily "retired" without pension. As a non-Jew, von Wiese fared better, but a year after the Frankfurt meeting he had to report that both his Institute and his journal had been shut down. Mannheim and von Wiese may have been the antagonists in a remarkable competition during the last five years of the Weimar Republic, but neither of them was among the winners in their generation.

Notes

1. Schluchter (1980: 236-241) dates the lectures and discusses their provenance. Buckmiller (1980: 20) summarizes the "pedagogical" objectives and programs of the Free Students. He points out that the organization sponsored lecture series in order to experiment with teaching situations directed towards cultivation rather than specialization, as well as democratic modes of conduct. For the sake of this "collective self-education," he writes, they organized "scientific sections. . . that were supposed to close the gap among individual disciplines and to further, to the greatest degree possible, the development of a personality of many-sided cultivation."
2. Note that we refer to "calling" rather than "vocation" in connection with Weber's lectures, although standard English translations prefer the Latin term, and we will naturally cite published versions by the translator's titles. Weber himself associates *"Beruf"* with "calling" in the first sentence of the chapter dealing with the concept (Weber 1958: 79; Weber 1922: 63). In "Science as a Vocation," Weber begins with a discussion of the scientific calling strictly in the sense of a career, but then changes direction: "But I believe that you actually wish to hear of something else, namely the inward calling for science" (Weber 1946: 134). The rest of the lecture, then, deals with the concept in its ethical sense. Whenever Weber directly addresses his audience in these texts, he should be understood, we think, to be speaking responsively to the members of the *Freien Studentenschaft*, whose cultivational aspirations were known to him from informal discussions. See Schluchter 1980.
3. It is instructive to compare Weber's approach to science teaching with the strikingly similar educational advocacy that John Stuart Mill derived from his philosophically moderated reading of Humboldt. See Mill 1977: II, 140-147.
4. See the articles by Kahler and Troeltsch in Lassman/Velody/Martins 1989: 35-46, 58-69.
5. In a letter supporting a Rockefeller grant to the *Hochschule für Politik* in 1932, the key official of the Foundation's Paris office writes: "as a teaching institution the Hochschule. . . is important in the promotion of the fundamental attitudes

which . . . count so heavily in the development of scientific work in the social field. . . . [It] has the objective attitude and scientific spirit in problems in the social sciences" (E.T. Gunn to E.E. Day, March 10, 1932. RF). The institution began with short courses and evening programs for officials, teachers, and employees of interested groups, but its two- to three-year certificate program became important enough to supply 2/3 of its audience by 1932. Students seeking university degrees submitted their theses and sat for examinations at the University of Berlin.

6. The institution was an important breeding ground for "realism" in thought about international politics. Arnold Wolfers, later the head of the Johns Hopkins Center of International Studies in Washington, was the Director, under Jäckh, and responsible for the research program underwritten by the Rockefeller Foundation after 1931. Jäckh's own blend of liberal politics and national advocacy made him a welcome spokesman for several years in the United States and at the Royal Institute for International Relations in London. The archives of the Rockefeller Foundation contain a series of German political analyses written by him, in part in confidence to the officers of the Foundation, ranging from the re-election of Hindenburg in 1932 to the first months of the Hitler regime. He portrayed himself as a confidante of the President, as well as of the three chancellors before Hitler, and he characterized Hindenburg as a heroic and loyal servant of the Weimar constitution, presenting all the dealings with Hitler as steps in a successful struggle to separate the "national" wing of the National Socialist movement from the Bolshevik and socialist one. "Papen," he explained in an address at Chatham House, London, in February, 1933, a few days after Hitler became chancellor, "is the man in the position of real power," having progressed far in "his historical mission to win over national-socialism for the service of the state." He wrote: "Hitler is chancellor in name, and Papen in reality. Hitler is in office, but not in power. . . . Far from being 'dictator' of this cabinet, Hitler might be termed, with very little exaggeration, its prisoner." Jäckh, it should be said, resigned as President rather than to dismiss his non-Aryan and Left staff, when the school was taken over, but he negotiated a settlement with Goebbels and Hitler that left the research division free, with himself as its President. "The national socialist Government has shown full appreciation of my decision. . .," Jäckh reported to the Sixth Conference of Institutions for the Scientific Study of International Relations on June 1, 1933, "and was therefore induced (after a private and intimate conversation which I had with Chancellor Hitler) to conduct the formalities of liquidating the Hochschule in a correct and generous spirit." Not immaterial to that generosity, as Jäckh reported after the war, was the generous financial support by the Rockefeller Foundation, amounting to 25 percent of the school's budget in 1932, and the commitment by the Foundation to continue its support through the first year of National Socialist rule. (Rockefeller Foundation Archives. RF1.1./ 717/19; Jäckh and Suhr 1952). Jäckh began as a journalist in Württemberg and moved to Berlin before World War I as head of the Alliance of German Craftsmen, evidently under the patronage of the industrialist, Robert Bosch, whom he served as a political advisor during the war years and into the 1920s (Heuss [1946] 1994). Among their joint ventures was support for an initiative by Alfred Weber and Friedrich Naumann in 1917, attempting to persuade Ludendorff to offer a peace settlement at the cost of claims on Belgium in return for Alsace Lorraine. The letter to Ludendorff was later signed as well by the heads of the three German trade unions at the time (Heuss [1946] 1994: 268). In the 1920s,

Jäckh led Bosch into association with New Commonwealth, an international organization promoting a global police force, that had been launched by a British coal magnate, Lord Davies.

7. In the notes assembled for a memoir that he did not live to write (SLB), Salomon recalls that he joined together with Georg Lukács, Emil Lederer, and Gustav Radbruch in 1912/13 "in the adventurous idea of doing something for the aesthetic future of film" by offering to write movie criticisms for the local newspaper. Salomon's relationship to Mannheim was complex. He recalls Mannheim and his wife with gratitude for many kindnesses and credits him (and Lederer) with intervening with Johnson to secure him his position at the New School in 1935. In the same notes, however, he also emphasizes their "fundamental disagreement" about the tasks of sociology, notably in the period of exile, where his own "theoretical-contemplative" attitude clashed with Mannheim's "pragmatic-political" one. This specification of their differences is put in doubt, at least for the Weimar years, when Salomon recalls with special pride that his acting editorship of the periodical, *Die Gesellschaft*, gave him an opportunity of publishing a "collective issue against Mannheim's *Ideologie und Utopie*—against the weakening of radical thought." In a review of the second volume of the *Jahrbuch für Soziologie* (1926), edited by Gottfried Salomon-Delatour (SLB), Salomon pairs Mannheim's essay on "The Sociological and Ideological Interpretation of Cultural Phenomena" with an essay by Salomon-Delatour called "Historical Materialism and the Theory of Ideology." He calls the former "the most important contribution to the methodology of cultural sociology appearing in recent years," but reserves judgment until Mannheim explains whether the social or immanent interpretation is supposed to give the appropriate determination of the essence of a cultural product. He is more reserved about the second contribution, proposing to wait until this first installment is continued. Leaving personal relations aside, the main point is, on the one hand, that Salomon sided with von Schelting against Mannheim on the question of value-freedom (see draft review in SLB), but, on the other, that he oriented to Mannheim in his programmatic statements about the relationship between political education and intellectuals. In a review of Carl Schmitt's admiring monograph on Hugo Preuss, written in 1931, Salomon quotes Preuss on the indispensability to a state under rule of law of a cultivated intelligentsia "over the walls of the party barracks" and concludes: "This role of the intelligentsia corresponds largely to the place that Mannheim assigns them in *Ideology und Utopia*, . . . the 'free-floating intelligentsia' that alone has a chance of true consciousness," adding only that at the time of writing it would be the SPD that could better represent German cultivation and spiritual freedom than any of the other parties, a point with which Mannheim would not have disagreed in 1931.

8. Salomon is more vehement than Mannheim in drawing the line between, on one side, elitist versions of humanism, whether presented as return to classical models or as Nietzschean breakthrough to a "New Man," and, on the other, the possibilities of a heroic model for a cultivation congruent with the democratic age. Salomon 1926b comprises a laudatory review-essay of Edgar Zilsel's Marxist critique of the concept of genius. In 1930, Salomon skewered a book by Friedrich Glum: "The Secret Germany," concluding that this pseudo-aristocratic concept was nothing but a utopian cover for bourgeois hostility to the labor movement. For the political uses of classical humanism in the end phase of the Weimar Republic, see Ehrlich/John 1998.

9. Salomon in effect accepts Weber's argument against Marxist *Weltanschauung*,

notably as it might be represented by Georg Lukács, as distinct from what we are calling his "Marxistic sociology," which he claims in 1926 to find effectively prefigured in Weber's own work. In addition to calling Weber a bourgeois Marx, he also refers to him as a "bourgeois Marxist." Salomon 1926a: 151. In the three-part series on Max Weber with which Salomon introduces himself—and Weber—to American scholars in 1934-5, he aligns himself wholeheartedly with Weber against Marxist "revolutionary sociology," a term he also uses against Karl Mannheim in his sharply critical but personally warm obituary notice, published in 1947 (Salomon 1934, 1935a, 1935b; Salomon 1947). Cp. Salomon 1936 (a reserved but not harsh review of Mannheim 1935).

10. Salomon's review of Alfred Weber's *Ideen zur Staats- und Kultursoziologie* (1927) in *Die Gesellschaft* (typescript in SLB) offers an especially forceful statement of his conviction that the "idealist" and "irrationalist humanist" reliance on "culture" as a lever against "civilization" cannot be defended. He compares Weber unfavorably not only with Marx but also with his brother Max, whom he credits with avoiding the infusion of ideologically charged value programs in the study of bourgeois civilization. There are some striking parallels between the details of his critique and Mannheim's arguments against Alfred Weber in their joint seminar (Mannheim [1929c] 2001), and a likelihood, to judge by Weber's reply that he identified Mannheim's position with Salomon's published views. See below.

11. Salomon's critique of Mannheim does not take away from the extent to which he shares Mannheim's diagnosis and analysis of the ideological field, despite his interesting decision to refer to Carl Schmitt rather than Mannheim at the key point. His reference here is evidently to Schmitt's *Political Theology* (1922) and *Die Geistesgeschichtliche Lage des modernen Parliamentarismus* (1923), since he follows his citation of Schmitt with a warning against turning to intellectualized history (*Geistesgeschichte*) instead of to a sociological understanding for the explanatory context. Since the conclusion of his implicit encounter with Mannheim is a veiled reference to "Marxistic" claims about the comparative scientific advantage of the proletariat, as put forward by Max Adler, whose conception of sociology he seems to be following, it is striking testimony to the power of Schmitt's reputation that Salomon preferred him to Kautsky or other Marxist writers as authority for the "dynamic" character of political ideas.

12. Stoltenberg 1926. A survey of sociology in Germany prepared by the Rockefeller Foundation staff in 1932 cites its German consultant, Fehling, as numbering the sociologists of importance in Germany at thirteen. The Foundation's inquiry found only three institutes and three seminars engaged in research worth noting, including von Wiese's sociological division of the Cologne Social Science Institute and Mannheim's Sociological Seminar in Frankfurt. The members of the older generation are not mentioned. Praised highly in this report, Mannheim's seminar is assessed more skeptically in Fehling's preliminary report on the grounds that "Mannheim's most advanced students go in for the historical-philosophical investigations." This official is clear, in any case, that the Rockefeller Foundation should not give active support to an institution in which Jews are so prominent, to avoid giving offense (RF 1.1./717/20/186 and RF RGB-1932/717/77/617). Alfred Weber's Institute at Heidelberg, it should be noted, is highly rated and strongly supported by the Rockefeller Foundation. The survey lists it under economics, but notes that the director, Weber, is a sociologist and that the institute covers all of the social sciences.

13. Strictly speaking, Wiese and Mannheim belonged to different generations, espe-

cially in the sense of Mannheim's study of the subject ([1928] 1993). In view of the generational challenge Mannheim will attempt to mount, König finds it ironic that von Wiese published Mannheim's paper in his closely held periodical (1987: 343).

14. Von Wiese wavered little in his insistence on the unpolitical character of sociology, even in an article published in 1936, when his consistency weakened his plea to the National Socialist cultural authorities to reconsider their dismissive treatment of the general sociology he represented, as manifested by the suspension of his journal and institute. He acknowledged that the flowering of sociology during the Weimar years had been furthered by the belief among friends of sociology close to Social Democratic ministries that there were close affinities between the discipline and Marxism, as well as by the designs of religious parties to foster a confessional sociology; but he insisted that these were "misunderstandings" and that genuine basic sociology has no necessary connection to its erstwhile political sponsors. The conception that sociology inclines against individualism simply by virtue of its focus on the social he treats more equivocally. On the one hand, he reserves the position that this judgment too is a one-sided distortion, but on the other, he pleads that this consideration should carry special weight now that socialism has been freed from "all ties to economic materialism, the principle of class-struggle, and its anti-national concomitants" (von Wiese 1936:16). If von Wiese may properly be assigned to the group of social scientists who spent the Nazi years in "inner emigration," it should also be noted that he was prepared to make arrangements with the authorities. He was never in opposition. For von Wiese and other sociologists in the Third Reich, see König 1987; Klingemann 1985; Klingemann 1986; Klingemann 1992; Zinn, 1992; Kettler/Meja 1995: 202-208.

15. We translate *"Lehre"* as "doctrine" rather than "theory" because of the emphasis on terminological refinement and logical classification. In this respect, as in some others, von Wiese's systematic writings resemble the black-letter treatises of positivist legal writers. As with those writers, too, there is the assumption of an order that is simply given, whose elements are to be expounded without considering questions of justification or change. The uses of treatises in the two cases, however, are too dissimilar to permit over-emphasis on the similarities. Hans Kelsen, for example, whose pure theory of law may be seen as a completion of the positivist legal project, used an empirical approach with strong Marxist elements when he turned to sociological analysis. See Kelsen 1920.

16. In his history of sociology, von Wiese treats Simmel as an inspirational but unsystematic genius. "In the main," he writes, "the relations doctrine takes up the threads of scientific research where Simmel let them drop in 1910 in favor of philosophical studies" ([1931] 1960: 135). This is not a claim that is widely accepted (cp. Tenbruck 1959).

17. Von Wiese had a better reception among the relatively small circle of American sociologists at the time who were eager to introduce a theoretical and systematic component into the wild variety of conceptually improvised empirical undertakings characteristic of American sociology in the 1920s and 1930s (cp. Kettler/ Meja 1995: 200-207, and literature there cited).

18. As von Wiese's colleague and successor at Cologne, René König limited himself to brief, context-specific evaluations of the systematic work, but his incidental remarks, for example, about von Wiese's contributions to Vierkandt's 1931 *Handbook of Sociology*, especially the lengthy article on the relations doctrine, which

he considered altogether unwarranted, are harsh (König 1987: 261). He suggests that the sixteen-page article should have been reduced to a one-page account in the context of Theodor Geiger's article on "Approaches."
19. See also Mannheim 1936: 78-87. Mannheim speaks of a gliding transition from the non-evaluative to the evaluative conception of ideology and he contends that this movement is evident not only in his own thinking but also more generally in the thought of his time: "We shall be forced eventually to assume an evaluative position" (83).
20. In this context, Mannheim challenged the ideal of contemplation in a manner reminiscent of Georg Lukács.
21. Nina Rubinstein preserved a fulsome letter of thanks for some flowers sent to Mannheim in 1930 during an illness. Mannheim addresses it to the "Mannheimer from Heidelberg," playing on a geographic pun originating with the students who accompanied him to Frankfurt. He claims that the gorgeous flowers propel him to recovery and inspire a resolve to have them all "ascend with him to a comparably exalted harmony [of nature and culture], quitting our discordant phase of skepticism." Below his signature, he announces that the teacher and sociologist in him cannot rest without assigning some questions about the distinctive qualities, historical precedents, and functions of groups like the "Mannheimer from Heidelberg." He exhorts them, "We shall have to transform the sociology of function [*Funktionssoziologie*] ever more into a sociology of mission [*Missionssoziologie*]." "Each of you is to write three pages on this," he demands. (NR: "Den Mannheimern aus Heidelberg," May 15, 1930). This passage and the text next following is adapted from Kettler/Meja 1995.
22. Mannheim speaks of a *lebenswissenschaftliche Methode*, a construction that would be mistranslated by any terms suggestive of "scientific" living. The point is rather that life defines the relevant sense of "science" or disciplined knowledge. That is why the concept is translated here as "life-based" method. See Mannheim 2001.
23. Von Wiese is insistent on the criteria for participation in the meeting, since the objective is to pass resolutions for submission to government ministries and the authority must be clear. Only individuals whose contracts of employment expressly mentioned sociology could participate and vote. Thirty-three teachers (*Dozenten*) were invited, and twenty-one attended, together with a number of assistants, without voting rights. Von Wiese takes no account of the fact that active membership in the German Sociological Association was in any case differently defined, and that there was probably this additional reason for the separate meeting of this ad hoc group.
24. After Mannheim's welcome to the group, according to the agenda published by von Wiese, von Wiese gave the initial report on the situation and he also reserved to himself the reports on the two most controversial issues, the curricula and examination requirements, as well as the qualifications for appointments in sociology. Mannheim and others reported on technical questions relating to specialized examination regimes (von Wiese 1931/1932: 442).
25. See below, p. 112f.
26. The compromise resolution, crafted by Alfred von Martin, read: "Sociology is to be taught, by means of lectures and tutorials (*Übungen*), in its theoretical foundations as well as in its concretization through historical and especially contemporary materials, and finally in its aspect of empirical observation and description" (von Wiese 1931/2: 130). Von Wiese found this acceptable because it retained

from his earlier resolutions of this question the formula of theoretical sociology as foundation.

5

The Challenge of Fascist Social Thought

Mannheim's opposition to the "intellectualism" associated with liberal thought, through his emphasis on irrational, ideological elements in even the most rational forms of social understanding, raised the question of his relationship to proto-fascist currents of thought in Weimar Germany, especially since he agreed with them in rejecting the privileged epistemological claims made by Marxists on behalf of the proletariat. On one level, the matter was quite simple. Mannheim unconditionally rejected the idea of an extra-rational route to binding truths, whether through revelation or through some alleged representation of national will, blood, or soul. Moreover, he was loyal to the Weimar constitution, hostile to the political schemes of the Right. The fervid fascist celebration of the deed, the myth, and the leader were all alien to him.[1] His thinking was both structural and reflexive, and in these respects, antithetical to the representative Fascists he examines in *Ideology and Utopia*, notably Mussolini. Writing in 1927-9, in his essay on politics as science, Mannheim treats Fascism as a temporary aberration, a blind perspective dependent on a transitory crisis of obstructed social change, the extreme disorientation of its clientele, and the astute manipulative technology of its outsider "putschist" elites, comprising deracinated intellectuals. Lacking a historical vision, it barely figures in the anticipated synthesis among liberal, conservative, and socialist political perspectives (Mannheim 1936: 119–123; Kettler/Meja 1995: 112–117; Loader 1985: 105–106).[2]

In the context of the debates about sociology as an academic subject, however, and especially about its place in cultivation, the writings of key authors that Mannheim identified with fascism after 1930 came too close to his own conceptions to be dismissed. The two most important figures for Mannheim are Hans Freyer and Carl Schmitt, although Heidegger is an acknowledged presence in the background. What Freyer and Schmitt bring is, first, an excoriating exposé of liberal thought and institutions, second, a radical diagnosis of crisis, and third, an elevation of political action to the highest urgency and consequently, especially for Freyer, a functional subordination of pedagogy to political education. "Cultivation [*Bildung*]," writes Freyer, in language that Mannheim could not easily dispute, "is the awakening and acquisition of an historical awareness of the situation" (Freyer 1931c: 625). Freyer's key concept of "actuality" (*Wirklichkeit*)—as in "sociology as a science grounded in actuality" (*Soziologie als Wirklichkeitswissenschaft* [1930])—figures importantly in Mannheim's own accounts of the method applied in his teaching. Mannheim's attempt to distinguish himself from these writers brings to the fore his aversion to radicalism, as well as his bent for mediated solutions, including a willingness to find common ground even with the proto-fascist writers whose ideas rest ultimately on the rejection of mediation and compromise.

Yet it is important to maintain historical perspective in thinking about the relationship between Weimar thinkers like Mannheim, on the republican Left, and figures who became important voices for National Socialism in the Hitler period. First, there was more political fluidity during the 1920s than Mannheim's thesis of the reign of total ideological awareness would lead us to expect. Like Schmitt, Freyer displayed hostility to the parliamentarist coalition during the war, and he joined heartily in the general trend from the enthusiasms of the youth movement to the "community of the trenches" of the "front generation" (Muller 1987: 46; Muller 1991: 697–698; Wolin 1992: 429, 433). Yet he was not simply a man of the Right. His call to the chair of sociology in Leipzig in 1924 came as a compromise between conservatives and socialists, after federal intervention against the left-wing coalition state government made it impossible for the Social Democratic minister of education to carry out his plan of appointing the Marxist Max Adler over the opposition of the faculty. Freyer evidently appeared acceptable to the moderate Left because he had referred to himself as a socialist after the war and because he was supported by the Prussian minister of education, Carl Heinrich Becker (Muller 1987: 137–141).[3] And this acceptance was in the polarized political atmosphere created not only by the harsh military repression in Saxony but also by the struggles in Bavaria, including Hitler's attempted putsch.

During Freyer's Leipzig years, moreover, he was both colleague and mentor of the socialist Hermann Heller, who came to the University as Privatdozent while continuing to serve as head of the Municipal Office of Adult Education (*Volksbildung*). Heller became the most prominent socialist constitutional lawyer of the Weimar years, always in close touch with Freyer, who was one of the few Leipzig professors to offer him his continued support. Freyer and Heller had been close since 1920/21 (Müller/Staff 1984: 80), and this earlier friendship may, in fact, have helped introduce Freyer to the Social Democrats in Saxony. The connection was not only personal. Even in exile, Heller always acknowledged his indebtedness to Freyer's principal philosophical and sociological writings (Müller/Staff 1984: 53, 130, 218, 434), and Freyer built an important part of an influential article on "The Contemporary Crisis of Cultivation" (Freyer 1931c), to be discussed below, on the ideas of the new "adult education movement" (*Volksbildungsbewegung*) on terms that reveal a reciprocal influence from Heller.[4]

Second, then, on the larger question of relations between thinkers on the Left and figures like Schmitt and Freyer, it should be noted that even sympathy with Fascism was not necessarily identified with an alignment with right-wing conservatism.[5] Mannheim's contention in *Ideology and Utopia* that nationalist and imperialist themes became prominent in Mussolini's fascism only in the second phase, beginning in the mid–1920s, turned on the early importance assigned to corporatist doctrines, which were treated with respect as a mode of syndicalism, even by opponents on the moderate Left. Respect for the "Soviet experiment," after all, was not refused because of the dictatorship there. The critique of parliamentarism was also by no means a monopoly of the conservative right. Schmitt's radical analyses of Weimar institutions were attractive to a whole generation of socialist writers, notably Otto Kirchheimer, Franz L. Neumann, and Albert Salomon (Scheuerman 1997). Mannheim himself reaches for the unusual term "sublime" twice in a single paragraph to characterize Schmitt's thought, when speaking of him to his students.

Third and most important, these writers were no less philosophically sophisticated and reflexive than Mannheim himself. In the lecture cited above, Mannheim expressly recognizes that Schmitt lays out the full range of intellectual alternatives. Freyer was engaged in the same complex negotiations as Mannheim with both Hegel and Max Weber during the decade of the 1920s, and Freyer was in fact the author of important and respected books on both fronts. This challenge, as Mannheim tells his students in 1930, came very close to him indeed. The encounters between Mannheim and the writers he took as exponents of basic fascist ideas, accordingly, were painstaking and non-polemical, although he also indicates that somehow more is at stake. After a preliminary exposition of the basic fascist gesture, which he characterizes as a conscious attempt, prefigured by Nietzsche, to turn back from the height of insight into reflexivity's uncertainties to a simple code of decision and action, Mannheim addresses his class in a pathetic language he uses nowhere else, as he explains his reasons for pressing on with the encounter:

> It is the radical disturbance created by the relative truth in fascism. I will tell you in advance that, for me, fascism can never be this final solution [*Endlösung*]. But if I am a sociologist, I must allow the other alternatives to come as close to me as possible. In a dialectical movement, I want to show how far the relative truth of the alternate possibility extends.[6] (Mannheim [1930a] 2001: 41)

Fascist intellectuals welcome the sophistication embodied in sociology of knowledge, according to Mannheim, but they use it to assert that there can be no politics at all without a violent reversal of this sophistication, and thus no political education without the inculcation of primitive oversimplifications. This paradox, brilliantly formulated by Heidegger, Schmitt, and Freyer, exerts a certain fascination on Mannheim, even while he recognizes it as an "atrocious" threat. As is suggested by this adjective, Mannheim's struggles with thinkers close to fascism have an urgency, even in 1930, that is not present in the competition with von Wiese. Yet it is fundamental to Mannheim's position that intellectuals may find a way to talk to each other, given sufficient self-understanding. In the concrete situations of intellectual life, accordingly, the encounters were with the authors of the brilliant formulations rather than with the authors of the threat.

Freyer was a major figure at the Frankfurt meeting of sociology teachers in 1932. The competition between Mannheim and von Wiese was evidently overshadowed, at least for a while, by the standoff between von Wiese and Freyer about the relations between historical

The Challenge of Fascist Social Thought 113

and systematic sociology. The issue was fundamental for Freyer and the opposition between them was nearly total. As is evident from his published 1931 introduction to sociology, Freyer argued that social ordering, unlike cultural formation, was a function of dynamic action in historical time. Unlike the objective, supra-historical forms of culture, social formations emerged from life, from the conduct of those who produce and reproduce them, and thus had to be understood as continually subject to change.[7] These forms were inherently historical; they existed in time (1931a: 7–10). Von Wiese, he contended, sought to study these social forms abstracted from their life flow. By presenting sociology as a specialized subject, whose only object was the relationship of forms of sociation (*Vergesellschaftung*), von Wiese was concerned only with classification and abstract reduction. Such a formal sociology was ahistorical; it was not oriented to the problems of the present, which were part of the historical flow (1931a: 98–100; also 1930b: 57–68; Muller 1987: 175–176). In short, von Wiese divorced his sociology from existing reality and abdicated its political responsibility. For Freyer, formal sociology could comprehend, at most, the historically generated forms that reproduce themselves across changing times, with the reproduction always taking place for reasons that require historical explanation. Sociology itself is a historical formation, and its point of departure must consequently be a reflection on its place in the historical constellation of the present. Sociological knowledge is historical knowledge and historical knowledge is inherently present-minded, an event of its time.

As noted earlier, Alfred von Martin found a formula to suspend the conflict between Freyer and von Wiese for the sake of a united appeal to the authorities, but the underlying issues in conflict were virtually identical with Mannheim's objectives in his case for current issues studies. On a methodological level, Mannheim's argument, and especially the intimate connection he draws between contemporary and historical studies, are not easily distinguished from Freyer's published writings on the subject (Freyer 1930b; Freyer 1931a; Freyer 1931c).[8]

Mannheim signals his determination to draw a hard and fast line, nevertheless. Alluding to favorable references to his own theories of ideology and utopia in Freyer, he quotes the flamboyant climactic sentence of Freyer's major work (Freyer 1930b: 207) to distance himself from fascist volitionism and decisionism:

> Interesting as we may find the attempts to extend our argument about the existential connectedness of thinking by tendencies employing the doctrine to legitimate their ever more questionable principles, we also consider certain conclusions that have been drawn from it to be dangerous. And when this theory goes so far as to give rise to the exaggerated assertion that "a will that is true is sufficient ground for true knowledge" ["*Wahres Wollen fundiert wahre Erkenntnis*"], the door has been opened to every kind of arbitrariness in theory. Who would not step into the intellectual arena armed with the conviction or pretense of "a will that is true"? And who in such a situation would not be pleased to be excused in future from having to make a properly substantiated case and to be permitted, instead, to invoke his inspiration and genuine conviction? Taken this way, the task imposed by insight into the reality of the existential connectedness of thinking is misdirected, because the insight no longer serves self-criticism and distantiation from existential bonds, as originally intended. Instead, it legitimates every kind of partisanship. (Mannheim [1932a] 2001: 150–51)

Yet this programmatic statement fails to capture all the dimensions of Freyer's thought that, in conjunction with the political developments between 1928 and 1930, make fascism so much more important a presence in Mannheim's 1930 course than it was in *Ideology und Utopia*. To understand why Mannheim comes to treat the antithesis between fascist social thought and his own reflexive sociology as the prime constituent of the "dialectics" he puts forward to his students (Mannheim [1930a] 2001), it is necessary to review Heidegger, Schmitt, and Freyer in some detail.

During the second year of the Republic, in the midst of the controversy about Becker's university initiatives, Martin Heidegger assaulted the "classical" German cultivation ideal in a series of lectures at Freiburg, while Mannheim was there to study with him.[9] It is in these lectures that Heidegger first laid out the philosophical position that to some extent became paradigmatic for the radical right and that Mannheim would treat as the point of departure for his engagement with fascist thought in his Frankfurt course (Laube 2000). Mannheim's judgment in 1930, three years before Heidegger's open adhesion to Nazism, on the inner links between fascism and the "existentialism" that Heidegger derives from Nietzsche reinforces Karl Löwith's conclusion ten years later:

> In the light of Heidegger's substantive adherence to the National Socialist mood and mode of thinking, it is inappropriate to find fault with his political decision by itself, not to speak of glossing it over, instead of explaining it on the basis of the principles of his philosophy. (Löwith 1986: 40)[10]

Mannheim does not go so far. After all, he also thinks of existentialism as the dominant—and perhaps most advanced—philosophy of his time. Mannheim's position in the "Competition" talk was shaped, as has been shown, by Heidegger's conception of a struggle over the "public interpretation of reality" (*die öffentliche Auslegung des Seins*). The parallelism he now identifies between Heidegger's thought and fascism, operating at a lower level, does not keep him from adapting more of the characteristic Heideggerian concepts to his own uses, notably the conception of human agency as "enactment" (*Vollzug*) and "disjunction" (*Umbruch*) as key terms in his own phenomenological social diagnoses. The terminology of life-based method (*lebenswissenschaftliche Methode*) that he introduces in his 1931 lecture courses conjoins two terms that figure decisively in Heidegger's proposals for university reform (Milchman/Rosenberg 1997: 82),[11] although the concept is significantly transmuted into a sociological one. Heidegger's "decision" (*Entscheidung*), moreover, he reserves, at least in the context of the 1930 course, for the act that, in his view, the proto-fascist thinkers wrongly isolate from reflection and fatally idolize. When Mannheim casts fascism as the decisive antithesis in the dialectics of his own thought, he is thinking above all of the deeper theoretical currents that the more blatant ideologists of the mass movement contemptuously disdain after the seizure of power. Mannheim would explain the relative isolation eventually imposed on Heidegger, Schmitt, and Freyer by the Nazi cultural machine as a normal example of relations between parties and "their" intellectuals; he would not think that it bears on their dedication to the fascist regime—or their shared responsibilities for its actions. Mannheim is fully aware, consequently, that his deep interest in these writers' thought requires him to recognize and to minimize the political risk.

Rather than trying to overcome the crisis generated by scientism and historicism, Heidegger called for the recognition that crisis was the primordial state of all genuine science and history. "The level which a science has reached," he wrote, "is determined by how far it is *capable* of crisis in its basic concepts" (quoted in Milchman/Rosenberg 1997: 81). In the situation of crisis, when everything was being questioned, the opportunity presented itself for a new rigorous knowledge (*Wissenschaft*) grounded on a radical decision (*Entscheidung*). "Radical questioning" was the motto of Heidegger's philosophy classes, a program implemented with glittering virtuosity, and it was followed by a totally new rendering of old texts and problems (Milchman/ Rosenberg 1997: 77–79). Such a decision for the new was also a parting of the ways (*Scheidung*), a radical "destruction" (*Destruktion*) of the old traditional learning, by which he meant a "de-structuring," or "dismantling" (*Abbau*) of established forms: "The *Destruktion* of the intellectual-historical tradition is tantamount to the explication of those motive-giving originary situations from which fundamental philosophical experiences spring" (Bambach 1995: 191, 209–215).

In the context of historical science, Heidegger denied that there was some given objectivity that could be reconstructed in Rankean style, "as it actually was." Instead, following Nietzsche, he argued that the act of deciding was a creative one that transformed history by appropriating from the past what was needed in the present. It is in that moment of decision that one would encounter the authentic actuality (*wirkliche Wirklichkeit*).[12] This decision took place in what he termed a "situation of historical enactment" (*vollzugsgeschichtliche Situation*). To decide meant not to behold the real world as a contemplative subject but to participate in the immediate enactment (*Vollzug*) of reality itself, a "worlding" of the world (Bambach 1995: 208, 214, 220). Heidegger told his students,

> The difficulties of access [to the problems of philosophy] do not occur sometime or somewhere nor are they enacted by someone. We live within them here and now—at this place, in this lecture hall. You before me, I before you. We designate this fixed situation of a shared environing world... with the title: *University*. (Quoted in Bambach 1995: 208)

Heidegger's university was not, first of all, a place of reflection but of decision, and a "site for the transformation of human existence" (Milchman/Rosenberg 1997: 78).

Already in 1919, in his first lecture course as a *Privatdozent*, as Milchman and Rosenberg report, "Heidegger linked the renewal of the university to a 'genuine revolutionizing in the spirit.'" "Renewal of the university," he asserted, "means the rebirth of genuine scientific consciousness and life-relationships" (*Lebenszusammenhanges*)" (quoted in Milchman/Rosenberg 1997: 82). Although sympathetic commentators like Milchman and Rosenberg (1993, 1997) implicitly question whether this conception necessarily led to the practical gloss that Heidegger put on it when the opportunity presented itself for him to attempt such a renewal, as rector of Freiburg under National Socialist auspices, the language remained the same. The decision for existence (*Dasein*) came first, and this was now revealed to be the unity of the *Volk* under its *Führer*.¹³

Heidegger's idea of cultivation as a two-step process of consummating the radical destruction of the meanings established in the past and volitional enactment of new meanings mandated by the authentic reality of the unmediated present also informs Freyer's writings, where the conception is expressly related to both sociology and political life. Like Salomon and Mannheim, Freyer proposed a sociology that would be political both in the sense of putting the dynamic element of politics in the center of social analysis and in the sense of constituting a political factor in its own effects. This performative dimension of political sociology, moreover, was inherently educational.

Writing on the assigned topic of the "present-day crisis of cultivation" in 1931, Freyer began with a rejection of the premise underlying the conventional formula he used in his title. There is no crisis of "cultivation" in Spranger's sense because the concern with his kind of cultivation no longer troubles actual life, however unprecedented the public involvement with educational projects. The sense of crisis in this respect derives, rather, from the demise of the humanistic ideal and the lack of insight into a new one. In its belief that the individual develops through a self-enclosed organic process from a germinal inner tendency (*Anlage*) the cultivational ideal no longer matches the existing reality. Freyer noted that Humboldt believed that cultivation was nothing but the blooming of the individual soul, out of which and within which the world could be configured. The totalities of personality and spirit existed in the relationship of microcosm/macrocosm, so that the unities of culture and cultivation formed the norm for one another and the individual could grasp the larger whole from his own individuality (1931c: 597–598; 601–604). Most important, this self-development was understood as the highest good in itself. Humboldt abandoned his life of practical achievement, Freyer recalled, in order to dedicate himself to his own cultivation. Although talk of cultivation flourishes, none of this really makes any sense today, not even as an ideology. While Friedrich Schlegel meant it literally when he wrote, "The greatest good and the sole utility is cultivation," we think that we are reading "an aphorism in the spirit of romantic irony, where concepts are necessarily somewhat in the air" (1931c: 598). We can understand these ideas as historical productions, he contends, urging the readers to conduct the "thought experiment" for themselves, but they have no currency for us. Freyer speaks of them lacking "validity" (*Gültigkeit*), but he only means that they are experienced as obsolete.

Freyer wrote that historical-sociological analysis can account for this absence of experiential "validity." The cultivation ideal entails a focus on individuality whose plausibility was a function of unique historical circumstances affecting persons occupying a distinct social location. At the end of the eighteenth century in Germany, the state was divided among multiple local dynasties, conjoined with members of the leading aristocratic and clerical estates (*Stände*) in combinations that were internally without conflict, but also largely ineffectual. Encompassed by the new absolute dynastic regimes, the two estates admitted to public roles splintered and lost all sense of their respective honor. In contrast to France, the third "estate"[14] had no political aspirations; it lived largely outside the state and had no public will. Nor was there a political will of the *Volk*, except in idealistic philosophical speculations, since the dynastic state had no congruence with the *Volk*. Thus the social realities of the time between the decline of estates and the rise of classes made the individualism of the cultivation ideal realistic for many members of both the second and third estate: that was their life. In this atmosphere, the ideal of cultivation served as a substitute for political will. In the nineteenth century, this social reality gave way to a new one as industrial capitalism established itself and society divided, first into the classes whose relations are correctly depicted by Marxism and later, in the twentieth century, into the economic interest groups of the new, pluralist world (1931b). Under these changed historical conditions, practical ideals of cultivation multiplied and the unified humanistic ideal served simply as the illusion (*Schein*) of a specific social segment, the cultivated bourgeoisie, with no real unifying power. Eventually, it simply became one among many options and manifestly an anachronism in its universal claims. In the interim, notably at the end of the nineteenth century, when cultivation became paired with possessions as the marks of entitlement, it served as "a typical bit of bourgeois ideology. . . one of those lies that are by no means only lies, but also a strength" (1931c: 611). Under conditions of class struggle, this bourgeois ideal was briefly opposed by a proletarian one, but the confrontation soon gave way to the present-day proliferation of incoherent alternatives. The crisis is not constituted by the obsolescence of the old ideal but by the obscuration of the new one.

A solution for the crisis, however, could not be found merely by identifying new, timely contents and appropriate forms for cultivation. Freyer's next analytical step depended on the central place that he assigned to the well-established sociological distinction between "critical" and "positive" ages, first introduced by Henri Saint-Simon a hundred years earlier. A critical age lacks the consensus on the interpretation and evaluation of the world which defines a positive one. Unlike Mannheim who more nearly resembles John Stuart Mill in treating the critical present as a novel opportunity for instituting a constitutionalized openness (Mill 1963; Mannheim [1930a] 2001), Freyer sees no hope without a new positivity. This yearning for closure is one of the most decisive differences between him and Mannheim.[15]

Both the function and the social location of the humanistic ideal of cultivation were designed for positive epochs and could not function in a critical one. Freyer cites contemporary efforts in adult education (*Volksbildung*). In an attempt to extend the life-enhancing effects of humanistic cultivation to a population segregated in diverse social locations, Freyer observes, educators draw on the efforts of sociography and contemporary issues studies in a vain attempt to identify the dimensions of meaningfulness appropriate to the various social locations, to build on experiences and attitudes, as the older cultivation built on the realities of individualism. But there are no such dimensions in the social locations constituted by industrial society. The critical age is thoroughgoing in its impoverishment of social existence.

Freyer next reviews an argument that recalls both Salomon and Mannheim, at the point where they are nearest to Max Weber's concept of value-freedom (1931c: 619). Let cultivation recognize the profoundly "realistic" character of the modern age, the argument goes, and let it provide deep and detailed insight into those social realities, and notably, as in Marxism, into the objective tendencies of development, endowing men with the capacity for orientation. Freyer summarizes:

> And the person who is cultivated under these circumstances would not be the person at home in the world of ideas, the person who has created a universe out of his individuality, but the one who stands in his age with a spiritual overview, the one who really has an overview of the real forces and factors of his age, without illusion. (1931c: 621)

Freyer rejects this conception as insufficiently geared to the disruptive force of the crisis. It is insufficiently responsive to the reality that we are all "mass" torn along by a torrent of change and that we clash as we move. There is no representative standpoint. Freyer expressly cites Mannheim's concept of the "free-floating intellectuals." They may exist; but they are not important. Moreover, the appearance of calm suspension refers only to their intellectual activities as such. More fundamentally, they are caught up in the dynamic and conflict-ridden uncertainties of existence, like others (1931c: 619–622).

An ideal of cultivation for a critical epoch had to be directed not toward a spiritual whole to be represented but rather toward a political whole to be enacted (*vollzogen*):

> The person assembles his spiritual forces where his will also stands, by virtue of his decision.... He expands his willed position into a consciously spiritual position, and thereby makes it free. A spiritual existence, then, that is not constructed like a figure of mediation but rather one that operates like a searchlight.... The sovereignty of spirit bestowed by cultivation is not the sovereignty of someone who has incorporated much or everything, but rather the sovereignty of the will that has equipped itself with historical consciousness of the situation. (1931c: 624)

Freyer acknowledges that the existence of wills in conflict means that there will be conflict among cultivational designs as well. Cultivation is not there for mediation; nor is it directed against radicalism. Freyer speaks contemptuously of those who think that cultivation exists to create a twilight in which all cows are gray. Everyone talks about decisions, he notes, thinking perhaps of Weber, but they do not take the concept seriously enough. Freyer plays on the two senses of the word *Bildung*:

> If cultivation is the awakening and gaining of a historical consciousness of the situation, then cultivation always exists on the basis of a certain position, in other words a decision.... Cultivation of the *Volk* [*Volksbildung*], one can say, ultimately means formation of the *Volk* [*Volkbildung*]. (625)

Cultivation is thus at one with active political consciousness, although it cannot do the work of carrying it into effect. "That can only be achieved by struggle [*durchgekämpft*]," Freyer concludes.

Freyer's recourse to this militant rhetoric at the end is no less revealing than the unexpectedly generous and pacific wishes for a dialogue with his opponent that immediately precedes it: "Just as nations can understand one another without ceasing to be what they are or willing what they will." A year later, with authoritarian rule established in Germany and the possibility of a Rightist takeover clearly on the horizon, Freyer shows little interest in providing for dialogue in an article in which he applies his conception of cultivation to the university. When he speaks of the university as ultimately the "highest school of the state," he has in mind a political mobilization that will brook no opposition.

He begins by counterposing his ideal of cultivation to the liberal perspective, which proclaimed the autonomy of science from the state. Alluding to Max Weber, he points out that this leaves value judgments and political decisions to prophets and demagogues. This separation of science from a larger reality created questions about how the university was to be structured. Some academics (Freyer cited a piece by Paul Tillich in the *Frankfurter Zeitung*) wanted a complete separation of pure theoretical science from the disciplines that trained students for a profession. Freyer argued that this was a false dichotomy, that science was one in all its parts and that the university was one essence with two natures. He denied that specialization had destroyed this unity (Freyer 1932: 520–524, 528–529). Rather than to divorce itself from the larger political reality, he contended, the mission of science was to understand its relationship to that reality. In fact, science and politics were part of the same cultural unity, for the spiritual substance of a time lived in all of its expressions of life. The spiritual foundations on which our life rests were also the presuppositions (*Voraussetzungen*) of science. Science was distinguished from the rest of culture by its methodological rigor, but while the method was different, the content was the same. The task of the university was to reveal what was true and what was false in an epoch. In doing so it would, at the same time, unite its theoretical and practical aspects (1932: 678–679).

To achieve this, science had to get more involved in the life of the nation and the state. It could not simply dismiss politics as ephemeral at the risk of becoming shallower. To renounce its proper task would not mean the purification of science but its resignation. This did not mean that science had to enter into a coalition with the existing state. It was necessary to distinguish between the idea of the state and the actual empirical state. While the two could coincide, this need not be the case. And Freyer left little doubt what he thought about the Weimar

Republic in this respect. As science clarified its relationship to an era, it would understand that it shared its presuppositions only with the ideal state. Its task was to help that ideal state to become a political reality, to help give voice to the forces of political will seeking to transform political reality by separating the valid from the arbitrary, the necessary from the chance, the substantial from the accidental. Science, then, could not forsake ultimate decisions. As an example, he cited sociology, which had made the decision to put the present at the center of its investigations, in full awareness that the present could only be known to a decided will (1932: 674–677, 683, 688–689).

Ultimately, Freyer asserted, science had to educate students for practical activity. This meant a schooling of the will by spiritually deepening the force of decision. The old humanistic idea of cultivation (and the free-floating intelligentsia) had to be replaced by a political cultivation in which the person became rooted in the nation and was responsibly bound to the decision of the state. The old forms of education that focused on the totality of personality had to be replaced by those that disciplined the will for the tasks at hand. Students had to attain a sense of concrete duty, to be prepared to sacrifice, to dedicate their total person to nation and state (Freyer 1933: 8, 16–18, 37, 39).[16] As is evident from this conclusion, the common ground among Freyer, Mannheim, and Salomon established by their shared dedication to political education as a constitutive element in sociology as subject matter and discipline is mostly on the surface. They differ profoundly in their conceptions of the teachable and, above all, in their conceptions of the political.

For Freyer, whatever concessions he might make to the language of diplomacy, politics is combat, and the aim of the struggle is domination (*Herrschaft*) (Freyer 1933). Political education thus turns into precisely the indoctrination and mobilization that Mannheim rejects. Carl Schmitt provides the political theory for this proto-fascist group of writers. His most influential essay is *The Concept of the Political* ([1928] 1976), and the most famous among his many pithy terms and aphorisms is his claim that politics is constituted by the distinction between friend and foe. Such a decision defined the state as an entity, within as without. The ultimate form that this political distinction took was war between nations and their states. Such a war, which meant the negation of the enemy, had to be understood as a matter of national survival, not rational economic interests. Politics in this sense negated the notion of humanity, for humanity could not wage war with itself. A peaceful world, the goal of liberal humanists, would be a world without politics. And liberalism with its humanistic premises was not a real theory of the state or political principle. Liberals were incapable of waging war, for they simply turned their "enemy" into a discussion partner ([1928] 1976: 26, 33, 35, 43–44, 46, 48–49, 54, 61). This decision of friend and enemy that lay at the basis of the state was one of closure. Rather than extending itself to and interacting with different worlds, something Mannheim saw as essential in 1930, the political decision established strict boundaries.[17]

In the year that *Ideology and Utopia* appeared, Freyer and Schmitt presented papers to a conference of German philosophers in which they agreed that the only viable cultural unity in the modern world was the *Volk*, an entity that became a historical subject through the agency of the state. They argued that the two basic units of both liberalism and the humanistic ideal of cultivation, the individual and humanity, belonged to different frames of reference and thus their conjunction was unable to overcome the pluralism of social interest groups. The individual could only become a politically ethical subject by recognizing his duty to the state, which collected and awakened the forces of the nation. In doing so he was bound to the collective national consciousness that was unified and responsible (Freyer 1930a: 106, 108–112; Schmitt 1930: 31, 34, 37–38, 42). The Weimar constitutional regime, accordingly, was not properly a state, not if taken on its own terms, in any case.[18] A state requires sovereignty—the corollary of the friend-foe decision—and a parliament of conflicting, bargaining interest groups could not be sovereign.

In earlier works ([1922] 1985; [1926] 1988; [1928] 1976; 1928) Schmitt had constructed the principles of this attack on the liberal parliamentary system. Schmitt argued that the liberal parliamentarism of the late eighteenth and early nineteenth centuries was based on a set of assumptions—"shared convictions as premises, the willingness to be persuaded, independence of party ties, freedom from selfish interests"—that contradicted the current reality. In other words, there was an organic public opinion, a set of political values shared by all those who contributed to that opinion. Parliamentary discussion occurred between individuals who disagreed about what these shared values meant and tried to convince one another through rational argument but who did not challenge the basic unity. It represented a "conflict of opinions" but not a "conflict of interests" (Schmitt [1926: 9] 1988: 5). Liberalism believed that this conflict of opinions would ultimately create harmony (truth) as differences were reconciled through discussion. Discussion in public opinion was represented in the government by discussion in parliament, so that the relationship between the two was that of macrocosm/microcosm. Basic freedoms (speech, press, assembly, etc.) were necessary to promote such discussion ([1926: 44–46, 59–60] 1988: 35–36, 47–48).

> The *ratio* of parliament rests, according to the apt characterization of Rudolf Smend, in a "dynamic-dialectic," that is, in a process of confrontation of differences and opinions, from which the just political will [*richtige staatliche Wille*] results. ([43] 34)

By the beginning of the twentieth century the organic public had fragmented under the pressure of the capitalist economy so that there was no longer a public opinion but a number of specific interest groups represented by political parties. There was no underlying organic totality represented there that would result in a common governmental will through discussion, but rather a conflict of irreconcilable interests that could not be resolved through discussion. Liberal parliamentary discussion had become simply a façade for this social pluralism ([1926: 10–11] 1988: 6; 1928: 248).

Although the main themes of Schmitt's critique of parliamentarism are similar to the conservative arguments of von Below and Spranger, for example, Schmitt departed from those academics by rejecting their call for a restoration of traditional institutions, the humanistic ideal of cultivation, and the authoritarian constitutional state (*Rechtsstaat*). Schmitt became fascinated with the conception of a political order in a constant state of emergency and the figure of the dictator. The constitutionalist state, whether monarchical or parliamentary, he saw as the articulation of an obsolete bourgeois design and he rejected it in favor of a state based on a new decision, plebiscitarian in process and dictatorial in form.[19] For Schmitt, the sovereign stands outside of the normally valid legal system, distinguishing himself as sovereign by deciding on the emergency situation without being subject to any controls. This decision, free from legal normative ties, becomes absolute. In making the decision, the sovereign thus defines the situation in its totality and "the power of real life breaks through the crust of a mechanism that has become torpid by repetition" (Schmitt [1922] 1985: 6–15).

Using the rhetoric of struggle common to Left and Right, Freyer translates the image of violent breakthrough central to both Heidegger and Schmitt into the language of revolution. He proclaims the imminence of the *Revolution from the Right*:[20]

> A new front is forming on the battlefields of bourgeois society—the revolution from the Right. With that magnetic power inherent in the battle cry of the future even before it has been sounded, it draws into its ranks the toughest, most alert, most contemporary men from all camps. It is still assembling, but it will strike. Its movement is still a mere collection of spirits, lacking awareness, symbols, or leadership. But overnight the front will arise. It will reach beyond the old parties with their petrified programs and antiquated ideologies. It will successfully call into question, not the reality of the stultified class antagonisms of a world that has become petit bourgeois on both sides, but the conceit that this is politically productive. It will do away with the ossified remnants of the nineteenth century and clear the way for the history of the twentieth. (Freyer 1931b: 5, translation slightly revised from Muller 1987: 194)

The revolution of the Right, Freyer argued, would be the action of the *Volk*, willing an end to the pluralism of interest groups that emerged with liberal industrial society. The revolution is of the Right because it intends the emancipation of the state from the unpolitical reign of society. The state and the community of the *Volk* were made latent by the history of the nineteenth century, but that history had now liquidated itself. Its central drama had been correctly pictured by Marx. But the Left had forsaken its revolutionary task through the decision of the proletariat, led by unions, to abandon class warfare and to be absorbed into the existing system, in return for the rewards of the welfare state. The latter was simply a surrogate for the compromises that took place between various interest groups, now including the proletariat. All conflict was reduced to negotiation and organization (1931b: 32–33, 36, 40, 42, 55, 56, 60).

Once the setting of public life had become completely that of society, the possibility of something that was not society, something completely revolutionary arose. That something, the *Volk*, which authors the revolution from the Right, was a non-social, communitarian formation (*Bildung*) with its own will and law.[21] It was not a combatant within industrial society but against that society. When the *Volk* becomes a political force it becomes the state. The latter is not a housing (*Gehäuse*) for the existing society, as the old nation-state had been, but the steel-hard point of the revolution against it. At key points, Freyer's language recalls Heidegger:

> The state is... the awakening of the *Volk* out of timeless existence [*Dasein*] to power over itself and to power in time. The old nation state, with its arbitrary boundaries, its fixed proprietorships and inherited lands, over which it rested like a glass cover, has badly falsified our thinking about the state. We think of the state as contrary to revolution, contrary to the emerging future, almost as contrary to life. This concept is to be thoroughly deconstructed (*abzubauen*). Here is a state that is completely historical action and identical with the revolutionary principle. (1931b: 37, 44, 61, quotation on 65)

In concretizing the force field of the *Volk* against industrial society, the state made the *Volk* the master of its world, the political subject of its history. The state is the will of the *Volk*: "Not a milled mass but a living space that knows itself as a unity becomes a will." The individual person became free when he became part of the common will of the nation, when he gave himself to the state (1931b: 65, 67, 69–70, quotation on 69). Two years earlier, he had already invoked Hegel to characterize the ethical consequences of this breakthrough: "The 'objective and subjective wills are reconciled and are one and the same whole.' 'Morality' has become 'Duty.'" (1930a: 114). Now he quotes, disavowing mere piety to Hegel (*Hegelei*), the state becomes "a concrete reality," "the realization of freedom" (1931b: 69).

Freyer's "revolution from the right," like Schmitt's plebiscitarian dictatorship, combined a maximum of dynamism and combative drive with an inner state of closure and popular unanimity. The imagery, as noted, is an idealized mobilization for war. And revolutionary Marxism, no less than Nietzsche, is an important imaginative resource. Having recalled the Marxist interpretation of the nineteenth century, Freyer writes,

> It is doubtless an audacious myth, that the estate of factory workers, simply because it was the last in rights and the first in misery during the nineteenth century, would be deputed to bear the sufferings of the world, while the bourgeoisie, just because it owns the means of production, would be the deputy for the world's sins. It is an audacious kind of chiliasm to believe that nothing needs to be done but to burst the chains of the class relationships in order to reopen the history of human freedom after several millennia. But the blatant reality of modern class struggles and its materialist interpretation have in any case given us final clarity about the makeup of revolutions, how revolutions look. (1931b: 13)

Revolutions need not be violent, Freyer writes; they may be made by the electoral ballot. But they are always essentially the same. In language that echoes the apocalyptic visions of Georg Lukács, Freyer contrasts the infinitely promising new realities and the old lies:

> Beneath the husks and in the forms of an existing society, the elements of a new one have taken shape. Everything that the existing order says, thinks, and knows about itself has become false. It lies as soon as it opens its mouth.... Still more. Everything that the existing order may be has become false. It does not even have to open its mouth or to set its thoughts in motion in order to lie. Its foundations do not bear anything; they just pretend. Its law has no validity; it simply functions. (1931b:14)

Like Schmitt with the law, Freyer attempts to reconcile these mythopoeic visions of total confusion and total renewal with a faithful regard for the sociological tradition and a subtle management of his own sociological analyses.[22] It is this combination that conditions Mannheim's relationship to the work.

For Freyer, sociology was not an abstract, "free-floating" system but rather occupied an existential location; it was a science of and in reality (*Wirklichkeit*) (1931a: 11). Sociology was ultimately dedicated not to a neutral systematization of social forms or to the inner enrichment of the individual, but to the realization of a political agenda to transform the present:

> Not the enrichment of the understanding subject through the variety of forms, but rather insight into the conditions of one's own existence, deepening of one's own decision, building a foundation for one's own reality—that is the meaning of theory here. (1930b: 90–91)

Taking up a theme that also attracted Mannheim, he linked sociology as a practice to a characterization of Saint-Simon, one of its originators, as having lived an "experimental life." Rather than remaining in his study and creating an abstract system, Saint-Simon became immersed in the current social realities. He understood that sociology was connected to a given historical world and tried to observe the crisis of the present in order to supersede it. In short, the purpose of sociology was to clarify and aid Saint-Simon's own immediate life experiences. This programmatic approach to sociology, its dedication to solving the present crisis, was what Freyer admired in other early sociologists, such as Comte, Stein, and Marx (1931a: 17–18, 27, 50). In the liberal capitalist society of the late nineteenth and early twentieth centuries, he concluded, such an approach had largely disappeared, as von Wiese's sociology demonstrated. While Freyer shared Spranger's and Curtius' opposition to "sociologism," in the sense of a theory that purports to explain the constitution of spiritual entities by social causation, he was no less firm in his insistence that sociology was nevertheless decisive for an orientation to practical life. In the competition between Mannheim and von Wiese, his position was clear.

For Freyer, sociology as a science of reality, was also an "ethical science" (*Ethoswissenschaft*), one directly implicated in political values. In a society charged with impending change, the will to change is a paramount of reality; and knowledge of society requires an active deep insight into that will (1926: 126; 1930b: 90–91; 1931a: 147–148). The sociologist of reality understood that all volition occupied a certain place in the historical stream. For political goals to be realized, it was necessary to grasp how the concrete will was connected to the existing reality. Sociology was able to cut across other disciplines and saw society as an individuality, as a whole with a psychic (*seelisch*) foundation. While sociological abstractions were useful, they always had to be layered into (*Einschichtung*) historical reality, that is, "bound" (*Bindung*) to the reality of a specific historical time. In its active participation in the course of historical change, sociology was connected to the philosophy of history, something that von Wiese had adamantly denied. "Consciousness of his mission" was an important quality of the sociologist (1931a: 12–14, 16, 21–23, 26–27, 88, 130, 146). The discipline attempted not only to understand social reality, but also to transform it. It was a practical science, but not merely in the American sense of a purely applied science that attempted to solve specific technical social problems, working out, in effect, the programs of the established, failed welfare state (1931a: 147). That amounts to a kind of bureaucratic science that sought to preserve the existing order. Sociology as an ethical science, in contrast, implies a utopia, Freyer wrote, "in the sense given the word by Karl Mannheim: reality transcending orientations that partially or totally explode the present order of existence" (1930b: 298).

In writing about the discipline of sociology, Freyer first distinguishes between outright political and theoretical writing. The former proceeds from a tactical perspective, with the work serving as a form of direct political action, like the *Revolution from the Right*, while the latter aspires to a more inclusive knowledge, given an essential animating will. Second, Freyer acknowledges that the will implicit in society is in dispute in a critical epoch and that there will therefore be multiple sociological theories, oriented by contrasting utopias. In such a time, sociology had to investigate existing ideologies and utopias, following Mannheim, with regard to their interrelationships and positioning within social reality. Such recognition could mean "restraining" (*bändigen*) one's own volition toward the future to properly assess its place in the present (1930b: 301–302; Muller 1987: 169–170). But this was done to serve the utopian will, not to undermine it. Freyer rejected Mannheim's aim of exposing ideologies or utopias (1930b: 262). Social connectedness is not only inevitable; it is also the source of the ability to penetrate certain critical regions of social existence (1930b: 112–113). In these respects, the distinction between ideology and theory fades into insignificance. The aim of theory is to formulate the "historically valid will of the present, and that means the historically valid will to its transformation" (1930b:113). The decisive question is only the quality of the will that informs the thinking.

Several points stand out when considering Mannheim's work in the light of these proto-Fascist writers. First, is the important contrast between his conception of competition among ideologies and their conception of warfare. When competition is construed as dialectics—especially in Mannheim's "soft" use of that concept—the idea of collaborative accumulation and compromise emerges, an idea that is anathema to both Freyer and Schmitt, for whom the adoption of a perspective is ultimately a matter for unconditional decision, not reasoned judgment. Schmitt is especially clear in the program he developed for analyzing the sociology of a concept, where this turns out to be an insight into the deepest metaphysical designs that inform the group's practices as well as their understandings, so that the one cannot be said to be the base and the other the superstructure (Schmitt [1922] 1985: 58f.). While Mannheim appreciates the importance of liberalism as total ideology in the constitution of Weimar institutions, for example, he aspires to a synthesis, however incomplete, generated by a *Realdialektik* among liberal, conservative, and socialist perspectives; and he thinks that this can be restarted from its present impasse through the critical operations of sociology of knowledge. This is precisely the prospect that both Schmitt and Freyer flatly reject. One must decide for one total view, and ultimately treat those who choose the others as foes. Anything else is itself mere liberalism, rendered incoherent by its indecision.[23]

Second, an important element in this contrast is the assessment of the intellectuals, Mannheim's sociological placeholder for the possibility of synthesis. Freyer deprecates their importance and autonomy, while Schmitt rages against them, especially after 1933. In a short piece by Schmitt that appeared in a Nazi publication he attacked exiled German intellectuals, clearly including Mannheim, as traitors to the *Volk*. Such intellectuals, whom Schmitt identifies with nineteenth-century liberalism, wanted to be part of the nation, without being completely dedicated to it. They claimed a connection to the nation (*Volksverbundenheit*) through their souls, while preserving a certain detachment in spirit using cover terms such as "freedom of spirit" and "independence of science." They used the distinction between "heart and brain" (*Herz und Hirn*) to make the claim of cultural leadership. National Socialism rejected this stance. For it, all human spirit and all productivity took place within a comprehensive total whole, the *Volk*, from which the creative spirit could not be separated. The "free-floating" character of the exiled intellectuals, who rejected a bondedness to the *Volk* (*Volksgebundenheit*), resulted in unconnectedness at best and more likely political betrayal. Such intellectuals were aliens to the German nation. Here ones sees Schmitt using a Mannheimian distinction to deny Mannheim's agenda. Mannheim believed that by admitting to an existential connectedness (*Seinsverbundenheit*), intellectuals could gain distance from their respective sociopolitical groups. As a discursive collective group, the intelligentsia with its various social connections would not be bound to any one of those positions (*Seinsgebundenheit*); it would fulfill the promise embodied in its being relatively free floating. Schmitt answered that such ambition was misplaced, that intellectuals should bind themselves to a position, that of the *Volk*, which formed a unity.[24] In Mannheim's 1930 lectures, he emphasizes distantiation as an irreversible feature of modern societies, not least in order to show that the intellectuals' sense of relative detachment was part of a broader phenomenon, and to raise the value of their ability to build on an understanding of this experience, for the benefit of all. The response to Schmitt and Freyer is that intellectuals who do not confront their condition of distantiation are deceiving themselves.

Third, then, is the question of utopia. Freyer, as we have seen, seizes upon Mannheim's concept of utopia in *Ideology and Utopia* to back his insistence on the volitional, emotionally charged core of social knowledge. Perhaps he even meant to point towards Mannheim's expressions of regret as he traces utopia's declines in energy from the time of its paradigmatic historical appearance in the chiliastic movements of the Reformation. Some commentators have suggested that Mannheim intended a close parallel between chiliastic utopianism and fascism, although Mannheim's account of fascism in "Politics as a Science" is quite different, and the question arises whether Mannheim's expressed fears that the end of utopia means a loss of political vitality might entail some sympathy for fascism, or at least explain a certain affinity between him and Freyer.

The concept of utopia had been vital to Freyer since his first, formative writings. Immediately after the war, Freyer published an article on utopias in which he addressed the relationship between the vitalistic conception of life as a flowing stream and the Hegelian conception of timeless cultural objectifications.[25] While the creative forces of the individual were released in the free flow of this stream of history, this came at the expense of orientation. The individual attained such an orientation from an objective cultural order. A positive epoch is one where such an order is in place and congruent with the life experiences of men. Eventually these cultural forms would lose their effectiveness in containing the stream of spiritual life and the stable cultural orientation would dissolve. When history entered the critical epochs in which the objective cultural forms were unable to contain the flux of life, the need for a revolutionary transformation of culture arose (Freyer 1920: 321–325; 1931c: 609, 617–618). This transformation became the goal of the utopian.

Freyer defined "utopia" as the vision of, and will toward, a new cultural reality. Athough past utopians viewed their constructions as scientific, and although Freyer believed that social science played a useful role in understanding the place of the utopia in the historical process, the primary force of the utopia was will, not knowledge. In short, the utopia was not a blueprint of the future but the will to actively transform the present (1920: 330, 343–344).[26]

Both Mannheim and Freyer emphasized the volitional nature of utopia, its need to transcend the present by imposing a unity of values. Both believed that to be successful in the twentieth century, the utopian will had to be clarified by a sociological diagnosis of the existing contexture. But while Mannheim, in *Ideology and Utopia*, emphasized the inability of the utopian will to realize its goals on its own terms, and allowed it only the capacity to drive history forward but not to "overcome" it (Loader 1985: 104–105), Freyer emphasized the possibility of utopian success. The most important feature of a utopia for him was its ability to achieve a dynamic equilibrium of the forces it constituted, allowing its adherents to experience the unity of the whole and imposing a stable cultural reality on the flow of life. In a utopia "the stream of history is dammed up" (1920: 325, 332, 328). Utopias served to transmute critical epochs into positive ones.

Mannheim respected Freyer's studies of utopia. He cites the early article in his own 1928 publication and even accepts as authoritative a later work by Freyer on the subject, written in 1936. Nevertheless, Mannheim's pages on the theme in the 1930 course, the only passage where he expressly speaks of developing a theme from *Ideology and Utopia*, seem clearly designed to clarify the distance between his own position and Freyer's. He now treats utopias as only a first, provisional expression of a discrepancy between the established contexts of meaning and the experiences of individuals. Utopias provide a standpoint from which those discrepancies can be comprehended, and a measure of orientation under conditions of meaninglessness. By their nature, however, they are undermined by practice. They cannot make sense of the actual conflicts and complexities that men encounter. They are then displaced, either by sociological insight or by one or another of the more differentiated, responsive modes of meaning-giving. Fascism, like orthodox Marxism, may be a form of "reprimitivization" because it attempts to close an inherently open system, but it is quite unrelated to the originality and ingenuousness of utopia.

Proto-fascism, as represented by Freyer and Schmitt, faced with the pluralistic modern world, did not seek to retreat into the imagined harmony of some past age. Unlike conservatism, it sought neither the return to the "golden age" of the imperial state nor the reestablishment of classical humanistic cultivation. Instead its proponents acknowledged that strife was an integral part of the modern world and attempted to prepare their students to participate in that strife by strengthening their sense of duty and sacrifice. To do so required an act of closure, the sealing off of the *Volk* as a unity of will, which meant the expulsion of those enemies who did not share that will and warfare with other willful unities that challenged the *Volk*. This conception was indeed the direct antithesis of Mannheim's project in 1930.

Mannheim speaks presciently of fascist intellectuals as destined to become "hysterical persons" because they attempt to live in denial of what they know. Because their posture allies them with segments of the masses who are unable to tolerate the loss of old certainties, they become dangerous persons too. Up to a point, he accepts Freyer's thesis of the present as a "critical" phase, in Saint-Simon's sense, but he denies that it is either necessary or ultimately possible to force the movement to a renewed "natural" phase by a gesture of reprimitivization.[27] His main argument comes down to the claim, reminiscent of Saint-Simon himself, whom Freyer cites as a model, that the crisis will open the way to its own resolution by means of the very critical intelligence that brings it about. From the standpoint of intellectual history, the disagreement between Mannheim and Freyer about the uses of Saint-Simon depends on whether one looks to the Saint-Simonians before or after their turn to religion (Manuel 1956; cp Mill 1963). The issue is tied to their eventual differences on the concept of utopia, with Mannheim returning closer to the position shared by liberals and orthodox Marxists.

For Mannheim, both his being attracted by Freyer's opening to fascism and his firm rejection of it recall an earlier moment in his intellectual development. The cultural criticism developed in the Lukács Circle during the First World War drew on Nietzsche and Dostoyevsky to project an inexplicable reversal in the process of intellectualization, a breakthrough of the soul. Lukács brought these ideas to Budapest from Heidelberg, where he and Bloch briefly represented them in the Weber Circle, and he carried elements of this conception into his revolutionary Marxism. Mannheim backed away. The memory nagged at him, mostly in the form of his recurrent invocations of the unresolved problem of "ecstasy" and his curiosity about Christianity, but his refusal to let the problem disrupt his theoretical designs remains firm (see the exchange of letters with Eduard Heimann, translated in Mannheim 2001).[28]

In the late Weimar context, Mannheim's rejection of utopian ways out of the crisis entails a careful balancing of accounts with Marxism. Although Mannheim comes at Marxism in Heidelberg by way of his rapt encounter with Lukács' *History and Class-Consciousness* ([1923] 1968), his uses of the Marxist tradition come ever closer to the "Marxistic sociology" that Albert Salomon and others developed in conjunction with Emil Lederer and Gustav Radbruch at Heidelberg. While Lukács shared the Rightists' determination to find a radical breakthrough in the struggle against the rationalized, technological, capitalist society, and demanded a recognition of communism as the authentic revolution that reclaims the ground falsely usurped by Freyer's ostensible revolution from the Right, [29] Mannheim became ever less persuaded by the activist mode of Marxist thought represented by

Lukács. Marxist social analysis became a resource of the politically educated for him, a contributor to functional strategies of managed social transformation.

Notes

1. Building on a widely shared perception of an initial social-radical phase in Mussolini's rule, Mannheim treats fascism apart from what he characterizes as its eventual "turn to the right," when it allies itself with conservative social forces and takes up familiar right-wing themes of nationalism and empire. Mannheim evidently sees no need to engage the latter elements.
2. Unlike liberalism, conservatism, and socialism, fascism is not included in Mannheim's typology of utopian mentalities in *Ideology and Utopia*. Perhaps Mannheim intended some analogies between fascism and the similarly ahistorical chiliastic thought (Loader 1985: 105–6), which he discusses at length, but for present purposes it is important to notice that he did not consider fascism important enough to make an express theme of it.
3. Freyer's conception in *Revolution from the Right* (1931) was strongly anti-capitalist and called for "state socialism."
4. See also Freyer 1933a: 26. Freyer cites Hermann Heller, as well as Max Weber and Carl Schmitt as authorities for the contention that every effective political system is necessarily a system of domination (*Herrschaft*), not a legal or contractual construction. Heller, it should be noted, represented a dissident element in the Young Socialist and socialist adult education organizations, introducing nationalist cultural themes derived from the youth movement. His faction lost influence, but he became an important young academic star, especially as a spokesman for the socialist legal mainstream against both Carl Schmitt and Hans Kelsen (see Müller/Staff 1984).
5. In his *Revolution from the Right*, Freyer disavows any identification between the incipient revolution he is proclaiming and "nationalist Romanticism, counter-revolutionary activism, idealistically costumed mediocrity, or the famous state above the parties," as well as imitations of [Italian] fascism, *action française*, or Sovietism in some Germanic disguise. Writing in 1931, after the electoral breakthrough of the NSDAP, he still speaks of the revolutionary movement as being without leadership.
6. Mannheim evidently has an unusual personal interest as well in intellectuals attracted to Fascism. Almost certainly referring to individuals close to him from the Lukács Circle in Budapest, like Emma Ritook, and quite possibly echoing the diagnostic manner of his wife, who was a psychologist, Mannheim tells his 1930 class: "[We] are confronted with the phenomenon of an advanced consciousness reversing itself to a more primitive stage. This gives rise to special kinds of hysteria, especially in the intellectual stratum. If one were working on fascism and counter-revolution, it would be essential to investigate the social location of this intelligentsia with great care. I have had a chance to look more closely at this situation in Hungary, where the intelligentsia is quite generally affected by this psychic manifestation and exhibits the whole range of such hysteria, and where a certain form of hysteria suddenly appears as an illness whose etiology has not yet been investigated." Mannheim's younger cousin, Ernest Manheim, studied sociology with Freyer in Leipzig and wrote his Habilitation under his sponsorship.

Writing an American reference for Manheim in 1936, Mannheim emphasizes that Freyer, "although a Nazi" continues to support his former student (LWP 7:10).
7. Apart from his sociology and some writings in rhapsodical mythic modes, Freyer was best known for his work in cultural philosophy, based on Hegel and Dilthey. His *Theory of Objective Mind* has just appeared in an English translation and has been welcomed by reviewers as a major contribution.
8. It should be noted that Freyer credits Alfred Weber with a key contribution to his own understanding of the links between historical and contemporary studies (Freyer 1931a: 115). For Mannheim and Alfred Weber, see below.
9. Reinhard Laube reports that Mannheim is registered as a member of Heidegger's seminar on "phenomenological exercises" in the Summer Semester of 1920. He suggests that Mannheim probably attended Heidegger's lectures during the same semester, although his name does not appear on the attendance list (Laube 2000). Laube's surmise is confirmed by Mannheim's citation of unpublished lectures by Heidegger in his 1922 treatise on cultural sociology (Mannheim [1922–24] 1982). For Heidegger's extraordinary fascination for his students, see Löwith 1986: 42f.
10. Milchman and Rosenberg (1993) make a persuasive case, with reference to Heidegger, for distinguishing between the meaning he attempted to impose on National Socialism through his participation (Freiburg National Socialism) and the interpretation that triumphed in the regime. Much the same could be said, to varying degrees, about Schmitt and Freyer. This view makes it possible to comprehend both their unquestionable political alignment with the Nazi takeover and their eventual marginalization by the party. There is nothing exculpatory in this reading of the record, since it does not absurdly argue that these worldly intellectuals were somehow the only people in Germany unaware of the movement's violent racism, which only Schmitt ever seconded in his writings. Nor does it imply that their fascism was somehow innocuous. They must take full responsibility for their political choices, as well as for their willingness to play the minor supporting roles they were eventually assigned. On Freyer (and Spranger) as professors abroad representing Nazi culture, see König 1987: 392. Löwith (1986: 112–115) describes Spranger's performance in Japan, and expresses his dismay at the combination of the old idealism, familiar from his acquaintance with him in Germany, with preposterous claims about German-Japanese cultural identities, transparently in the service of the Axis pact.
11. Milchman and Rosenberg (1993) write: "This conjoining of science and factical life, which had been severed by the relentless trajectory of modernity, and the insistence that the university was the site on which this conjoining of *Leben* and *Wissenschaft* would occur, characterized Heidegger's *Denkweg* right through the period of the rectorate."
12. Compare Mannheim [1930a] 2001.
13. Milchman/Rosenberg 1997 make a useful contribution by situating Heidegger's rectorial program in 1933–34 in the context of his earlier advocacy of radical university reform, but they do not relate his position to the wider Weimar controversy about the universities, notably the quarrel centered on Becker's policy in Prussia.
14. Because of the class connotations of the term, we avoid "bourgeois" at this point, although Freyer speaks of "*Bürger*." The absence of class identity, objective or subjective, is central to Freyer's analysis, as is the transformation of the situation when the third estate becomes the bourgeoisie, in the course of the nineteenth century.

15. It is arguable that Mannheim often wavered on this point, especially after 1933, but his antipathy for the kind of uniformity that fatally attracted Freyer makes it unjust, as some have done, to label him as another "Utopian of the Right" (Floud 1966).
16. Freyer was rather traditional when it came to the actual implementation of political cultivation. In an article published after the Nazi seizure of power, he proposed a "political semester" that consisted of a series of lectures with three goals: to awaken the sense of political greatness ("Frederick the Great Battles for Silesia"; "Bismarck Founds the Empire"), to provide insight into the dynamics of political happening ("The Establishment of the English World Empire"; "Prussia and Germany"), and to provide the factual foundation for understanding the current political situation of Germany ("The System of Versailles"; "The German Nationality in Middle and East Europe"). The political semester would supposedly provide unity for the university otherwise divided according to specialization (1933: 21–23).
17. Regardless of what one makes of Schmitt's sophisticated legal theories, the position certainly resonates with the ideology of Nazism. The essence of the Nazi state was the racial definition of friend and enemy. It engaged in a war of annihilation, allegedly for its own survival, against its enemies foreign and domestic.
18. Schmitt's writings as a political theorist are not identical with his writings as a theorist of public law and the Weimar constitution. Above all, his legal writings are interventions in legal controversies, attempts to shape the law in concrete instances. These are not inconsistencies, but a difference in levels of discussion that makes it ill-advised to meld arguments from the two contexts without careful consideration (cp. McCormick, 1997).
19. As McCormick (2000) shows, this argument first reaches its full force in Schmitt 1922, where Schmitt abandons his earlier critical distinction between a Roman-style "commissural" dictatorship under Article 48 of the Weimar Constitution and unlimited "sovereign" dictatorship. In his earlier work on the subject, he had favored President Ebert's deployment of the former against the pro-Soviet total conception (1921). Now Schmitt wrote approvingly of the counterrevolutionary philosophy of state: "As soon as Donoso Cortés realized that the period of monarchy had come to an end because there no longer were kings and no one would have the courage to be king in any way other than by the will of the people, he brought his decisionism to its logical conclusion. He demanded a political dictatorship. In the cited remarks of de Maistre we can also see a reduction of the state to the moment of the decision, to a pure decision not based on reason and discussion and not justifying itself, that is, to an absolute decision created out of nothingness" ([1922] 1985: 65–66). In his legal writings on the subject (1924, 1931), Schmitt states the case more judiciously, until just before Hitler's seizure of power (1932). The sequence of writings on dictatorship culminates in Schmitt's notorious justification of Hitler's 1934 murder of his erstwhile political allies, "The Führer protects legality." Schmitt's shifts throughout correlate with changing political opportunities: his 1931 essay, for example, is written for Schleicher's rule and the 1932 essay is aimed at von Papen (cp. McCormick 1997; Caldwell 1997; Dyzenhaus 1997; Scheuerman 1997).
20. Insofar as the National Socialist movement was identified with attacks on the "treachery" of Versailles, anti-Semitism, and, above all, the charismatic leadership of Hitler, Freyer implicitly kept his distance. He expressly denied that the "revolution" had as yet found its leader (1931). His attacks on the Weimar welfare

state are categorical but civil in tone, with a respectful treatment of his opposition. The conception of "liberating the state" also runs counter to the "movement" rhetoric of the NSDAP. Muller (1987: 189) nevertheless suggests that this work was understood at the time as a defense of National Socialism if not of Hitler.
21. On the historical survival of *Volk* as a communitarian substructure in society, see Freyer 1931a: 133–4.
22. For the operation of this dualism in Schmitt, see McCormick 1997, a path breaking work.
23. Schmitt elaborates his position against "dilatory compromise" especially in his conflicts with other jurists about the Weimar constitution. His paradoxical conclusion in that context is often an insistence that the Weimar constitution in fact embodies a decision for bourgeois liberalism, by virtue of its guarantees of property rights and rule of law, whatever verbal concessions might have been made to Catholic or Socialist ideologies. He uses this approach to defend conservative political interests, as with the presumed constitutional prohibition against expropriating the royal houses. Some of the young Socialist jurists who are attracted by his anti-liberal radicalism, among other things, occasionally try to turn the argument the other way, with the Weimar "decision" construed as favoring socialism (Kirchheimer 1932). Another of that group, Franz Neumann, who will be one of Mannheim's students in exile, argued as Mannheim might have done, that the constitution sets up a dynamic process that will integrate antithetical elements in a "rule of social law," taking up Hermann Heller's key concept (Neumann 1932). Schmitt's constitutional arguments, as we have seen, are ever more overshadowed by his fascination with dictatorship.
24. Unlike Freyer, Schmitt graduates from these coded denunciations of intellectuals remote from the *Volk* to contemptuous denunciations of thinkers who are radically disqualified from bonding by virtue of being Jewish. His enthusiastic condemnation of "Jewish jurists" includes not only close colleagues and universally respected founders of German legal thought, but also a jurist he had held up as a model in a lavish tribute only a few years before (Sinzheimer 1938). This history does not stop him from speaking in a patronizing way of Mannheim after the war (Schmitt 1950).
25. Muller (1987: 49) documents the importance of the late work of both Georg Simmel and Wilhelm Dilthey for Freyer.
26. For a longer discussion of this article, see Muller (1987: 53–55).
27. It should be noted that Mannheim in 1930 grants that he cannot categorically exclude the possibility that "life" will tolerate (or even demand) a fascist moment. He does not think so, he says, and he is certain that it cannot be more than an interlude, in any case, but the possibility exists where there is paralysis of action. This is not, in his view, a concession on any theoretical issue in dispute. Nevertheless, Mannheim's reluctant uncertainty on this point may help to explain some distressing evidence of later ambiguity, even about Hitler. See Kettler/Meja 1995: 262. For Mannheim's refusal to read the "crisis" as fascists or conservatives did, even in the weeks before Hitler's rise to power, see Mannheim [1932b] 2001.
28. In his critique of Mannheim's *Man and Society in an Age of Reconstruction*, Heimann charges Mannheim with abandoning the effort common to the Tillich Circle of which they had been both been a part to ground a fundamental difference from fascism on deep spiritual commitments. His purely rationalist concept of planning, according to Heimann, weakens his position even in the isolated passage where he tries to separate himself from Fascist proponents of planning by

criticizing Freyer's subordination of planning to power (Freyer 1933; Mannheim [1935] 1940). Freyer's position, Heimann suggests, is less passive in the face of technology and therefore by no means inferior to Mannheim's: "The demarcation from fascism cannot be discovered by denying it the capacity for solving the intellectual tasks entailed in its rule. The actual demarcation lies in belief in spiritual values—belief in truth, justice, and love. The demarcation from fascism cannot be discovered by denying it the capacity for solving the intellectual tasks entailed in its rule. The actual demarcation lies in belief in spiritual values—belief in truth, justice, and love." For the background of this critique, see the excerpts from the "Frankfurt Conversations" of June 30, 1931, Tillich 1983; Mannheim 2001.

29. For a careful comparison between Lukács and Carl Schmitt, highlighting similarities no less relevant to a comparison with Freyer, see McCormick 1997: 31–82

6

Marxism and Sociology

In their respective surveys of German sociological theory, both von Wiese and Freyer give Karl Marx an honored place among the forefathers of German sociology. It is fair to say, in fact, that Marxism dictated much of the agenda for early twentieth-century sociology in Germany. Most generally, in keeping with intellectual developments among major intellectual representatives of the socialist movement, as they appropriated the legacy of Friedrich Engels' late writings, Marx was valued for insights into the importance of neglected economic variables and for the analytical constructs of class struggle and capitalism. He was taken as the originator of historical materialism, a kind of positivism. The holistic theory of history, however, and especially the conceptions of revolution and the unity of theory and practice were typically attacked as hostile to both human spirituality and science; and the political program was alternately denounced as a dangerous utopia entailing a nightmare of violence and bureaucratic repression or as a mere ideology to promote petty labor interests, to which was added, after 1918, unforgiving fury over the Left's struggles against the war. The political history of the first Weimar years, notably the effects of the Russian Revolution and the eruptions of street violence in the campaigns for and against a revolutionary alternative in Germany, exacerbated the academic hostility to revolutionary Marxist thought. This is the context in which Karl Mannheim attempted, as a unestablished junior academic, to call attention to *History and Class Consciousness* by his erstwhile mentor, Georg Lukács, a work that celebrates precisely—and exclusively—the elements of Marxism excluded by the respectful reconstruction of Marx as a one-sidedly economic determinist sociologist.[1]

The consequences of Mannheim's undertaking, considered intrepid by some of the students who were first drawn to him in this context, were undoubtedly cushioned by the fact that Lukács was himself a minor Heidelberg celebrity during the years before the revolutions, a welcome member of the Weber Circle, a scientific interlocutor and possible habilitant of Alfred Weber, and an early confidante of Salomon, Lederer, and others now making their way in postwar Heidelberg. Max Weber greatly admired Lukács' literary essays and was eager to help Lukács gain habilitation as a philosopher, but he insisted that Lukács would have to abandon his essayistic manner of working, in favor of scientific rigor.[2] In Heidelberg, as in his native Budapest, Lukács was an independent voice of radical cultural criticism, who had developed his own subtle strategy for addressing the "tragedy of culture" that Georg Simmel had diagnosed. With Ernst Bloch, he explored the possibilities of chiliastic religious and utopian thought, notably the work of the mystics, as a way of imagining the breakthrough they felt must come. He was an aesthetician, reworking Hegel's design without Hegel's metaphysical grounding, but he decried aesthetics as a symptom of the soul's impoverishment. But it was a crisis of infinite promise, he thought, with Dostoyevsky flashing on the horizon as a thunderbolt in anticipation of the cleansing cultural storm.

Still a schoolboy, Mannheim approached Lukács in 1911, and he soon found himself admitted as one of the youngest to the intimate circle around Lukács that was institutionalized during the war years, first, as the "Sunday Circle" and, second, in 1917, as an advanced lecture series in cultural studies, for which the twenty-four-year-old Mannheim gave the introductory program lecture. The group competed among the younger intellectuals with a social-scientific society headed by Oscar Jászi, but there were no significant political conflicts between them, since they were unified in opposition to the authoritarian Hungarian regime, as well as to the narrow-minded, clerical, and anti-Semitic domestic opposition. Mannheim took part in both groups (Kettler 1971; Karádi/Veszér 1985; Gluck 1985; Gábor 1983). Although the culturist group tended to be unpolitical, their sympathies were loosely on the Left. In a diary of his youth, there is a detailed account by Mannheim of his first visit to Lukács, on June 23, 1911.

Mannheim reports, "I told Lukács how little I trusted socialism" because "socialism, and particularly the elements of historical materialism in socialism, did have a soul destroying effect, and the soul must emerge again." Lukács' reply is prophetic of his later development:

> He said that lately he had regained his trust in socialism, because it had a branch going back to spiritual origins, the one originating from Hegel. If we read Marx, we could see the affinities. I should not forget, he told me, that this was the first movement since the mystics that really penetrated deeply and mobilized everything. We could be witnessing a unique process. In the old days there was the Bible and this had created sociology; now it would turn out the other way: sociology would create a new faith for humanity. (Sárközi 1986: 436–37)

Nevertheless, Lukács' sudden entry into the Communist Party in the winter after the war came wholly unexpectedly to his circle, most of whom did not join him in this politicization of their shared cultural radicalism. During the short-lived Bela Kun Soviet regime, between April and July of 1919, however, Lukács used his position as commissar of culture to incorporate Mannheim and the others in the ambitious educational program of the regime. The university was divided between a small highly specialized scholarly institute and a pedagogical academy, notably intended to train teachers to fight illiteracy and to carry the new political enlightenment. As noted earlier, Mannheim taught in that pedagogical program for the brief semester of Soviet rule. With the collapse, they all had to flee. Like Lukács, Mannheim spent the first months of his exile in Vienna, and there was evidently some continuing contact between them, although Lukács and his closest political comrades were deeply immersed in matters in which Mannheim did not share. Mannheim's first publication in Germany was a review of Lukács' *Theory of the Novel*, published in the influential journal, *Logos*, but the strongly admiring review makes no mention of Lukács' political conversion and theoretical reorientation in the preceding two years.

He praises Lukács, first, for recognizing that each of the many ways of knowing a given object is autonomous and has its own logical structure. An aesthetic view of an object's form, for example, requires that the elements of form are recognized as spiritual entities, interconnected by relations appropriate to such entities, and not by the causal linkages required if the object were to be explained as a physical field of force. Such pluralism respects the Idealist concern for logical order and structural analysis, but it avoids the reductionism inherent in the modern search for universal abstract laws that has led Idealism in its neo-Kantian form to assimilate all knowledge to the model of science. Second, Mannheim celebrates Lukács' attempt to find a level of interpretation able to account for the emergence of the plurality of inquiries and reveal the reasons for the variety of logics. Mannheim speaks of this level as a metaphysical one, but agrees with Lukács that it will take the form of a philosophy of history. This form accords with modern Romanticism, with its acute sensibilities for historical experience, but avoids the subjectivism and relativism with which Historicism has come to be linked. Mannheim thus lays out the two central issues of reductionism and relativism that occupy his philosophical speculations and that he carries forward into his subsequent sociological work. The autonomy of the various domains of knowledge counters the reductionist tendency to bring everything down to a fundamental unified science of the analytically simplest parts, like psychology or materialist sociology. The "metaphysics" projected differentiates itself into these autonomous activities, and its theory interprets them "from the top down." The possibility of such an integrative philosophy, in turn, counters relativism, while acknowledging diversity and change. There is nothing of Marxism here. It was the publication of *History and Class Consciousness* that first led Mannheim to reexamine his relations with Marxism.[3]

Lukács offers an interpretation of Marx strongly influenced by his own immersion in the German literature of cultural crisis, as well as by his own deep involvement with German idealist philosophy, notably Hegel and Fichte. True to the critique of rationalization epitomized in Alfred Weber's distinction between culture and civilization, he rejects Engels' identification of Marxism with recent advances in the physical sciences, especially Darwinism, and he construes the doctrine as above all an organon for political practice, ultimately as a realization of the classical ideal of "man as an end in himself" and as the militant articulation of a new culture (Lukács [1920a] 1973). The communist revolution, he concludes, is the breakthrough he had been seeking in his radical cultural criticism, and it is everywhere actually present, most notably in Lénin's Russia and in the Communist Party. Participation in that revolution, however, requires strict subordination to the organizational and strategic requirements of the class that is uniquely situated to do the work of theory and practice, under the guidance of its conscious minority.[4] There is no basis except such identification for social understanding or action.

It is important to be clear about this central feature of Lukács' Marxist theory, since it severely limits what Mannheim can draw from him, once he has questioned the revolutionary character of the crisis, qualified the privileged epistemological status of proletarian consciousness, and rejected the notion of any party as unique embodiment of tranformative action. There is a certain plausibility in the notion that Mannheim takes over the structure of Lukács' theory, simply substituting sociology for class consciousness and the intelligentsia for the proletariat, but Mannheim and Lukács are agreed that the holistic Marxist framework, as such, cannot accommodate such a shift in emphasis (Lukács 1920b; Lukács [1933] 1982). When Mannheim refers to himself as a Marxist, as he occasionally does during the last Weimar years, he is more nearly referring to the comparatively respectable Marx who is recognized as among the founders of German sociology and whose ideas can be appropriated selectively than to the revolutionary Marx envisioned by Lukács. The latter conception feeds instead, precisely because of the way in which Lukács constrains his activism by organization, into Mannheim's later critical depiction of an orthodox Marxism that inhibits the freedom integral to thought for the sake of action (see below). Orthodox Marxism, like fascism, eventually appears to him as a mode of reprimitivization, a retreat from the uncertainties inseparable from the openness of dynamic sociological thought. In effect, as Mannheim sees it, the unity of theory and practice dissolves, as the needs of practice are permitted to restrain theory.

The Marxism of Georg Lukács, in short, is essentially indifferent to the problems of sociology in the university, both of which fall under the strictures that he applies to organizations of intellectuals whom he considers inherently dedicated to reproducing their privilege in a bourgeois society (1920b), if they do not abandon their own organizations for those of the proletariat. Revolutionary struggle, Lukács says, is the appropriate means of education (*Erziehungsmittel*) (Lukács [1923] 1968: 84). Mannheim's dedication to the scientific discipline and to the university as the loci of cultivation, as well as his conception of political education for the sake of synthesis in thought and moderation in action put him at a great remove from Lukács. Yet Mannheim remained inspired by Lukács' heroic attempt to carry the legacy of classical German idealism into the anti-idealist Marxist account of social structure and social change, the aspect of Lukács' thought that brought him into constant conflict with the party to which that thought had brought him.

Lukács begins as a self-professed "orthodox" Marxist. The canon is authoritative, except for the more scientistic writings of Engels, and the historical drama is transpiring as Marx depicted it in the *Communist Manifesto*. The crisis of capitalism is grounded in the contradiction between means and relations of production, but its manifestations appear in every dimension of life, the political and cultural ones above all. In a passage reminiscent of both Freyer and Mannheim's emphasis on the questions of the day as point of departure for social understanding, Lukács writes,

> Only when man becomes capable of comprehending the present as becoming, in that he recognizes within it those tendencies out of whose dialectical contradictions he becomes capable of creating the future, only then does the present, the present as becoming, come to be his present. ([1923] 1968: 223)

Such dialectical knowledge, however, is not to be gained by scientific training as such, since "Only he who is called and willing to bring the future into being, can see the concrete truth of the present." Such calling does not depend on the accidents of individuals and their daemons, as in Max Weber, but in social location. It is embedded in the class consciousness of the proletariat. Only the classes historically situated to shape a social world have a class consciousness at all, Lukács argues. The bourgeoisie and proletariat are the only historical classes in this sense, with the bourgeoisie on the defensive and the proletariat on the offensive, and the imaginings of other social formations are simply cloaks for their despair. Yet the actual beliefs and professions of members even of the historical classes cannot be equated with class consciousness. Implicitly drawing on Max Weber, Lukács writes,

> Class consciousness . . . is the rationally appropriate reaction which is. . . imputed to a specific typical condition or situation in the process of production. (62)

The need for imputation arises for Lukács, above all, because of the widespread absence of active revolutionary awareness in the organized working class. Lukács is famous, above all, as the theorist of "false consciousness."

While Lenin had been largely content to blame the opposition of the Second International to his world-revolutionary project on the material privilege enjoyed by the "aristocrats of labor" in command of the trade unions and on the economic advantages enjoyed by the working classes of imperialist countries as a whole, Lukács developed a more elegant theory reminiscent of theories associated with Weber's rationalization thesis but expressly grounded on Marx's thesis of the fetishistic reification that is a concomitant of capitalist commodity production. Reformers and revisionists, he says, pride themselves on facing the "facts" of social complexity, notably the improving conditions of the working class and the rise of new middle classes, practical priorities of working people, and the expertise needed to operate a technologically advanced economy. But this characteristic empiricism is itself a manifestation of that transmutation of human actions into external objects which is the constitutive process of capitalism, as Marx showed. Corresponding to the passivity attending this "realism" in the economic-social sphere, Lukács contends, is a bland utopianism regarding the state and its politics. Constitutions and parliaments and legal systems and party competitions are all taken at face value, as is the supposed neutrality of the state machinery. Working-class organizations are held captive to the mechanisms of reification, even when they follow a course that appears to them as oppositional, unless they are somehow led by their own actions to make the leap to the revolutionary perspective.

A distinctive notion in *History and Class Consciousness*, less attractive to fellow Communists than to activist thinkers of quite different political coloration, is that determinism ceases to operate at the depth of the crisis and that the proletariat acts in "the realm of freedom" when it enters unconditionally on its revolutionary course. Everything depends on its maturity and class consciousness. The Russian Revolution succeeded because of Lenin's mastery of practical knowledge. The Hungarian and German revolutions failed for lack of such magisterial leadership. Like Lukács' other deviations from the more mechanical scientific model of Marxism, this conception brought him harsh criticism from official party intellectuals, but it also helps to explain his attractiveness to Mannheim and others brought up in the atmosphere of the Weber debate.

Most important in both of these respects is Lukács' continued alignment with the party of "culture" against the party of "civilization," technology, and specialized sciences. In an essay of 1920, not included in *History and Class Consciousness* but certainly known to Mannheim, if only because it was the text of a lecture on a ceremonial occasion in Budapest that Mannheim could not have missed, he uses Alfred Weber's terminology, much in Weber's sense, while disdainfully separating himself from bourgeois plaints that the collapse of capitalism spells the end of culture. "The culture of the capitalist epoch had already collapsed," he writes, "before the economic and political collapse made itself known" (65). The reasons for this, however, are revealing in their lack of disrespect for the contents of that culture, in its classical high phase, before the maturation of technology and industry.[5] As a complex of products and capacities that have value beyond the satisfaction of basic human needs, culture depends on the availability of free energies. That is why cultures belonged to ruling classes in the past. As capitalism advances, however, it subjects its ruling class as well as its subjects to the requirements of production. More specifically, Lukács cites the dire effects of turning cultural products into commodities, the disruption of unified creation by division of labor, and the constant demand for novelties. Culture must grow organically, oriented to man as an end in himself. The counter-image of culture that Lukács applies as a criterion to condemn these effects is fully in accord with the views of Spranger and Curtius. In tacit recognition of such parallels, Lukács traces the roots of cultural collapse to a contradiction between culture and the organization of both production and society. Although the contents of cultural productions are generated by social reality, their forms may be transcendent, derived from the human creativity that brings them forth. There is a relative autonomy at work here, and the producers of culture suffered from the contradictions afflicting their work. As a result, Lukács says, the remnants of genuine culture under capitalism were harshly critical of capitalism, without being able, by themselves, to achieve any change. Pessimism and despair prevailed. However, Lukács concludes, "Emancipation from capitalism signifies emancipation from domination by the economy." There will be a new culture because there will be an escape from the imperatives of commodity production and technology culminating in a new organicism.[6]

Five years after the publication of *History and Class Consciousness*, Mannheim and Alfred Weber conducted a joint seminar on the book. Although Mannheim nominally figured in the debate as the advocate of Lukács' book, his reading showed the great distance between his own position and the conservative cultural ideal that continued to work in Lukács—and that Mannheim tried to impute to Weber instead. The background for the seminar was provided by Alfred Weber's comments in Zurich, after Mannheim's lecture on "Competition as Cultural Phenomenon." Weber had reacted strongly to Mannheim's paper, labeling it "intellectualistic" and reminiscent of historical materialism.[7] Addressing his independent Heidelberg protégé directly, he says,

> What I find missing in your discussion is a recognition of spiritual creativity as a basis for action, for example for the action of social classes. What I reject is the reduction of all these things to, in the final analysis, intellectual categories to which have been added several—if you will excuse me—sociological categories taken from the old materialistic view of history. You have spoken of positions of social power, of aspirations that result from them, of a public interpretation of existence which is combined with these positions of power and aspirations, but not of other factors in this context. Is all this anything more than a brilliant rendition of the old historical materialism, presented with extraordinary subtlety? Basically it is nothing else. (Meja/Stehr 1990: 89–90)

During the debate that followed, a number of thinkers ranging from Werner Sombart to Norbert Elias supported Mannheim against this reduction of his argument (Meja/Stehr 1990: 53–56, 90, 91–92). But no less telling for Weber than Mannheim's alleged "historical materialism" was his alleged "intellectualism," which meant for Weber the fragmentation of the cultural sphere into rational constructs, designed by thinking and integrated by ideological principles, and manifesting spirit rather than soul (Mannheim 2001). He credits Mannheim with a "sublimated intellectualism that uses such categories to present, with extraordinary gracefulness and refinement, problems that pertain properly to the soul" and he says with regret that despite these subtleties the intellectualism has the same effects and results as "the vulgarized intellectualism represented by the old materialist theory of history" (Meja/Stehr 1982: 376). Imposing "intellectualistic" categories upon culture, whether centered on groups' material interests or on their need to offer a public interpretation of the world congruent with their social being means the destruction of the larger organic sphere of meaning. Not rational analysis but "spiritual creativity" is the essential faculty for synthesis. By "spiritual creativity" Weber meant the ability to create a cultural totality of meaning, to bridge the gap between the soul of the individual and the larger unified whole. And like the formulators of the humanistic ideal of cultivation, Weber assumed that such an organic totality existed, something that Mannheim had come to reject.

The differences between Mannheim and Weber, as well as the relevance of Marxism to these differences, would not have come as a surprise to either man in 1928. Weber had written Else Jaffé after he first saw Mannheim's preliminary habilitation proposal in 1921 that Mannheim's all-embracing methodological prospectus ruefully reminded him of Lederer and Lukács, since Mannheim, too, promised to deviate from his own theoretical line (Demm 1999: 30). Both of the men that Weber links to Mannheim were, of course, Marxists, in one sense or another, and closer to Mannheim than Weber could ever be.[8] Using a Latin formula, Weber cleverly projects them as a sort of astronomical cluster, with one attracting the other: *"Trahit* Lederer Lukács. *Trahit* Lukács Mannheim" (Alfred Weber to Else Jaffé, February 13, 1922, Barch, NL A. Weber/90, p. 84; cit. Demm 1999: 30). Although Mannheim had carefully sought his advice, Weber fully expected Mannheim to follow his own way. He highly commended the completed project, supervised in the end by Emil Lederer and substantially narrowed since the original design, although he expressly faulted its closeness to the Marxist scheme of base and superstructure (Demm 1999: 470–1). Alfred Weber was a genuine liberal, willing to respect and to debate differences, and Mannheim, of course, made the possibility of finding common ground for synthesis central to his position. They were both committed to the "spirit of Heidelberg," which, as Demm points out, "distinguished itself precisely by its numerous adversarial debates and open discussions, both in seminars and in scientific circles" (Demm 1999: 43–44).[9]

Accordingly, the debate about Marxism between the noted professor and upstart *Privatdozent* continued collegially some months later in a joint seminar back in Heidelberg, the protocol of which is included in our collection of translations (Mannheim 2001). The seminar began as a discussion of Lukács's *History and Class Consciousness* and quickly returned to the themes of Zurich. Both men agreed that Lukács was right to maintain that consciousness is historical, that historical knowledge must have a volitional component and that history forms a totality. However, they were in sharp disagreement over the meaning to attach to what Weber approvingly calls Lukács' "demand and attempts at de-absolutizing the rational and intellectualism."

At the outset, Weber announced his vitalistic premises, declaring himself a "Bergsonian." For him, "the highest arbiters and the orientation poles of existence were determined meta-intellectually—as Plato's metaphysics, for example, is based on vision rather than on rational coherences of validity." "Intellectualistic" thinking is purely instrumental and "has no part in the setting of ends." Such thinking tries to present "ideas" as nothing more than a type of thinking when in fact they are "acts of deportment of the soul, whereby a subject . . . creatively unites itself with the object." Explaining his earlier characterization of Mannheim's position as "intellectualistic," he contends that Mannheim works with the bourgeois disjunction between thought and being, introduced by Descartes, while he insists on recognizing "other fundamental powers of existence." "What is at issue here," he contends, "are the ultimate attitudes of soul, the ultimate attitudes of the soul towards existence." And he implies that Lukács may be closer to his own position than to that of Mannheim.

Mannheim disagreed with Weber's depiction of his position as "intellectualistic." For him, this term applies properly to "a theory of thinking that maintains that correct judgments can be discovered on the basis of something immanent in thought," and it has as its underlying image "a conception that all possible truths and correct judgments that are thinkable are all present, valid simultaneously." He is satisfied to think, since the issue is not being forced on the agenda by the present situation, that the physical sciences may have this character, although he concedes, as a Marxist, that there may come a time when it will be necessary to reconsider that assumption. The question between himself and Weber, he contends, is not "intellectualism" but contrasting conceptions of rationality. As paraphrased by the rapporteur:

> He wants to posit a different conception of the rational in place of this intellectualistic one, one where that which can be thought at a given point in time is inwardly connected to the thinking historical subject's condition of being, and where the only thinkable thoughts and truths are those that coincide with the point one has reached in being. (Mannheim [1929c] 2001: 113)

When Mannheim comes to specify this thought, however, he departs from Lukács in quite dramatic ways. First, he expressly corrects him on the question of whether only the proletariat has a chance of knowledge. "Every . . . standpoint," he says, "has such a [chance] for its own part. . . . up to the threshold of the concealment that it enacts in its thought, and this boundary always lies at the point of its own basic wants in the social process." Mannheim drives the point home:

> When he uses the word "bourgeois," it does not mean the same as it does in the language of a fighting socialist, for whom it designates *eo ipso* a class condemned to go under, but rather an intellectual standpoint that has a function necessary for the future and not fulfillable by any other standpoint. (118; cp. Laube 2000)

Second, Mannheim labels the rationality that he sees as vital to the historical process a "functionalist" one, which is constituted by the connection between the basic wants of a given standpoint and the "achievable." This reanalysis of "dialectic" would surely have amazed Lukács. Mannheim sets this "functionalist" rationality over against a "morphological" rationality that he imputes to Weber, a rationalization of organic forms designed "to rescue the irrational." He credits the latter with insights denied the former, but insists, even compromising his effort to avoid the stigma of intellectualism, that the Marxism he supports is right to "analyze and functionalize. . . as far as possible":

> It must do this because it represents a fighting class that depends on the ability to master being. Because it is activist thought, it must be intellectualistic. And for this aspect it possesses maximal chances for truth—i.e., for knowledge of everything that is subject to rationalization and mastery in history. (117–118)

Mannheim's "defense" of Lukács eventuates in a remarkable openness to technological thinking, if also in a uniquely reflexive mode, since it is not grounded in the presumed universality of the science on which technology rests but in self-aware working-class orientations. This rationality, he contends, aims at historical change while Weber's rationality is dedicated to resistance to change. It is a question of two distinct standpoints. For himself, he claims a position capable of appreciating both, while reserving the right to recognize one of them as more adequate to the historical moment.

Weber objected to Mannheim's depiction of him as a conservative "Romantic," concerned above all to encapsulate, contemplate, and protect a realm of perfected cultural formations. He asserted that his reflexive approach also allowed for actualization and experimentation. He allows a place to intellectualism as an instrument for meeting the material needs of existence (*Dasein*), but he denies that the mentality appropriate to these processes of civilization has any comprehension of culture. Not thinking, but an intuitive action of the soul opens the way to inner participation in the formations comprising culture. Civilization has its just, progressive claims, but there is no meaning without culture.

The discussion sparkles with philosophical displays, some of them deeply suggestive, but the remaining difference most interesting here, as in Zurich, relates to education and cultivation. The question is, how does the individual soul orient itself in the world? Does it do so by achieving some sort of unity with the larger organic, meaningful whole? This was the assumption at the basis of the humanistic ideal of cultivation, one shared by Weber. Or is more self-reflexivity required, by which one contextualizes one's perspective in relation to various competing volitional/spiritual currents, so that one might participate in the reconfiguration of meaning? This was Mannheim's position by the time of the joint seminar. The question had been among the first he addressed in his youthful intellectual life. With Lukács, he had argued that the soul cannot commune directly with cultural formations in a time of spiritual objectification, but that there is no alternative to proceeding intellectually in the critical and analytical mode appropriate to the times until a great incalculable overturn transpires (Mannheim [1918] 1970; Kettler 1971).[10] When he was not persuaded, with Lukács, that the Communist revolution represented that turning point, he began to reconsider the stark disjunction between soul and spirit, between culture and civilization. In the last analysis, he thus broke with Lukács on the need for, or reality of, revolution. There could not be a deeper breach, whatever affinities remained between their theories of history. Weber could not accept that culture might be comprehended as a modality of civilization any more than Lukács could accept that mediation between proletarian and bourgeois ideologies might generate a synthesis and grounds for further human development. Access to the highest human achievement—what Lukács called, in language he may have recalled from his time with Alfred Weber—the idea of man as an end in himself—had to be unmediated and complete. For Lukács, this required the steps from proletarian class consciousness to revolution to "new culture." For Weber, it came back ultimately to cultivation in the classical sense, understood much as the classics did, however pessimistic the prospects might be.

Mannheim, in contrast, was surprisingly cool. He certainly saw the pedagogical implications of the issue between them. At the beginning of the second day of the seminar, he uses two models of pedagogy to exemplify the contrast between the irrational and the rational, as he would like it understood. "Thinking that is rationally determined has achievement and the achievable as its paradigm," he says, "while the paradigm of the irrational, in contrast, is growth and the growing.... The reaction of the subject to the rational is cognition, while that to the irrational is to let it have a productive and formative effect on himself." In the older pedagogy, he continues, paraphrasing the cultivational ideal as it might be stated by Spranger or Curtius, "the teacher originally works on the student out of his own substantial being, in order to build education up out of the student's center, so that the student develops himself creatively." This is no longer the case. "That which works creatively and substantively is retreating, as the orientation to the rationally achievable and controllable comes ever more to the fore." The point is that Mannheim registers the transition without regret. He moves from the newer pedagogy to psychoanalysis, which "has worked out a rational method for treating things of the soul." Without irony, he points out that this science seeks "first to analyze things of the soul into certain basic elements and then purposefully to recompose the latter."[11] Undermining his opponent, he recalls, first, that it is Alfred Weber's brother Max who offers the methodological paradigm for such rationalizing of the irrational, and he claims, second, that Alfred Weber's morphological cultural sociology is performing the same function, although more from necessity than out of hope for achievement. Mannheim recalls that this was the main thesis of his conservatism study. Defensive rationalization to protect irrational substance is still rationalization. Mannheim values Alfred Weber's sociology of culture and learns from it, but he denies that it can do what Weber hopes (cp. Loader 1997; Demm 2000; Blomert 1995; Blomert 1999). The old unmediated contact between an elevated soul and an organic culture is no more possible in sociology than in pedagogy. Mannheim's reference to Max Weber is not only a reminder of the common ground between the two speakers—to the students too—but also an implicit reference to his claim in Zurich to be engaged in a renewal of Weber's norm of value-freedom. In their political professions, too, Mannheim and Alfred Weber highlighted their commonality.

When Mannheim remarks, "What is common to all of us is the determination not to let ourselves be swallowed up by capitalism,"

Alfred Weber responds that, as far as he is concerned, "the question he addresses to history is the same as that of socialism: he does not want capitalism either." His closing remarks in the seminar, in fact—as he rejects what he calls Mannheim's attempt to "relationize" him and refuses, in turn, to "encapsulate" Mannheim in some morphological shell, as Mannheim expects him to do—return to the claim of a shared political project. The protocol closes: "The standpoint that he [AW] represents offers no less a complete embrace of precisely the proletarian standpoint, because he grew up [in that standpoint] on the basis of an origin in [the proletarian standpoint] and a going beyond it." It is not discreditable to the two scholars to suggest that there was an element of playing to the expectations of their students in their competition to identify with the proletarian standpoint. Whatever may have been the case with Weber, the core group of students close to Mannheim at the end of his Heidelberg stay, with the important exception of Elias, were engaged politically on the Left (Kettler/Meja 1994). The context of the seminar was moreover defined by two student papers on Lukács, at least one of which was certainly enthusiastic, and the two interventions by post-doctoral students present were clearly friendly to the Marxist project. For Weber to speak of his origin in the proletarian standpoint rather embroiders his sincere early dedication to reformist social policy, and for Mannheim to call himself a Marxist in the context of that discussion raises not a few doubts, in view of the key positions he abandons, at least as they are essential to the Marxism of Lukács.[12]

There is another important dimension however, and it points towards a major current in Mannheim's thought, a productive relationship to Marxism that is not mediated by Lukács in any important way. At the opening of the first of the seminar sessions, according to the protocol, "[Professor Weber] distinguished the Marxism expounded by Lukács in his book as 'dialectical materialism' from the philosophical position of historical materialism as a positivistic method of viewing history, which must be judged empirically according to its fruitfulness for specific research tasks and not philosophically, like the other" (Mannheim [1929c] 2001). Weber was satisfied that Lukács also raised the key questions that Mannheim and he then discussed, but it is important to note that Mannheim never challenged the distinction and that he addressed himself to Weber's questions. Without attempting to decide the question here whether Mannheim ever fully finished dealing with the problems of "dialectical materialism" raised by Lukács, we can safely conclude that Mannheim's references to himself as a "Marxist" in the seminar and his praise of Marx as master sociologist in his introductory lectures refer more nearly to "historical materialism," the approach that was represented in sociology by the Austrian Max Adler, who was to have been the occupant of the chair eventually awarded to Hans Freyer, and notably by his primary Heidelberg mentor, the actual director of his habilitation essay, Emil Lederer. In both cases, Mannheim's interest attached not to their philosophical attempts to engage the issues of Lukács' "dialectical materialism," for which Mannheim turned instead to existentialist and phenomenological thinkers, but to their methods and to their substantive historical theses subject to empirical testing.

Adler would have been an awkward model for Mannheim to acknowledge during the Heidelberg years, although he cites him respectfully in his 1921 treatise, both because of his uncongenial philosophy and because of the sharp conflict between him and Alfred Weber. Max Adler was an Austrian socialist best known for his attempts to reconcile Marxist social theory with Kantian philosophy. During the first years of the Weimar Republic, he was recognized by the German Sociological Association as an acceptable spokesperson for Marxism, which could not be simply excluded under the new circumstances. In 1920 and again in 1924, he was invited to offer a major presentation. The 1924 meetings of the association took place in Heidelberg, and they featured Max Scheler's seminal talk on sociology of knowledge (*Soziologie des Wissens*), introducing the concept. Adler was Scheler's co-referee, as Mannheim was von Wiese's four years later. Punctuated by angry heckling from Alfred Weber, Adler argued that Scheler's philosophical speculations on relations between cultural contexts and modes of knowing lack reference to dynamic social forces, and that Scheler's teachings, typified by his plea for Western openness to Eastern capacities for suffering and contemplation, reveal the inability of "bourgeois science" to face realities damaging to its world. Adler recalls that his distinction between "bourgeois" and "proletarian" social policy (*Sozialpolitik*) had already caused an uproar the day before, and he continues: "For there is such ressentiment associated with the terms `bourgeois and proletarian' among bourgeois scholars, that it is scarcely possible to have a calm discussion." Someone rises to the bait and calls out, "And what about proletarian scholars?" Adler calmly—

even pedantically—insists that "proletarian science" is not interest-bound and that scientific method is universal: the difference lies in proletarian readiness to comprehend the social forces making for progressive change. His distinction explains, he contends, the sudden fascination in bourgeois-educated publics with the decline of culture, as well as the Orient—"even in those circles where Orientals are not in general so very popular." Moreover, bourgeois scholars now extenuate the old "Yellow Peril" and even flirt with it, "because it might help to avert the Red Peril, if also at the cost of white independence." Alfred Weber interrupts to charge rabble-rousing ("*Volksversammlung!*") and is answered by protest and applause. Adler proceeds with his contrast between "stationary" and "evolutionary" thinking, and he evokes another angry response when he mockingly recalls the contrasts between contemporary political imagery and that of the recent past. It is now good form, he notes, to speak about the cultural "muck" (*Schlamm*) of the times, while the same intellectual leaders had failed to notice the muck in which hundreds of thousands died, but spoke instead of the "genius of war." At this point, Scheler and Weber both burst out in rage, and the hall is in an uproar. From the chair, von Wiese cautions the speaker to abstain from value judgments. Adler agrees but observes that while it is not considered a value judgment to see nothing but muck in revolutionary outbreaks, it is an altogether different matter when war and oppression are at issue (Adler [1924] 1982). This was far from Mannheim's style.[13]

Adler's work, nevertheless, played an important part in freeing historical materialist teachings from the stigma of reductionist economism. First, he insisted on the right of Marxists to expand the range of Marxist thought without being held to a scholastic standard of interpretation, especially by their opponents. His Marxism rejects orthodoxy. Citing an article that he wrote jointly in 1904 with Rudolph Hilferding, Adler explains what he means by Marxism:

> Not a dogmatic formula or a compilation and systematization of Marx quotations, but the *method of thinking* founded by Marx. . . . We do not represent Marxism as something that has always been literally correct, but that as something that is *capable* of being right. What counts as Marxism for us is everything that must be thought, even if it appears nowhere in Marx and Engels, as a logical consequence of their basic views, and for their grounding as well as further development. Only such a Marxism has meaning for me, because it is a living teaching and a generative spiritual force. (Adler [1924] 1982: 140)

Second, Adler inveighed against a materialist rendering of the relations captured in what he repeatedly insists is only the metaphorical construction of base and superstructure. Arguing against Hans Kelsen during their joint appearance before the German Sociological Association in 1920 on the topic of "State and Socialism," Adler says,

> It would mean the violent death of any understanding of the materialist interpretation of history if one did not recognize that there is in it no dualism between a spiritless economic material and a spiritual life erected upon it. Economic relations are nothing but relations of production and exchange, which means that they are relations among men and thus *spiritual relations*. Consequently, a single band of a spiritual nature encloses everything from economic phenomena to the heights of mystical contemplation. (Adler 1922: 86–7)

Economic activities become socially relevant only through their mediation as a mode of social experience, and "rightly understood, the teaching. . . that 'the economy' is the basis for the entire superstructure of social consciousness means only that the concrete historical filling up of the forms of social consciousness receive their decisive impulses from the sphere where the maintenance and reproduction of life is secured" (Adler 1922: 88). "There are no material relations," he says elsewhere, "because work itself, when it is oriented to material production, as well as the distribution of its products and consumption is impossible without the purposive and evaluative activity of human beings" (Adler [1924] 1982: 134–5). In his 1924 treatise, Mannheim cites a passage to the same effect from one of Adler's earlier books and asserts that "it is for this reason that Max Adler's interpretation of Marx is completely correct and fully adequate" in this respect (Mannheim [1922–24] 1982: 223). Marxism appears as a theory of social-psychological linkages among historical layers of social formation, subject to empirical investigation and testing. Not the revolution, but the dynamic social effect of aggressive class action in the social spheres of law, politics, and ethics, as well as economic organization, becomes the central figure, in keeping with the Austrian Marxist political conception.

In Germany, Adler's work especially inspired the younger postwar generation who published in the journal established by his erstwhile co-author, Rudolf Hilferding.[14] In Adler's spirit, *Die Gesellschaft* was an outlet for empirical appropriations of Marxism without a sacrifice of political radicalism. Historical materialism became an open terrain instead of a closed doctrine, expanded to include developments and disputes internal to such fields as law and art—even economics—without forcing the "Marxist" analyst to disconnect from the constitutive discourses of the respective fields because of doctrinaire reductions, and expanded also to concentrate on new developments unanticipated by the Marxist classics without the prejudgment that these must prove to be without significance "in the last analysis." In a simple sense, Adler can be said to have been the godfather of a new generation of academically gifted intellectuals attracted to the Social Democratic parties of central Europe for political reasons and eager to experiment loyally with the categories of the party doctrine, while they pursued the academic or professional recognition—and careers—opened up by the postwar political changes.

In the intermediate generation, among the figures who emerged in the prewar decade, few were as important to this group, both as intellectual mentor and as power broker, than Alfred Weber's wayward habilitant and admired colleague, Emil Lederer. Lederer was born of Jewish parents in Bohemia in 1882, a year before Lukács, and received his first degree in economics, in the Vienna institute of the marginal utility theorists.[15] He was brought to Heidelberg in 1910 to serve as principal assistant by Edgar Jaffé, the directing editor of the foremost social science journal, *Archiv für Sozialwissenschaft und Sozialpolitik*, and he became one of the directing editors in 1922, together with Alfred Weber and Joseph Schumpeter. Weber oversaw his habilitation and picked him as his own teaching replacement when he was briefly called to active service early in the war. Lederer received a first academic appointment at Heidelberg in 1920 and Weber was able to see him installed as a full professor in 1923 to replace a major conservative voice, Eberhard Gothein. A member of the prewar Heidelberg cluster that also included Lukács, Radbruch, and Salomon, he was close, after the war, to both Becker and the cultural minister of Baden; and he served as promoter to Salomon, Hans Speier, Adolph Löwe, among other productive scholars working in various Marxist idioms. And he was Karl Mannheim's very effective patron saint, from the time of Mannheim's arrival in Heidelberg to the time of his establishment as professor in Frankfurt (Blomert 1999; Demm 1999; Demm 2000; Kettler/Meja 1995; Woldring 1986: 24–30). There is some danger that Lederer's intellectual accomplishments may be neglected because of his history of potent sponsorships and weight in academic politics. But Alfred Weber's respect for Lederer and his extraordinary appeal to a vital generation of students were not earned by his political skills.

With his credentials as a technical economist and his strategic position on a key journal, Lederer was in an extraordinary position to normalize Marxist approaches to social inquiry in the university, at least in those institutions not fully controlled by conservative and nationalist academics. He represents the most important exception to the rule of successful university resistance to the changes intended by Becker and his counterparts in cultural ministries controlled by the Weimar coalition parties. During the early 1920s, his courses were exclusively devoted to Marxism, socialism, and socialization; and these topics continued to predominate in his teaching.[16] His habilitation thesis addressed the issue of the salaried, the newly arising middle stratum of private and public officials, as well as the wider array of white-collar and service occupations, a question important to socialist debates since the time of Bernstein's provocative citation of this phenomenon among others that rendered Marxist social theory, in his view, largely obsolete. Lederer challenged this view, in a detailed statistical study, and his writings on the topic, having liberated the topic from the polarization derived from the Revisionism debate, initiated an important extended discussion among socialist scholars (see Blomert, 1999).[17]

Lederer's empirically conditioned and selective adaptation of Marxism is evident in an influential article published in a political science journal in the year of his habilitation, "The Economic Factor and the Political Idea in the Modern Party System" (Lederer 1911). Lederer does not challenge the older liberal conception of competing political parties as expressions of clashing fundamental political ideas, since he observes that the parties do indeed find themselves impelled to advance their electoral prospects by urging universal principles, but he questions the continued saliency of this phenomenon to the conditions he sees emerging. The rise of an organized economy has seen the incorporation of individuals according to class interests in organizations that are playing an ever more powerful part in determining the effective social policy outcomes. The classes represented are defined by economic location, but they are differentiated far more finely than might be suggested by Marxist macro-theory, from industrialists and industrial workers to numerous varieties of economic locations in the middle ranks (*Mittelstand*). Their various justifications and mobilizing doctrines are ideologies in precisely the Marxist sense. They are increasingly colonizing the parties as well, converting parliament into a forum of interest group politics, although the legislative process is no longer decisive for public policy outcomes. Marxist categories best serve to explain the interrelationships. The effective defunctionalization of parliament also points towards new forms of representation, perhaps a self-governing society remote from the stage of state domination.[18] On this view, Marxism serves as a kind of theory of the middle range, to stretch Merton's label, best applicable to a given phase of historical development.

This sense of Marxism echoes in Mannheim's cautious answer to Alfred Weber's inquiry, during the joint seminar, whether he considered the Marxist conception universally valid. The protocol records,

> Dr. Mannheim gives preference to the validity of the Marxist conception of history for the capitalist epoch, and he is prepared to concede economism a preferential heuristic value for pre-capitalist epochs as well, because we have gained, as a result of our mainly economically determined problem situation, a good eye for the significance of the economic in history as a whole. By this method, we make visible in the longitudinal section of history precisely the configurations that are practically most important for us today. (Mannheim [1929c] 2001: 114)

Mannheim cites Lederer's 1911 article in the introduction to the long excerpt from his habilitation work on conservatism that he published in the journal co-directed by Lederer, Weber, and Schumpeter (Mannheim 1927: 422), where he also published more than half of his scholarly articles between 1922 and 1930, but Lederer's basic conception informs the study as a whole. Lederer is unrestrained in its praise, while Weber's favorable report includes the following pregnant reservation:

> The theory of base and superstructure that Mannheim has not completely outgrown—although no historical materialist—still seems to me to manifest itself too much in the theses of the work. (Cit. in Demm 1999: 470–1)

Lederer clearly liked what made Weber uneasy, precisely because Mannheim's structural analysis of conservative thought, implying the integrity of cultural formations, and his sociological explanation of the conditions of its social possibility utilized "genuine scholarly materials and a method free from subjectivity" in a manner "far beyond all aphorisms about the relationships between base and superstructure" (UAH. cp. Woldring 1986: 24–25). Lederer writes, "[Mannheim's thesis] opens up the problem of reality and 'superstructure,' but in a way that does not look only to reality in the sense of naked economic interests, but also to the forms of social appearances, the social structure of a time, and that supplies, on the other hand, a clarification and enrichment of the concept of superstructure that first makes it usable." The point is that the analysis is specific and qualified, not aphoristic.[19] And that is what makes for the uses of Marxism that Lederer's student, Albert Salomon, called "Marxistic" sociology (see above).

Lederer's interest in cultural sociology was not an incidental byproduct of his studies in the new class structure of organized capitalism, although this in itself turned his attention, for example, to the important link between cultivational ideals and the constitution of the intellectual occupations.[20] His contribution to the seminal volume for Max Weber in 1923 was the text of his 1922 presentation to the German Sociological Association, "The Tasks of a Cultural Sociology." According to Scaff (1990), Lederer moves beyond Marxism in this study, but this reading underestimates the versatility of the approach in Lederer's judgment. He certainly rejects the idea that cultural sociology should limit itself to the kinds of questions that limited historical materialism in the past. Lederer points out to critics of the enterprise that Alfred Weber shows that cultural sociology may not be equated with historical materialism. Lederer's distinctive position only emerges, however, when he charges the critics with using a false rendering of Marx to discredit the materialist theory of history:

> Marx provided nothing more than apercus for the materialist theory of history. How much untrammeled further development is both possible and necessary in order to make all of the scientific possibilities that repose in his basic thoughts bear fruit is shown by the works of Max Adler, which have been given much too little recognition until now,— to all of which we make reference here—by the problem set laid out in quite a different direction by Lukács [in his review of Benedetto Croce in 1911] and by the partly tacit theses in sociological studies whose topics consisted of the analysis of a specific phenomenon. [Lederer's Note:] In this connection, may I refer to my study: "The economic factor and political ideas in the modern party system": the attempt is made there to examine the structure of the political ideal of the present with reference to their dependence on the antagonistic economic currents of interests and to show the way by which the political idea of early bourgeois society turns into "ideology" in the current sense of the word. (Lederer 1923: 149–50)

Like Adler, Lederer shows the need to reconceptualize the social dimension of the relationship between "base" and "superstructure," so that the pattern of class relations relevant to a certain artistic style, for example, cannot be related to the economic locations of those classes without a great many intermediate steps. The linkages will not, in any case, be causal in a naturalistic sense, especially since cultural production is always a matter of independent creativity. The social equation operates most decisively in defining the social conditions for the actualization of the art work and its recognition[21] or the effective validation of the law, not in its concrete generation. As a practical matter, the concept of "production relations" is replaced in this work by "the times," with the primary sociological task being to delineate the social relations that constitute the "times" in the relevant sense. As Scaff points out, Lederer finds that contemporary art is distinguished by its actual detachment from the social "base," but Scaff does not give sufficient weight to the fact that Lederer subjects this phenomenon itself to a social interpretation. In his conclusion, Lederer returns literally to the Marxist[ic] roots:

> To be sure, this falling away of the social substructure is only one possibility, but it shows especially clearly what is meant by social conditioning [*Bedingtheit*]: not the reduction of cultural achievements to calculable consequences of material causes. Rather: their interlinkage [*Verknüpfung*] with the totality of social basic conditions [*Grundverhältnisse*], which may not be evaluated as less in liveliness, significance, creative force because they are rooted in turn in the relations of production. (Lederer 1923: 171)[22]

The Marxist framing of social inquiry—and especially in the area of cultural sociology—is not so much a self-contained research program as it is a response to a magisterial stimulus, a resolve to experiment with certain key figures (like the discrepancy between means and relations of production), and an emblem of alternatives rejected. It is a badge. In this sense, Mannheim was (often) a Marxist in his sociology. This Marxism was not a world view but a social-scientific heuristic.

In Mannheim's view, his Marxism, unlike the Marxism of Lukács or other orthodox adherents of the creed, did not even pretend to extend to all the vital issues confronting the "sociological attitude" taken as a world view, as he worked the conception out most clearly in the 1930 lecture course (Mannheim [1930a] 2001). Mannheim's "empiricism" extended to the evidences of "experience" in the sense of the phenomenological school, as well as "life" in the sense of the vitalism that Alfred Weber invoked by his reference to Bergson.[23] The reasoning that Adler and Lederer used to explain the rootedness of social and cultural formations in production relations does not preclude attention to experiences that do not fit present understandings of production relations. The integrity of aesthetic experience, after all, is presupposed by their non-reductionist conception of the art examined by cultural sociology. It is the work of social understanding to comprehend these experiences, not to censor a certain class of them as illegitimate because they are not recognizable as experiences of class interest, economic deprivation, or workplace tensions. If Mannheim's "Marxism" stood for the paradigm of "functional" rationalization, as he indicated in his exchanges with Weber, it embodied a demand rather than a completed achievement—or, indeed, one that could ever be completed. In this sense, he challenges Weber's self-understanding of his own theoretical work. The "morphological" apprehension of life and the soul in their immediacy is itself a mode of rationalization, if not (yet) a Marxistic one, and it does not entail, to make explicit something that is only implicit in the joint seminar and becomes explicit only in Mannheim's writings after the challenge of Freyer becomes clear in 1930, some sort of privileged "irrationalist" expressivity. "Life" and "experience" set the agenda, indeed, but it is thought that has to fulfill it, notably the sociological thought epitomized in "Marxism."

The relationship between the language of "life" philosophy favored by Alfred Weber and Mannheim's sociological program is well illustrated in a newspaper article later that year (Mannheim 1929c; Mannheim 2001) published by Mannheim to publicize the work of the newly founded Institute of Journalistic Studies at Heidelberg, where Weber had secured him a teaching position (Blomert 1999: 38–48; Demm 1999: 128–137). Mannheim poses the issue in terms reminiscent of his article on "Science and Youth" six years earlier (Mannheim [1922] 2001). The emphasis is on the rejuvenation of the sciences by opening them to new experiences, without, however, surrendering them to the flux. In this case, moreover, he can show, on the one hand, that the cultural disciplines, notably philosophy, have already expanded their conceptions since the time of Dilthey to recognize inchoate forms of lived experience, notably under the heading of "everyday life." To comprehend these newly recognized objects of study, however, Mannheim calls on sociology.

Because of the intimate links between the newspapers and the articulation of everyday life known as public opinion, Mannheim argued, the establishment of journalism as a university subject brought science in closer contact with "life." But the study cannot be limited to the practical aspects of the field, the skills and information needed for effective practice of the occupation. To comprehend the press and its relations with public opinion, it is necessary to put the matter in the wider contexture explored by sociology, as the decisive academic discipline for the rational appropriation of the new.

Sociology, Mannheim believed, was able to reconfigure itself conceptually through remaining open to the constantly new empirical content of the world of everyday life. Interestingly, as at one point in his discussion with Alfred Weber, he presented Max Weber's work as paradigmatic. Not Marx but Max Weber usually served him as the paradigm for sociology in appeals to wider publics. Like Albert Salomon, however, he did not let this invocation of Weber stand in the way of his simultaneous identification of sociology with Marxism in the extended sense, especially when addressing students. In any case, the sociology of public opinion appeared as a crucial integrating approach for the science of journalism, allowing for "the reciprocal penetration of practice and university science. . . to take effect." The prerational intimations of lived experience were opened to observation in the various stages of their articulation into forms, and the emerging forms were subject to study in their dynamic fluidity. Sociology refined its capacities for such study by engaging with practical experiences that a scholastic formalism could not even recognize, and a specific location in the world of practice is provided a new consciousness of its interconnections with the larger social context by sociology, and thus of its tasks and possibilities.[24] With the suggestion that study of public opinion and the press contributes to sociology, Mannheim has elevated a level of experience and a mode of its integration that Marx himself considered fit matter only for exposé and contempt, notwithstanding his lifelong involvement in the journalistic domain.

The limiting case of religious experience[25] is graphically developed in a recorded encounter in 1931 between Mannheim and three Frankfurt colleagues who subsequently became well known for their own radical transformations of Marxist impulses but who chose at that time to represent the Marxist world view: Theodore Wiesengrund [Adorno], Max Horkheimer, and Frederick Pollock (Tillich [1983]; Mannheim's interventions are translated in Mannheim 2001). In this case, moreover, Mannheim does not suggest how sociology might interact with "life," except by acknowledging the limits of its jurisdiction. Yet it is just as important to note that such experience is not permitted to overturn the understandings derived through sociological analysis. Mannheim refuses to let Marxist objections deter him from exploring his religious intimations, but he also refuses to permit these religious questions to interfere with his dedication to the interests of the working class, an issue posed by the objections raised in the course of the discussion to the religious socialism of the meeting's organizer.

On June 27, 1931, the theologian Paul Tillich, recently appointed professor of social education in the unorthodox philosophy department in Frankfurt, organized a day-long meeting between members of the informal Frankfurt discussion group who were his regular partners in intense talk about social and political questions and a number of Protestant theologians, several of whom were not a little skeptical of Tillich's secular involvements and social-philosophical religious thought (Tillich 1983). The immediate occasion was the soul-searching within the Church about the Christian mission in a secularized world, an inquiry given urgency by perplexity about the role of Protestantism in the face of the social and political conditions of the worldwide Depression. Interestingly enough, the impetus for the discussion, both in Frankfurt and in the Protestant churches at large, arose importantly from within the Foreign Mission community, especially in England, that had been ever more pressed to clarify the social and political role that it was quite manifestly playing, under imperial auspices and in the face of rising resistance. [26]

The participants included, in addition to "dialectical theologians" interested in Tillich, not only Karl Mannheim but also the classical humanist philosopher and university curator, Kurt Riezler, who brought most of these leftist thinkers to Frankfurt, and the three principals in the new Institut für Sozialforschung. Adorno and Mannheim are known to have been close personal friends of Paul and Hannah Tillich at the time, with "Teddy" as the petted philosophical protégé and family pianist and Karl and Julia Mannheim as regular companions in the Tillichs' explorations of the outer fringes of Weimar culture. The vehemence and openness of the debate indicate that the others too were clearly bound together by more than the organized proceedings being recorded.

In his own first intervention Tillich defines the overall situation as one in which the autonomization of culture and the rise of the proletariat critically challenge Christian thought and action. He separates those he has invited to encounter the Protestant theologians into three groups, each of which can contribute, he maintains, by frankly displaying its own position: a group that seeks contemporary orientation from philosophical traditions originating with the Greeks (referring to Riezler); a group of those who "take their point of departure from . . . the common experience of the proletarian situation and socialism, and who also make this fact central to all of their work" (referring to the Institute trio); and finally, using language clearly endorsing Mannheim's self-characterization at the time, a group "that begins by disinterestedly analyzing the situation, linking each of us in our diverse groups with our actual situation, and whose critique of what is going on in the other groups has gained decisive importance for me" (Tillich 1983: 322).

The common theoretical context, especially as Mannheim and Tillich try to lay it down, is defined by themes such as the "crisis of rationality." Mannheim's special mix of quite abstract socio-philosophical theorizing and very direct personal statements should be observed. In Mannheim's vehement interventions, doubtless colored by the conventions of paradoxical speech prevalent in the Tillich circle, he acknowledges and dramatizes the insufficiencies of a thoroughly secularized and rationalized world view, even while he insistently identifies his own discipline with it. He presents himself as one of those who would have to be converted, if Christianity had a valid claim to a contemporary mission, but he sees no reason to believe that this tradition could meet his needs. He finds stirring in himself, as he finds everywhere in the present-day world, certain primal religious impulses. Everyone is experiencing them on their own, however, and there are no signs of a common movement. Interestingly, Mannheim treats a sociological-Marxist interpretation of the phenomenon almost as a digression and by no means as adequate to explain it all. From a sociological point of view, Mannheim muses, much of this must doubtless be understood as a manifestation of reactionary polarization against the "progressive current we call the leftist political movement or enlightenment or industrialization," and in this reactionary character the religious tendency must clearly be opposed by all those "who desire a changed world." But there is also an primal religiosity that springs from an altogether different source, and this is the type that Mannheim finds worth discussing. It emerges in individuals like himself, "who do not want this element of vitality (*Lebenselement*) for anything politically retrograde, no restoration of a lost security, but who, quite to the contrary, want to comprehend the new man from this point of view." Mannheim does not believe that the old religion can articulate this religiosity. He thinks that he must rather find ways of expressing it in terms of his own situation:

> Every human being who has radically experienced rationalization as I have done, as a sociologist, tends to act like the vintner who smashed and demolished all about him as his vineyard was being destroyed by hail: 'we'll soon see who first finishes it off.' He wants to pursue rational thought to its conclusion, and he wants to get to the conclusion as quickly as possible. (Mannheim 2001: 135)

Certain forms of experience, encounter, and self-awareness do disappear with the rise of "this industrial, rational, sociological world." Mannheim continues,

> But the human being is more than this rationalized world, and these repressed elements are latently present in us and seek for a different form; and it is by no means a part of modern man that he represses these elements as well. (135)

Although the old mythologized language can't give it voice, the existential reality of primordial religiosity is still there after rationalization has gone as far as it can go. Mannheim attempts to account for the search by the teleological character of all form-giving: not the past, but only the anticipation of what is to come can actualize the new religious impulse. Invoking the concept that continues to work in his thinking in tension with his newly strengthened "functionalism," he writes,

> In the rediscovery of earlier elements, the point of orientation is never in the past, but in the new, in that which is emerging within us. This I call the Utopian element in us. The forward orientation is already constitutive in viewing any individual object. Not the past determines what can be extracted from the past, but rather it is something present in us, out of the contemporary predicament of our life [*Lebensnot*], to drive us forward. (135–136)

A Protestant theologian, he fears, can only offer him the most dangerous thing of all, words that are rooted in a different situation. Someone like himself, he repeats twice, "had better stammer" than abandon the struggle with his errors.

Such paradoxical complexities, reminiscent of the mysteries expounded in Lukács' Sunday Circle during Mannheim's Budapest years and somewhat anticipatory of his more sober appeals to Christian thinkers during his years as a member of "the Moot" in English emigration, are guaranteed to repel at least three of the other non-theologians present. Max Horkheimer speaks early and does not direct his remarks directly to Mannheim, whose *Ideology and Utopia* he had angrily denounced the year before, in his first published article. But he scorns all this talk of crisis, spiritual need, and primal religiosity. Capitalism knows full well what it is doing as it enters a new phase, and the need which brings suffering is much more real than all this talk about the profanation of culture. It is necessary to take sides in the struggle against this suffering, so that it can be overcome so far as humanly possible. Since natural scarcity has been proven a fallacy, the real question concerns the forms which organize humankind. Adorno's more explicit rejection of Mannheim on this occasion is more accommodating to the level of discussion, but no less impatient. Although Mannheim introduced his vineyard hailstorm in irony, to model "the conduct of us awful rationalists and modernists" the image was subsequently taken seriously and it has obscured the whole discussion. The functions of this supposedly destructive rationality must be looked at much more deeply, Adorno demands. Then it may well become evident that the functions which Mannheim is prepared to turn over to the daemonic are actually taken up and preserved in this rationality. Between them, Horkheimer and Adorno, joined more weakly by Pollock, state a fairly straightforward Marxist position, "brutally" (Horkheimer) dismissive of the meeting's central questions and premises.[27]

Mannheim is angered by the challenge in the name of an exclusive Marxism. He sets out to answer "the group that asked how it is even possible to occupy ourselves with primal religious impulses when men outside are hungry." "A readiness to help and the solidarity with the proletariat are a matter of course," he says, and this stand should naturally always be declared. But even if he agrees that this is "the most important thing," he continues, "the matter becomes dangerous when the attempt is made to put a stop to every concrete set of problems with this." Speaking directly in his own person, he insists on the "unconditional evidence" of the reality of the religious problems, if also in a secular form, because they are "burning," engrossing, and "set as a task." Countering Pollock's scornful observation that at most seven percent of all people can afford the luxury of worrying about such matters, Mannheim strikingly asserts that those who are able to do so must think of themselves as performing a representative function for those who are too much distracted by need. Others will reach these problems "once they have a higher income," and the fortunate "vanguard" must deal with these problems as their contribution to reforming humanity. Mannheim stresses this idea of a "representative function," and includes not only "deepening of the soul" but also "cultivation in an aristocratic manner" are such legitimate activities. He concludes this self-styled *captatio benevolentiae* with a reproach of his own:

> It is by no means necessary that the intelligentsia can only legitimate itself by a self-ironization as a spiritual canaille that can achieve nothing on its own for humanity. It should not degrade itself to this extreme. What I would rather hear and what I would rather continue to contribute is what the intelligentsia can offer in return, so as to be able continue using it in the common struggle. One must have the courage of one's position, for it is a vanguard position.

Later in the discussion, Mannheim draws on the language of the mediaeval mystics to characterize the "ecstatic" source of his own religious experience, but he insists that his modernity requires him to be accurate and that there is no personal God speaking in him, the only kind of God that would make any sense. Spiritualized divinities, Hegelian or otherwise, contribute nothing to his religious yearnings. But there is something wrong with all this and his intelligence cannot lead him to the conclusion that there is nothing behind it all. "That's why I am ashamed," he says, "to speak of it." The religious impulse thrusts itself upon him when he has been duly pounding away with the hail:

> As I carry out the business of the hailstorm, ever more radically, and penetrate the world with rational-functional thought, it is an exciting game to gain an immanent and sociological understanding of the world. But the more I drive the devil—or, as the case may be, God—out of the world, the more I discover that I have also driven out man.

His impulsion to religion comes with the recognition that his analytical framework is concerned only with the response mechanisms (*Reaktionsapparatur*) at work in the world. "Modern man needs that" because we have too little time for more than superficial transactional responses. "This has something to do with industrialization," Mannheim adds casually. Although all things become transparent to Mannheim through this analytical scheme, he avers, it also leads to repression of all the kinds of encounter that are so richly present in the world of religion. He cannot accept the available religious formulations of this world, but he will also not accept the impoverishment of human encounters, their reduction to functional responses. He wishes for a restoration of deeper encounter experiences and must find a way of expressing this undertaking without denying his modernity or accepting the premature gratification offered by the old theology. Modernity and rationality and sociology belong together, in short, and Mannheim will not deny his vocation to any of them, but the most thoroughgoing exercises of these vocations bring the recognition that something is missing. Religion knows about this something else, but no known religion can make it good in the present situation. Somehow Mannheim wants to show that sociology is indispensable to that which sociology reveals to the sociologist it cannot do, just as the most complete rationality is inescapable for moderns who cannot live by rationality alone.

The most penetrating of Mannheim's attempts to interrelate the issues of cultivation, elite, mass, rationality, and "ecstasy," in the sense of the self-confrontation explored in the Frankfurt Discussions of 1931, is to be found in an essay published posthumously and translated as "Democratization of Culture" (*Geist*) (Mannheim [1933] 1956: 171–246), which was evidently the final chapter of the "Sociology of Spirit," the volume whose publication was prevented by Nazi proscription of Mannheim. The editor notes that the paper was written in 1933, but adds that he has prepared a "free translation, clarifying obscurities and omitting redundant passages." The fact that the editor has punctuated the text with clearly identified editor's footnotes where he occasionally dissents from points in the argument nevertheless speaks for the comparative reliabilty of the text.[28] Unlike other essays in this posthumous version of the book, notably the crucial theoretical chapter expressly offering to replace Hegel's "phenomenology of spirit" with a "sociology of spirit," the "Democratization" essay is free of references to works published after its ostensible completion. The translation of the book's title as "sociology of culture" is especially regrettable, since the slightly mangled torso represents Mannheim's lost hope of a culminating "sociology of the spirit," which he expressly distinguished from sociology of culture in the introduction to his 1930 lecture course (Mannheim 2001), and posited as comprehensive meta-theory. This was to have been his master work.[29] As it is, it represents Mannheim's last word on the distinctly German phase of the debate about cultivation and sociology (see below).

For present purposes, it is enough to point out, first, that Mannheim attempted in this essay to make good the implicit promise made to Horkheimer, Wiesengrund-Adorno, and Pollock that the intellectual elite's monopoly of cultivation of spirit or deepening of soul was only temporary. Aristocratic cultivation was inherently elitist, but the social conditions for its existence had gone. Democratic cultivation—a complementary mastery of specialization and sociological orientation—had to take hold of the masses, or it could not exist at all. The "ecstatic self-distantiation" that corresponds to the deepening of the soul is similarly presented as a capacity for I-thou and I-myself existential relations that are at home in a perfected democratic society, where it must be universal to exist. This long study is the surprisingly hopeful complement to Mannheim's "stammering" interventions in Frankfurt two years earlier.

By 1935, Mannheim had drastically lowered his expectations for both the spirit and soul of democratic culture. The crisis is overwhelming. His *Man and Society in an Age of Reconstruction* sees only the "crisis of mass culture," and the response through planning cannot address "political education" in the democratic spirit of Weimar any more than it can attach any priority to the supposed "burning" needs of the soul. "Utopia" is a dangerous distraction, as is the exposé of ideologies. He circulated the book among his widely scattered friends. Eduard Heimann was one of Paul Tillich's closest associates and an intimate of Karl Mannheim and his closest university associates. We close our collection of translations (Mannheim 2001), then, with an exchange of letters between these two exiles, a reprise of the differences between Alfred Weber and Mannheim, but in a new, tragic key. What there is of Marxism is closer to the ideologists of the Five-Year plan that to either Lukács or Adler. A note of finality sounds through the debate. Heimann charges that Mannheim's abandonment of the formerly shared insight into the primacy of the "irrational," understood as religious experience, put him in the camp of the mechanistic and manipulative enemy. Mannheim, in return, makes the case for sociology as rationalization of the irrational. Mannheim writes,

> The lowest form of [the] enthusiasm for irrationality has been turned into a program by the Nazis, inasmuch as they attach higher value to the inability to think, the unrational (in contrast to the irrational), and blind submission than to tenacity in thinking, given that one has begun to think. That is the glorification not so much of the irrational as of the inability to think—the *ressentiment* typical of backward strata unable to meet the intellectual requirements of modernity. But I am also

against the higher forms of this kind of enthusiasm for irrationalism that think that certain contents of the soul or cosmic substances are destroyed by being thought about. It has always been my experience that real thinking enhances the capacity for experience and that faiths can only be elevated by the courage to think. Even when it comes to "the religious," I agree with Guardini, who spoke the following true word about Pascal, "He is far from the new-fashioned weakness of nerve that considers 'the religious' threatened whenever concepts are brought into play. He is not in the modern sense a believer in experience." (R. Guardini, *Christian Consciousness. Studies on Pascal*). I believe that thinking is one of the highest gifts of the human species, the most radical instrument for penetrating the world—directed towards the outer world no less than the world of experience—and emptying out results not from the fact that man thinks but from the fact that empty men think. (184)

In response to Heimann's reproach that his turn towards instrumentalism represents a denial of his own life and experience, then, Mannheim answers:

Now I will tell you why I am so insistent about observing men and society first of all at the distance of structural analysis and not at the level of biographical encounter, which is so much more capable of nuance. Because, in my opinion, it was precisely the sin of the German intellectuals that they did not look first at the fundamental general contours of things (as is naturally done by people who are impelled to action in public), but rather (corresponding to the conditions of privacy and intimacy characteristic of their existence) fled directly into nuances, and dissipated themselves there. (191)

There is a deep unhappiness here that is absent from Mannheim's writings even at the very end of the Weimar age. Yet it may be said that Mannheim's teaching at Frankfurt spares him from self-reproach in both of these respects. He did attempt to address the personal experiences of his students as the points of contact for the political education in the form of sociological cultivation that he sought to impart, but he invited them to situate themselves in a sociological, structural context; and he certainly insisted that they think.

Notes

1. It should be noted that official Communist Party intellectuals immediately criticized Lukács' work, especially for its hostility to "materialist" natural science and its disrespect for Engels. Lukács made communism deeply interesting to some young intellectuals, but he was repeatedly led by his primary political loyalties to disavow the work that had this effect. This pattern undoubtedly entered into Mannheim's depiction of the fate of intellectuals at the hands of party machines, especially in a phase of orthodox "reprimitivization." See Lectures IX and X in Mannheim [1930a] 2001.

2. Max Weber did not forgive Lukács his political conversion, it seems, since he refused to join a group of prominent republican intellectuals who petitioned for his safekeeping in Austria, when the Horthy regime sought his extradition. See Kettler 1971.
3. The effect is documented in the two unfinished treatises on sociology of culture that Mannheim wrote during his first years in Heidelberg, probably in conjunction with his proposals for habilitation projects, first for Heinrich Rickert and then for Alfred Weber. The respective contents, titles, and dates of composition of the two Mannheim treatises make it highly likely that they represent two preliminary stages of the habilitation work, with the eventual final product a much more narrowly focused and empirical study that reflects the intellectual habits of Emil Lederer, who actually signed as principal sponsor. In the earlier of the two, dated 1922, Mannheim criticizes Marx's theory of ideology for failing to distinguish between sociological explanation and normative evaluation of intellectual productions, finding a relativistic vicious circle. In the later work, datable by internal evidence as written two years later, he highlights the historicity and reflexivity of theory, including theory of knowledge, and accepts the possibility of a Marxist approach to ideology, as in Lukács, where there is a grounding in historical ontology to distinguish between an adequate and inadequate socially explainable social knowledge (Mannheim [1922–24] 1982; Kettler 1965). In their reports on the habilitation, both Weber and Lederer make reference to preparatory methodological studies. Weber mentions "countless methodological and critical preliminary works" (Demm 1999: 470) and Lederer describes the habilitation as "a continuation of a series of investigations that sought "to gain clarity about the objectives and capacities of sociology," attempting now in the instance of a concrete case to apply these ideas about cultural sociology. (UAH, H-IV-102/149, Bl.49-60 (= Universitätsarchiv Heidelberg, Akten der Philosophischen Fakultät, 1919-1932. cit. Demm 199: 32n142). See below. The existence of texts embodying two distinct approaches is almost certainly also explained in part by Mannheim's need to reorient from philosophy to sociology. On February 13, 1922, Alfred Weber wrote to Else Jaffé that Mannheim had brought him a grand design for his project, which he found too systematic and grandiose for his liking, but which he nevertheless encouraged him to complete. Two years later, in February of 1923, he told the same correspondent that Mannheim had asked him to recommend "ideas and redesign of his work, so that the philosophers could no longer complain that it is not sociological" and jeopardize his habilitation (Alfred Weber to Else Jaffé, February 21, 1923, BArch, NL A.Weber/92, p. 110f. The almost illegible correspondence was heroically deciphered by Eberhard Demm, and the citations and discussions are in Demm 1999: 30-31, as well as Demm 2000). We do not suggest that Mannheim wrote counter to his convictions simply to please one or another supervisor. As we have seen, if our surmise about the provenance of the texts is correct, neither Rickert nor Weber was in fact fully pleased, and their displeasure was certainly predictable. Still, Mannheim's experiments were conditioned by the intellectual occasions. *Ideology and Utopia* contains an elaborate set of conclusions from the encounter, notably in the discussion of the Marxist view of the relations between theory and practice (110-119) and in the important discussion of totality in the context of Utopianism (227). For a strongly polemical but acute orthodox Marxist appraisal by another former member of the Lukács circle in Budapest, a talented philosopher, see Fogarasi 1930. Fogarasi cites the malign influence of Lukács—out of favor with his Communist comrades, as so

often—to explain some of Mannheim's failings. He contends, incidentally, that Mannheim himself was a fallen-away Marxist, for which there is no independent evidence, at least in Fogarasi's sense of the term. Mannheim's Frankfurt teaching, in any case, strikes a new balance. See below and the texts translated in Mannheim 2001.

4. Lukács develops this argument in greatest detail in a book on Lenin ([1924] 1971), in which he finds evidence of the greatest mastery of practical science in every one of Lenin's actions. The conception of practical science draws on the humanistic literature on Machiavelli.

5. Among the decrees of the Budapest Soviet on its first or second day in power was a ruling by Lukács that theaters must play works of classical authors, insofar as there were not enough plays with revolutionary content (Kettler 1971).

6. Lukács never had any patience with avant-garde modernism. He figured as a pioneer in Budapest, as a young man, but his tastes effectively stopped at realism in theater and Cézanne, with Dostoyevsky and French symbolist poetry as the outer limit. As commissar of culture, he fought bitterly with the more experimental Budapest artists. See Kettler 1971. Already in a review of Hans Staudinger's book on the sociology of workers' cultural organizations in 1916, the first volume of Alfred Weber's series on cultural sociology, Lukács professes to share Staudinger's hope that "the economic organicism and synthesis of the work world will lead to a cultural synthesis, to a new mastery of the collective over the personal, solidarity (*Bindung*) above freedom," although he denies that Staudinger's factual report on the psychology of one group of workers gives any reason to hope for this result (Lukács 1915: 220). Lukács challenges the methodological looseness of the approach and questions Alfred Weber's programmatic design. Weber's rejoinder is placatory, pleading the youth of the enterprise.

7. In his account of the convention in the *Frankfurter Zeitung*, Mannheim diplomatically did not into any of the details of the discussion, saying only that it was "stimulating" (*erregte*) (Mannheim 1928).

8. Mannheim was received in Heidelberg by Lederer, who had been Lukács' intimate friend and whose wife was the sister of Lukács' great love. Mannheim lived next door to Lederer and enjoyed his complete social patronage. They were bound as well by intellectual ties, as will be shown below.

9. Under these conditions, and in view of the cordiality of the exchanges between Mannheim and Weber as they appear in the transcript, it is difficult to know what to make of Norbert Elias' recollection late in life that the occasion was in fact a bitter ideological squabble fueled by Mannheim's competitive spirit. Norbert Elias writes that there was a "smoldering conflict between Alfred Weber and Karl Mannheim, which flared briefly into public view at that Zurich sociologists' convention." Elias writes that Mannheim felt the need to challenge those with a higher reputation than his own and implies that such was his motivation for undercutting Alfred Weber's position in his talk (Elias 1994: 111, 114-115, 120). Like most such recollections, they are most interesting for the insight they offer into Elias' final version of his own story—in this instance, about his difficult relations with Mannheim. Demm is certainly correct in rejecting the probative value of Elias' testimony (Demm 1999: 36f.; cp. Blomert 1999: 161f.). It should be noted as well that Mannheim and Weber were united by a common political dedication to the republic, which was by no means common, either in Heidelberg or in the German Sociological Association. Weber attempted to engage the dislocations of the Weimar Republic in a more positive manner than many of the

thinkers discussed above. His concepts of "spiritual leaders" and "leader democracy" represented an attempt to establish an organic relationship between the cultural elite and the republican masses. In other words, he sought to combine the organic unity he believed characterized an earlier age with the pluralism presented by modern democracy. He saw the cultural sociology that he was in the process of developing as an important orienting tool in the creation of this unity (A. Weber 1918; A. Weber 1925; Demm 1990; Loader 1997).
10. Note that Freyer was addressing similar questions in the immediate postwar years, in his works on objective cultural formations, their devaluation in a critical age and consequent dependence on social dynamics.
11. The German word *Seele* is indeed used equally for the wide range of meanings associated with "soul" in both religious and philosophical thought and for the central unit of analysis in psychology. In the present context, where "soul" is still posed against "spirit," the translation is clear. In Mannheim and his contemporaries, "soul" is likely to contaminate "psyche" whenever "psychology" is not pretty firmly fixed as a specialized discipline.
12. If Demm is correct, the reference to Max Weber in this context may have had a meaning quite different from that ascribed to it in the text above. Demm reports that Mannheim was the center of a group of "eastern" students, most of them Jewish, who played "Max and Marx" over against Alfred Weber in 1921-2, according to Weber's correspondence. Demm 1999: 90. In the same passage, however, Demm names Eduard Baumgarten as the key figure among the students at that time, so the situation remains unclear. It is difficult, in any case, to make a reliable estimate, beyond the documentation, of Alfred Weber's reactions to Mannheim's citations of Max Weber as arbitrator between them.
13. Von Wiese complained plaintively, "that what is truly sociological has been given short shrift in many of the speeches. . . . Political passion forces quick judgment, and disturbs the calmness of observation" (Quoted in Käsler 1983: 248). There is no record of the impression that the occasion made on Mannheim, although he must have been present, since he addressed himself immediately to the central concept of Scheler's talk. It is worth wondering whether Elias' curious version of the atmosphere at the 1928 debates between Mannheim and Weber was somehow contaminated by memories of the earlier lively contretemps.
14. Adler may also have helped to legitimate Carl Schmitt among the younger socialists. He plays off Schmitt's doctrine of the "sovereign dictatorship" against Kelsen's critique of the Marxist conception of the "dictatorship of the proletariat," delighting in finding a non-Marxist formulation to pit against Kelsen's claims that dictatorship is only a legally limited emergency power (Adler 1922: 196. Cp. McCormick 1997; and esp. McCormick 2001).
15. Biographical information on Lederer is taken from Demm 1999: 21-24.
16. Nina Rubinstein, a member of the Menshevik "family" in Germany and daughter of the prominent socialist figure, Alexander Stein, recalled her father's insistence that she must go to Heidelberg to join the comrades studying with Lederer. In the event, she soon deserted Lederer for Mannheim (Raith 1999; Rubinstein 2000; Kettler/Meja 1993).
17. Lukács contributed to the debate in 1919, in an article published in *Kommunist*.
18. Lederer's prewar vision of parliament and interest groups corresponds to the portrayal current among anti-Republican politicians and refined by Carl Schmitt in the Weimar period, with reversed valences, to discredit the constitutional regime as inherently anti-political and lacking in state legitimacy. It is probably no

coincidence that Lederer's essay is contemporary with the pluralist writings of Harold J. Laski and the interest group theorization of Arthur Bentley. Lederer's views are further developed by some socialist writers, notably by lawyers close to the labor movement. See Fraenkel 1930. Cp. Luthardt 1986. Mannheim's conception of the political (in Mannheim 1929a) may be seen as, among other things, an attempt to mediate between the recognition of ideological conflict in Lederer's sense, and the activist concerns encapsulated in Schmitt's "politics" concept.

19. Lederer's eleven-page report is detailed in its account of Mannheim's complex argument, manifestly written out of deep familiarity and sympathy with the project. If anything, the rationale is more clearly stated than by Mannheim. Especially striking is Lederer's emphasis on aspects that Mannheim later neglects when he shortens the work for publication. This is the report not only of an advocate but also of an active mentor. It should be noted, however, that Mannheim did most of the work on the habilitation during Lederer's absence in Japan, where he served as visiting professor between March, 1923, and Summer, 1925. That is fully consistent with a decisive influence by Lederer in moving Mannheim from the general theoretical prospectus that Weber mentioned in February, 1921 and again February, 1923, to the much more empirical and focused study of conservatism. No correspondence between Lederer and Mannheim has been located.

20. Mannheim cites Lederer 1931 on this question in his unpublished work on the intellectuals. (1956: 144ff.)

21. Lederer cites Lukács' early "Theory of the Drama" in support of this point.

22. The thesis of the contemporary autonomy of art, and its social explanation in the conditions of modernity, is a key feature of Lukács' writings before his turn to Leninism, most elaborately in the "Heidelberg Aesthetic" which he was writing during his years of intimacy with Lederer. Lederer's preoccupation with the art historian Wölfflin in this work is a reminder that Mannheim published his article on problems of art and style a year or two before Lederer's piece. What we know about the intellectual collegiality between Lederer and Mannheim, as between Lederer and Lukács in the earlier time, makes it hard to believe that they were not exploring these questions together, notwithstanding the absence of citations in this case. This is quite apart from the exchanges through Alfred Weber and in his intellectual salon.

23. The contrast between this sense of empiricism and the sense current in English and American philosophy is an important element of ambiguity in the translation of Mannheim's *Ideology and Utopia* and its subsequent appropriation. Mannheim almost certainly played on the dual sense of the term in the "Preliminary Approach to the Problem," written in 1936 for the English-speaking audience. [This note is an extension of the analysis of the translation problem discussed in Kettler/Meja 1995 and Loader 1985.] Mannheim's adaptations of "American" research methods in Frankfurt, notably his encouragement of interview methods, were always directed to collecting testimonies of "experiences" rather than survey data in the emerging American sense. This is clear not only from Mannheim's own description of a survey project in the article on "Crisis," (Mannheim [1932b] 2001) but also from the recollections of a survey project on the condition of women in working class families he planned with his student, Margaret Freudenthal (Sallis-Freudenthal 1977; Freudenthal [1934] 1986; Kettler/Meja 1993).

24. An outline summary of Mannheim's course on the "sociology of public opinion and the press" in 1928, published in an annual report of the Institute illustrates Mannheim's design. The focus is on the sociological constitution of a public and

the generation of opinion, but especially interesting in the light of Jürgen Habermas' lifelong explorations, is a preliminary finding about the distinction between "objective facts" as understood by logic and the "phenomena that transmit opinions" of interest to sociology and other human sciences. The latter, according to Mannheim, must be understood as "the living speech of communications" (*die lebendige Rede des Verkehrs*) and therefore integrally social (GLA 235/3277).
25. Mannheim repeatedly uses a somewhat unusual German expression (*religiöse Erfahrung*) that is a direct translation of William James' central concept in *Varieties of Religious Experience*. Mannheim's subsequent interest in American pragmatism is well-documented, and it seems likely that he already found the approach congenial earlier, especially in his eagerness to negotiate between the Anglo-American and German senses of empiricism (cp. Louis Wirth's Preface to Mannheim 1936). See above, note 23. There are no citations of James in Mannheim's writings of the time, however, although Woldring (1986:12) points out that William James was on the list of writers studied by Oscar Jászi's Society for Social Studies during the years of Mannheim's attendance.
26. The "Frankfurt Discussion" was opened by Heinrich Frick, active in the Foreign Mission Movement, not by Tillich, and he cites as inspiration for his reflections a number of American Quakers and above all the English church activist and organizer, Joseph H. Oldham. It is not coincidental, then, that Mannheim will center the last eight years of his English stay on the activities of a Christian discussion circle, called the Moot, that was organized and led by Oldham and generated by the same series of ecumenical church meetings that stimulated Tillich and his associates on this occasion (Loader 1985; Kettler/Meja 1995).
27. Not quite three weeks after this discussion, Horkheimer addressed many of the same participants in a less "brutal" lecture on "History and Psychology" at the local Kant Society, a regular discussion group. According to the sketchy outline in the Max-Horkheimer-Archive (MHA IX, 210), Horkheimer faulted the limited anthropology of Marxism, especially its tendency towards "pan-economism" and cited the rise of the NSDAP as evidence of the need for a psychology able to comprehend the need for satisfying fantasies. In the discussion, however, he was strongly seconded by Wiesengrund (Adorno) in rejecting attempts by Riezler and Tillich to look critically at the philosophical grounding for the Marxist concept of history, which the latter charge with being uncritically positivist. Mannheim is recorded with a single interpellation, directed against Riezler's Heideggerian proposal rather than Horkheimer, but his point is not clear from the fragmentary notes.
28. Especially revealing in the present context is the editor's supplement to Mannheim's argument that the Hegelian dialectic "'neutralizes' itself" and precludes genuine open-ended discussion. The editor adds that "this is true of Marxist no less than of Hegelian dialectic" ([1933]1956:193n2); but the opposite is of course the point of Mannheim's transmutation of the Marxist conception of "material discussion" in *Ideology and Utopia* and his Frankfurt writings.
29. Mannheim evidently had tantalizing indications that his German publisher was prepared to publish the work, notwithstanding his outcast status, but these clearly came to nothing (Mannheim to Wirth, 24.6.33, LWP/7:11). The work intended as the grand integration of his studies in exile similarly was left to be completed by others at his death, and it similarly suffered some measure of adulteration by his greatest admirers, acting in good faith to strengthen his American-English reputation. It is a sad story that cannot be studied because the documentation is unavailable, although some may turn up in the Edward Shils papers, when they are sorted.

7

Karl Mannheim as Professor: *The Introduction to Sociology*

Mannheim's last year at Heidelberg was fateful in the history of the Republic. At the very end of 1929, after the onset of the Great Depression, the National Socialists, building on their participation in the campaign to repudiate the Young Plan, made an electoral breakthrough in Thüringen. A similar electoral success occurred in November, 1929 municipal elections in Frankfurt, where the party collected 10 percent of the vote (Hamilton 1982: 200). These regional shocks assumed more national proportions as the NSDAP began what would be more than three years of continual campaigning, highlighted by street marches, assembly room brawls, and furious drive-throughs in open trucks. They were a raging presence. In March, 1930, the month before Mannheim assumed his chair in the newly reorganized Social Science Faculty at the Johann-Wolfgang-Goethe University in Frankfurt, the parliamentary coalition supporting the Social Democratic Chancellor split fatally over the issue of unemployment insurance,[1] and the Republic entered a period of parliamentary gridlock. Increasing numbers of academic republicans, including Alfred Weber, talked of a retreat from the parliamentary system (Döring 1975: 99). In a 1931 pamphlet entitled *The End of Democracy?* Weber lamented that the National Socialists were better equipped to deal with the new reality than were the democratic parties, because they had developed a new vision and a new élan (Weber 1931: 7). In elections not long after Mannheim finished his lecture series, the NSDAP became the second largest party in the Parliament and the KPD the third largest. Both of these parties were openly opposed to the Republic as a parliamentary government, and it was the shared awareness of their rise, above all, that Mannheim presupposed in his discussions of fascism and Marxism in the 1930 lectures. Thus Mannheim moved to the modernist city of Frankfurt just when what has been called the "crisis of classical modernity" was beginning its most desperate phase.

The university stood as a tribute to the decade past. Defining the field more broadly than the technical disciplinary boundaries that marked von Wiese's domain, in line with Becker's conception, Wolfgang Schivelbusch has noted,

> In 1930, when Karl Mannheim was appointed to the chair in sociology and Max Horkheimer to the one in social philosophy, Frankfurt had become, ten years after the death of Max Weber, the uncontested successor to Heidelberg as the center of German sociology. (Schivelbusch 1982: 14; see also Stölting 1986: 117)

Schivelbusch's account of Frankfurt as the successor to Heidelberg goes on to use the same dichotomy that Mannheim used earlier in his letters from Heidelberg, the two poles of Max Weber and Stefan George, which he summarized as ideological critique versus myth, society versus cultivated elite, and rational concept versus "intuition" (*innere Schau*) (15).[2] But if the poles were the same as in Heidelberg, the context in which they were located was very different, for the city was no provincial sheltered valley, and the university was newer and less traditional. The city's economic base was in commerce and it had a long tradition of liberal political orientation. In right-wing circles it was described as "the city of democratic purity and Jewish tradition—even in the sphere of academia" (Kluke 1972: 572). The population was 4.7 percent Jewish, the largest percentage in Germany, and Jews played an important role in both municipal affairs and the university, contributing a sizable number of the liberal and socialist intelligentsia.

The modernist elements of Frankfurt came to the fore in the mid–1920s. In his 1924 inaugural address as mayor (*Oberbürgermeister*), Ludwig Landmann set the tone by declaring that Frankfurt was not only a commercial center but also a cultural one, displaying an "international cultural will." If Heidelberg combined its international element with its provincial setting to become a "world village," Frankfurt's ambition was to become a "cultural metropolis" (*Kulturmetropole*), and its outstanding national newspaper, *Frankfurter Zeitung*, carried this claim throughout the country, notably in its influential feuilleton section under Mannheim's friend, Siegfried Kracauer. What Landmann called the "spirit of Frankfurt" was part of a strong modernist orientation that had a second, separate newspaper, *New Frankfurt*, and that included such movements as the Neue Sachlichkeit, the Bauhaus School, and the paintings of Max Beckmann. This marked an abrupt break from the old civic culture that had been established prior to the war and that placed value on historical continuity. The first issue of *New Frankfurt* in 1926 contained an article that stated that the world was in the midst of a "mighty transformation" (*Umschwung*), "a turning-point in destiny and essence" (*Schicksals- und Wesenswende*), and that Frankfurt was a part of this. Orientation toward past history was devalued because it destroyed "our creative instincts." *New Frankfurt* was intended to be an organ of instruction for citizens as to how the "old Frankfurt" would give way to the new. In 1930, the year Mannheim arrived in Frankfurt, a counter-movement to the modernizing trend in culture appeared in the form of the "Association of Friends of the Old Town," which counterposed the traditional character of the old town to the new modernist trends. This "polarization" of the old and new Frankfurt was "very much apparent" in the last years of the Republic (Hansert 1992: 143–149, 152–154, 156–157, 160; Lieberman 1994).

The university was also part of the transition from old to new. Established just prior to the war with private funding, a good part of which was Jewish, it was initially a route for Jews to seek entry to the older civic culture of Frankfurt. But during the Republic the University became more markedly a force for modernization. Like the other newly established urban universities in Cologne and Hamburg, the university had a more heterogeneous student body than was the norm at the older universities and it was more receptive to new fields of inquiry.[3] By 1930, 9.5 percent of the student body was Jewish, sharing with Berlin the highest percentage in the country, and a fifth of these were not German citizens. Traditional student life, which centered upon men's student corporations, was challenged in Frankfurt by women students, working-class students and foreign students.[4] The university also opened many classes to townspeople without the conventional preparation of the *Gymnasium*. One Nazi flyer referred to the university as "a stronghold of Jewish impudence and Marxist insolence." Because of these factors, anti-Semitism and Nazi student activity were not as strong within the university[5] as they were in the city at large[6] and at other universities (Hamilton 1982: 199; Greffrath 1979:

63, 163; Kluke 1972: 565, 675; Hammerstein 1989: 163; Steinberg 1977: 4, 6, 15).

One would expect this university to be more in tune with the views of Haenisch and Becker, and that was indeed the case. Both men advocated financial support of the university by the Prussian government during the difficult economic situation of the first years of the Republic. They were fully aware that the university, with its strong connections to the city, served as a counterbalance to the more traditional universities that demonstrated little support for the Republic (Kluke 1972: 246–254; Pauck/Pauck 1976: 110).[7]

In 1928, Becker named Kurt Riezler as curator of the university. Riezler, unlike many academics, was dedicated to the Republic and believed that the university should be engaged in an "intensive spiritual dialogue with the vital forces of the present" rather than retreating to the traditional "nonpolitical" professorial stance. This is exactly what Mannheim had advocated, most recently in his article on journalism as a university science (Mannheim [1929d] 2001).

Riezler's own interventions in the "Frankfurt Discussions" suggest some deeper points of similarity between them, as well as some differences. He rejected the idea that the contemporary problem was posed by an objectified, soulless rationalized world, a sort of iron cage (to use Max Weber's term), emptied of meaning and inner significance. He considers that conception, constitutive of the older cultural criticism (including both the younger Lukács—and Mannheim— and Alfred Weber) obsolete. "We do not live in such a rigidified world," he says, "we live in a field of ruins [*Trümmerfeld*]" (Tillich 1983: 329). Under conditions of "nihilism," there is no confrontation between a settled "profanity" and a restorative Protestant religiosity. The combatants among the ruins, including the proponents of "efficiency" no less than the sociologists who undermine efforts to use old wreckage for new structures, are all faced with questions of finding some ultimate grounding for their activities. And "religiosity" in the broad sense of the discussion, may be at work among even the unlikeliest of the contestants. Soviet events, for example, cannot be explained on the basis of economic calculation: "Nowhere in the world has there ever been so much suffering deliberately inflicted and borne for the sake of a goal that none of them believe they will live to see, and not even for the sake of their children, who have been largely removed from their families." All it would take is the appearance of a talented Christian sectarian to transmute the rationalistic justification imposed by an arbitrary materialist ideology into a manifestly religious faith. Disregarding the details, the important point is that Riezler works out of a position close to Mannheim's more settled views.

While Mannheim dramatized a categorical clash between the rational and religious during the Frankfurt Discussion, this was an exaggeration evoked by his eagerness to meet Tillich's premise of crisis. In a letter written six weeks before the Frankfurt Discussion to his colleague, Max Wertheimer, evidently in continuation of a dispute at the Kant Society, he attempts to use language consistent with a rejection of a categorical divide between physical and cultural science to characterize the existential self-confrontation central to his image of a religious experience (Mannheim [1931c] 2001). As this suggests, his settled position is less well captured by the rhetoric of the confrontational occasion than by his shifting of the axes between "civilization" and "culture" in the joint seminar with Alfred Weber. The competition is among alternative world visions, with each comprising its own rationalized and "utopian" moments. His work during the next years will specify this conception, and the "profane" will never again simply confront "the religious."[8]

In addition to providing a friendly environment, Riezler may have contributed directly to these efforts. At a more immediate political level, Riezler shared the view of Mannheim, Lederer, and other moderate socialists that political parties, associations, and other social institutions served as a necessary intermediary network between the individual citizen and the nation as a whole. Riezler encouraged the work of the Academy of Labor at the University, an entity partially funded by the trade union movement and staffed by socialist scholars, notably the leading sociological labor law theorist, Hugo Sinzheimer (Kettler 1984). To signal his dedication to "the vital unity of nation [*Volk*] and state," on the other hand, one of Riezler's early acts as curator was to organize a celebration of the tenth year of the constitution in St. Paul's Church, a symbol of the liberal revolutions of 1848 (Kluke 1972: 475–476). In a term that did not come into its own until two generations later, he was a constitutional patriot.

Riezler appointed a number of faculty who deviated from traditional academic concerns, thus creating a friction between the administration and the entrenched disciplines. Riezler intended to make Frankfurt "a center of the German university culture." Two of his objectives in these appointments were new attention to interdisciplinarity and pedagogical strategy. In 1929, after much negotiation, he named Paul Tillich as professor of "philosophy and sociology, including social pedagogy." The same year Heinrich de Man was hired to teach "sociology with special emphasis on social psychology and social pedagogy." The innovative social psychologist Max Wertheimer was also hired in 1929 (Hammerstein 1989: 122).[9] In 1930 Max Horkheimer became professor of philosophy and director of the privately funded Institute for Social Research and Mannheim was appointed to Franz Oppenheimer's chair in sociology against the wishes of the faculty, after Lederer declined and Minister Becker was enlisted to force the result (Matthiesen 1990: 81; Kluke 1972: 540–545; Kettler/Meja 1995). The three names on the faculty's own recommended list were, significantly, Carl Schmitt, Leopold von Wiese, and Hans Kelsen, whose conception of the radical gap between sociology and pure theory of law had occasioned noteworthy clashes with both Max Adler and Hermann Heller (Hammerstein 1989: 128).[10] Mannheim, who was also enabled by Lederer's influence to bring both Norbert Elias and Adolf Löwe to Frankfurt with him, clearly fit into Riezler's plans to make Frankfurt a center of interdisciplinary studies (Matthiesen 1990: 81). That Mannheim understood this is evidenced by his claim in a letter of December, 1929, to Riezler that "sociology, especially in the form that I represent, assigns itself the task of establishing so-called 'cross-connections' among the specialized sciences" (Mannheim 1996: 38). The interdisciplinary spirit was very strong at Frankfurt and the rigid boundaries between disciplines often bridged. Professors visited one another's seminars and held joint seminars. The debates that took place in the classrooms spilled over into a number of intellectual circles (Pauck/Pauck 1976: 117–119).

We should not paint too positive a picture of the intellectual life of Frankfurt, however, for even in this modernist setting, the danger of National Socialism was active. Ultimately the depiction of Frankfurt's intellectual poles by Schivelbusch is misleading, as Mannheim clearly understood. As he had noted earlier in Heidelberg, the mythic position of the charismatic Stefan George was simply an escape from modernity, not an attempt to engage it.[11] Rather, it was the mythic position of the charismatic Adolf Hitler, as supported by men like Martin Heidegger, Carl Schmitt, and Hans Freyer, that formed the real opposite pole to Mannheim's version of the sociological attitude.

By the time of the "Frankfurt Discussions" led by Tillich, moreover, the Weimar social and political arrangements were being overwhelmed. Germany's unemployment rates had been on an unparalleled steep climb for two years, a situation devastating for the unions that had been principal actors in the "collectivist democracy"—the pluralist constitutionalism analyzed by Lederer and his socialist followers; communists and the hard Right consisting of National Socialists and Hugenberg's DNVP had paralyzed Parliament since their triumphs in the elections of 1930; and the government had been ruling by use of blanket delegations of legislative power and presidential decrees, approaching Schmitt's "dictatorship"; and furious assaults on the "Weimar system" dominated almost all media of public expression, including, increasingly, the streets. Universities and their graduates were not secure against these massive disturbances, and radical rightist tendencies swept student organizations and not a few lecterns. In his courses of 1931 and 1932, Mannheim paid some attention to these concrete developments. He diagnosed a crisis of social orientation among decisive collective social actors, due largely to breakdowns in processes of social selection and social mobility, that is, malfunctions in the rational order.[12] These exemplifications of the current issues studies that he justified at length in his 1932 talk on *Present Tasks of Sociology* (Mannheim [1932a] 2001) are to be understood, however, in the context of his introductory course of 1930, where he attempts to carry through the transmutation of sociology into a cultivation appropriate to the democratic epoch and its crisis.

Mannheim's programmatic comparison between that cultivation (*Bildung*) and the humanistic cultivation in the Humboldt tradition did not appear until its posthumous publication in an English version edited by other hands, but it was evidently written in 1933 (see above). Despite some shifts in emphasis, notably a greater pessimism about political effectiveness, its main points identify Mannheim's objectives in his course. Mannheim speaks of contrasting "cultural ideals," treating them as conscious counterparts of contrasting aristocratic and democratic mechanisms of the cultural processes that are manifested in language, politics, artistic styles, and philosophical currents, and that have seen a progressive shift from one to the other as social relations have changed in a cumulative development to modern times that Mannheim calls democratization of spirit. The theory of democratization is the meta-theory of Mannheim's sociology. At this level, Marxism plays little part.[13]

Modern times in the early 1930s meant the deterioration of Weimar democracy and the emergence of Nazism. The two were certainly connected, but was that connection inevitable? Here Mannheim challenged Max Scheler's earlier assumption that they were.[14] Scheler, following the lead of nineteenth-century pessimists, believed that while democracy might assume rational forms (*Vernunftdemokratie*), it would eventually arrive at its final form, "democracy of feeling" (*Stimmungsdemokratie*), which was ultimately chaotic and destructive. Mannheim was not unqualifiedly optimistic about democracy, allowing that it did not necessarily lead either to the advance of rationality in society or to international harmony. Both national aggressiveness and dictatorship could thrive on democratic soil, and one need look no further than Germany for proof of this. Mannheim labeled such a condition "massification." It was characterized by a lack of orientation on the part of the lower classes as they slipped away from guidance by established elites and found no alternative ([1933] 1956: 173, 196; 1932a: 37). The result was the irrational panic that he was witnessing.

Mannheim wrote that this potential for disaster arose from the two primary characteristics of democracies. The first is the acceptance of the essential equality of all human beings. No group of individuals is seen as qualitatively different from others, and thus no group assumes a "natural" position atop status and power hierarchies. Democracies reject vertical divisions of society. The second principle is the autonomy and vital selfhood of every individual in society. The free development of all of its individual members is what makes democracy creative and vital. However, when those individual powers are unleashed with no "natural" hierarchy to keep them in check, they always carry with them the danger of fomenting chaos. Insecurity, Mannheim wrote, is always a characteristic of modern democracies ([1933] 1956: 176–177, 246). This combination of equality and individuality necessitated some kind of order to prevent the threatened chaos. Mannheim believed that this order could come from the democratic selection of elites, the third characteristic of democracy. This selection stood in contrast to two others, an aristocratic one that was affiliated with the humanistic model of cultivation and a fascistic one with its faith in dictatorship.

The humanistic ideal of cultivation, Mannheim wrote, was aristocratic in that it assumed a certain distance between the elite who were to be educated and the masses who were not. At the same time it assumed that the elite stood in some kind of organic relationship to the rest of society, so that its values were those of everyone. Or in Mannheim's terms, it presupposed vertical (social) distance but not horizontal distance. The cultivated people who made up the elite were assumed to be well-rounded individuals who were educated in a relatively stable environment. The ideal had an antipathy to both the diverse and the dynamic and, thus, despite touting the individual personality, placed restraints on the individual ([1933] 1956: 229–234).

All cultivation presupposes self-distantiation, a measure of reflexivity that removes the individual from automatic integration into the ways of society, but aristocratic self-distantiation differs from the emerging democratic one, primarily because of the importance of social distance and the consciousness of unquestioned hierarchy, as well as other fixed attributes of elite location. Because the society in which it occurs is monopolistic (to use Mannheim's earlier term), aristocratic self-distantiation is temporal, directing the individual backward in time, rather than spatial. The individual is distanced from his everyday life, including the experience of work, by being educated in the ideals of a past age, especially the classical world. As noted earlier, such a distantiation promotes a static view of the world that is backward looking. There is no interaction with other social groups which are assumed to be inferior, deferential, and therefore culturally irrelevant. The humanistic ideal of cultivation in its historicist form admits change over time, while insisting on spatial unity and cultural homogeneity. The present is constrained by the past. Thus, because self-distantiation is subordinate to social distantiation, Mannheim sees it as inadequate and outmoded. It is incapable of orientation in the changing modern world.[15]

This is not the case for democratic self-distantiation, which Mannheim sees as the direct product of social de-distantiation. As the social gap between hierarchical groups decreases, the lower classes become more active participants in the decision-making system. They have to learn how to relate to their fellow humans in a way that is not given as the "natural" order. This means a certain degree of abstractness and greater communicability—a reformulation of Mannheim's earlier work, but with similar results. With democratization, people are forced to expand themselves beyond conjunctive relationships as they increasingly communicate with others who are strangers to their personal lives. Horizontal relationships replace vertical ones, existential distantiation replaces social distantiation. Qualitative knowledge, which is intelligible only to people who are part of the same conjunctive community, counts for less. Abstraction means self-distantiation, placing oneself in relationships where subject-object considerations are important ([1933] 1956: 209, 242, 187–188). Above all it means self-reflexivity, something that could no longer be achieved by the humanistic ideal of cultivation.

Mannheim does not disguise a certain regret for the obsolescence of the humanistic ideal. "Steeped in the values of antiquity," reserved for the man of leisure, restricted to the contemplation of manifestations of life only "as they are embalmed in the flawless creations of classic art or poetry," adverse to "risky experimentation with real-life impulses," remote from most men, and solitary, the ideal nevertheless "contains elements indispensable for a full and rich life, and cultural ideals of a more universal appeal should make use of these elements in changed form" ([1933] 1956: 230–232). The shortcomings are more than a matter of taste or timeliness, in the sense of fashion. The humanist confuses the élite sector with the whole world, while in fact "he lacks the most primitive understanding of elementary facts" beyond "the world of his own educated sector"; he pursues an object that is meaningless to groups "confronted by matters of life or death, safety or disaster, triumph or decline"; his aestheticism excludes the awareness of doom, however sublimated, that informs the greatest art itself, as well as the sensibilities of unsheltered groups; he lacks the capacity to connect with persons rather than objectified "works," notwithstanding his own ideal of the perfected personality; but, above all, his "endeavor to produce 'harmonious,' 'integrated' personalities" entails an "antipathy to the dynamic and unexpected," and thereby "profoundly misunderstood life." As he does not say, but as may be understood, especially in view of the Max Weber's references that follow, humanism makes it impossible to engage in politics, as that activity is depicted in *Ideology and Utopia*. "In defending the orderliness of the world," Mannheim concludes flatly, "humanism merely betrayed a desire to maintain a wholly artificial security, based upon entrenched economic privilege" ([1933] 1956: 232–234).

The contrasting ideal reveals its antecedents in Max Weber's thought. Both vocation lectures are recalled. Mannheim begins with "vocational specialization," defending it against humanist complaints. The orientation to work implies an emphasis "upon the concrete situation, calling for active intervention, in which the individual happens to find himself." Of course, specialization can be impossibly narrow, but democratic cultivation reaches out while remaining "organically linked" to one's everyday occupation. "Man can become 'cultivated' only through and within a concretely goal-oriented practice." "The man who follows this path," Mannheim observes, "will be able to live the things he talks about, while the man who follows the humanistic course will often repeat things that... have no personal meaning for him." In his 1933 essay, Mannheim is surprisingly flaccid on the question of political education, as such, as an aspect of democratic cultivation, contenting himself with a brief sketch of the practical education of "the politician's evolution from a narrow particularist to a responsible statesman" through movement to "higher policy-making bodies." This is perhaps the element in his design most devastated by his own political hopelessness at the time of writing, and perhaps affected also by his first cautious steps towards his later extravagant admiration for the political career of the modern English gentleman. More interesting is his claim that modern specializations require effective interactions with other specializations and thus foster the capacity for a structural view. Sociology then builds on this capacity and cultivates the wider orientation in life and in social reality.[16]

Mannheim believed that a new ideal of cultivation had to address ordinary people in their real lives so that they might achieve the necessary self-reflexivity. This could not be accomplished without somehow involving people's real circumstances. Empirical research could be useful in acquiring this information, as long as it was put into a meaningful context (1932a: 28–31). He reiterated this position in a newspaper article at the end of 1932 on "The Spiritual Crisis in the Light of Sociology" (Mannheim [1932b] 2001).[17] He argued that one could not simply examine the current crisis from an exalted spiritual position, but must examine the actual lives of ordinary people. What intellectuals experience as a crisis of ideals is really only a reflection of the spiritual and psychic processes of fitting into new situations in life. If ordinary people's lives remain essentially stable, larger changes in the nation do not create the feeling of "spiritual crisis" among them. Such people, who have carried out (*vollzogen*) their adjustment to their situation, will continue in their habitual patterns and "remain faithful to their customary world of belief." Crisis is felt only when one's own life is disrupted.

Mannheim buttressed his argument with information from a small "survey" he had done. While his survey appeared to be extremely limited and did not become the model for his later work, it does indicate a strong concern for the orientation of the ordinary person. Just as importantly, it indicates his understanding of the fragmentation of cultural and political life in the Republic. Clearly Mannheim did not deny that the time was one of crisis, but he argued that there was not simply a single crisis that could be reduced to high culture or class struggle or parliamentary majorities, but a plurality of crises to match the plurality of experiences.[18] And these crises had to be viewed sociologically in order to resolve them.

As people's lives became more irrational, the finely tuned operation of modern society became endangered.[19] The unwillingness of people to accept traditional solutions to the dislocations resulted in the disintegration of institutions. Mannheim believed that while this dissolution was fraught with danger, it need not be viewed in a completely negative way, for it represented an opportunity for self-reflexivity and growth. However, for this to occur one could not simply trumpet elitist slogans about cultivation, which had no connection to people's real lives, but rather provide the orientation that would allow the "new person" to emerge.[20]

Mannheim believed that the first step away from massification was the development of small communities that allowed the opportunity to arrive at responsible individual conclusions. Mannheim stressed that it was possible for the democratic individual to have the same rational powers of judgment that former elites had, that democracy could indeed be one of reason (*Vernunftdemokratie*), even if this was not automatic. Educating the masses in this new orientation for responsibility became the primary task of the new education. The section on current issues study in his 1932 address on the sociological curriculum developed this argument (see above). Mannheim described his position as one of pedagogical optimism ([1933] 1956: 183, 196, 199, 239; 1932a: 37).

For Freyer, as we have seen, the older humanistic ideal also had to be discarded in favor of one that was closer to reality. Sociology as a science of reality played an important role, but it was always subordinate to the development of the political will, whereby the person was rooted in the communal nation (*Volk*) and was responsibly bound to the decision of the state. Mannheim rejected this lurch to a mythical and melodramatic "reality" mediated by the arbitrary ideology of the Revolution from the Right, as he rejected the decisionist logical structure of the argument. Despite acknowledging Schmitt's depiction of the potential weaknesses of parliamentary democracy ([1933] 1956: 174, 191), Mannheim believed that the masses could learn to become responsible democratic citizens as they developed reality-oriented ways of thinking, where the reality is understood as a dynamic totality, subject to strategic interventions governed by adequate political judgment in a situation of conflict, an understanding comparable to the knowledge that Marxism aspires to provide. It is the task of sociology as a specialized discipline to uncover such knowledge; but the discipline can do so only in intimate conjunction with the fostering of a sociological attitude both among its practitioners and among the concentric circles of publics that are its audience.

Mannheim's inaugural lectures in Frankfurt, with the title of "General Sociology," took place in the summer semester of 1930. Our retitling of the work should not be taken to suggest a required sequence of courses for sociology students. There was no degree program in sociology as yet, and there were consequently no required courses. Students could choose sociology as an option in several degree programs, and they could arrange to write their dissertations under a sociologist.[21] Mannheim had sociology students only in the sense that a core group assembled around his teaching. His audience would have consisted not only of enrolled students but also of visitors, many of them women. Each of his lectures opened with a summary of what had come before sufficiently detailed to permit such visitors to follow the lectures without attending the full sequence. His opening talk, in fact, declares the independence of this introduction from the merely scholastic conception of the subject matter. Mannheim insists not only that methodological concerns cannot be permitted to inhibit the emergence of a study geared to unprecedented phenomena and a novel point of view, but also that "the impulse to traditionalization, stabilization, rendering-teachable comes from the scholastic element common to both the pedagogical enterprise (*Schulbetrieb*) and system-making." The progression of the argument through the weeks, accordingly, has the attractive form of an extended essay, rather than a systematic classification of topics.[22]

Opening with a distinction between the specialized study of sociology and the attitude that makes it possible and guides its uses, Mannheim addresses the modern transformations of life experience, notably the phenomenon of distantiation, that are its social genealogy. Sociology, it turns out, is not simply an academic subject, but a way of seeing for a decisive modern social type. Yet distantiation is experienced first as a crisis of disorientation, and there are several typical reactions, including utopianism, romanticism, and, most recently, existentialism, three terms to conjure with in the intellectual life of Weimar. Partly in conjunction with these intellectual reactions and partly as a more or less unmediated function of especially stressed social locations, the present is confronted with the phenomenon of reprimitivization as an escape from the crisis. The question is whether this can undo the distantiation that unsettles practical certainties. Mannheim distinguishes between two current forms of reprimitivization, fascism and Marxist orthodoxy. The former derives from the sophisticated existentialist response as well as a high level of sociological knowledge, and it represents a deliberate turning back from an achieved level of insight, a substitution of willed decision for knowledgeable uncertainty and judgment, while the latter freezes an attained level of knowledge, treating it as if it had a univocality and finality that social knowledge cannot achieve. The sociological attitude is then seen as best articulated in the dynamic thinking associated in the recent past with the unattached intellectual as an emergent type. The discussion ends in an appraisal of the appeals and coercions that both kinds of reprimitivizations exercise on the intellectual in the present situation and a plea for courage. The lectures are of course addressed to the class, but they are also, as the essay form implies, severely self-examining. Mannheim does not spare his students his ongoing difficulties with his authorities and critics.

He first addressed the arguments concerning the scope and character of sociology during the Republic, from von Wiese to von Below and Curtius. In fixing the concept of sociology, he said, one must understand that it applies to a multiform intellectual undertaking, comprehensible at three different levels. One level is that of a specialized science with a clearly defined object, society. Viewed at this level, sociology concerns itself with social processes and formations in general, and addresses questions such as "what is a class?" There is a certain ambiguity in Mannheim's characterization of this level. His statements about it clearly refer to von Wiese's postulates, but it is unclear whether Mannheim means to accord this conception a partial validity or to treat it as too restrictive to count. In the introductory remarks recorded only in the Wolff notes, Mannheim says that formal sociology is good as a sub-field, if it does not claim a monopoly, and he goes on to class it together with political and ethnographic, "primitive" sociology as the three parts of "material sociology," with the latter corresponding to a second great subdivision, the "sociology of the spirit," encompassing both cultural sociology and sociology of knowledge. One reason for thinking the Wolff notes may have been supplemented by Mannheim's original lesson plan is that this seems too systematic a scheme for the tenor of his lectures and that its distinctions never recur. In the full lecture notes, in any case, Mannheim says, "limited to such themes, sociology is without question an unassailable specialized science," but then proceeds instantly to convert the seemingly normative judgment into a slightly discreditable empirical one, explaining how sociologists have gutted their actual discipline to meet the expectations of academic prejudice. Essayists, one may say, enjoy the use of such ambiguities, and his listeners were left free to interpret his judgment of von Wiese as they liked. Mannheim, in the meantime, was equally free to incorporate a dimension of formal sociology into his own work. Complementarily, Mannheim's treatment of the first level can be taken as an instance of the dialectics he introduced as the distinctive method of sociology at its most comprehensive.

At the second level, sociology appears as a method increasingly used by all of the specialized human sciences. If von Wiese represented the falsely one-sided claims for the first level, von Below embodied the second, although neither man is named. Seen dialectically, each level obviously discerns an element of sociology, but neither comprehends the discipline as a whole—or, for that matter, the limited aspect towards which it points. Sociology properly understood has to be seen at the third level, as the multiform working out of a "new posture of consciousness," a distinctive "attitude" grounded in modern social experience. Mannheim is not modest about sociology as thus understood: "Sociology is a new kind of philosophy, I think. In its actual origins, it is a secularized philosophy. This process of emergence is the most important developmental process in the history of the human spirit." Implicitly, this conception shatters Max Weber's scientific asceticism and supersedes Lukács' claims for proletarian consciousness. Weber's accomplishments cannot be comprehended by Weber's methodological reflections, it seems, and what is valuable about the "proletarian perspective" is due to its special participation in this wider consciousness, which is by no means limited to this class or explainable by the relations of production. Perhaps there is a pedagogical explanation for Mannheim's vehemence at the point of introduction, given that the lectures are generally free of such effusions and that Mannheim does not seek to take advantage in argument from such extravagant philosophical claims. He is announcing that he is offering a scientifically grounded and constrained alternative to the *Weltanschauungen* competing for a youth in search of answers. Sociology understood at the third level is the discipline that subscribes to Becker's mission and becomes a means of orientation for citizens of the Republic. In doing so it offers a counter-model to other forms of political orientation, which Mannheim called "reprimitivization" and which included both the radical conservatism of Schmitt and Freyer and the varieties of orthodox Marxism, including not only Lukács and the communists, but also, almost certainly, the ideological stalwarts of the Social Democratic party organization.

The ambiguous paradigm for the sociological attitude, for Mannheim in 1930, as for Freyer in 1931, is Saint-Simon. But it is not Saint-Simon, the prophet of a closed technical perfection, who attracts Mannheim, but Saint-Simon the pioneer of an "experimental life," unbound by mental habits of class or station, and available to all of the ways of experiencing, seeing, and acting that are present in his time, while expanding the options precisely by virtue of this availability. The attractiveness of the same model to Freyer is a sign of Mannheim's risk-taking. As with the topic of utopia in general, the crux is in the uses of patient, rational reflection as controlling instance for the experimental life. The aperçu is meant to be an opening to meticulous analysis. Mannheim does not aspire to act as "prophet" in the sense deprecated by Max Weber, but as initiator into a demanding scientific practice unlikely to yield Saint-Simonian types of enthusiasm. Mannheim's essays, as Bacon put it, are intended to speak not only to men's bosoms but also to their business.

Yet it is impossible to work through these notes, fascinating as they are for both the historian and theorist, without feeling an occasional surge of sympathy for the critical preview of his lecturing manner submitted to Becker by the Frankfurt dean in 1929, in his attempt to avert Mannheim's appointment: "Professor Mannheim represents a tendency in sociology that is of little real value to our students. Our students need a sociologist with a background in political economy or legal studies. Professor Mannheim's orientation, however, is philosophical. His language, moreover, is hard to understand for people without the necessary philosophical education" (UF, Letter of Dean Hellauer to the Ministry of Science, Art, and Education in Berlin, 27.11.29).[23] Mannheim's subsequent courses moderated their demands on his hearers. Perhaps they also sacrificed something of the intimacy that Mannheim achieved, as a counter to the difficulty of his higher theoretical flights. Mannheim's students testified often to the personal fascination of his presence, and his colleagues did not rarely protest it.[24] Striking throughout the lectures is Mannheim's personal voice, narrating the story of his analyses in the first person in direct address to the students, evoked in the second person. The analyses themselves are often detached, of course, with frequent use of the passive voice and the impersonal "one" (*man*) constructions, but Mannheim always returns to say something about his reasons for going here or there in the argument.

In formulating the essentials of the sociological attitude, Mannheim depended on two important concepts, "enactment" (*Vollzug, vollziehen*) and "distantiation" (*Distanzierung*), which had a dialectical relationship to one another. Although we refer to the first of these terms as "enactment" in this discussion, the difficulties in its translation have resulted in our rendering the root word also as carrying out (or through), effectuating or executing, depending on the location of the specific use in the spectrum of connotations we believe to be intended. The term signals the use of both vitalist and Heideggerian language in Mannheim's Frankfurt writings, as well as his development of Simmel's conceptualizations. It indicates activities of the most diverse sort, from the "execution" of an individual act to the "enactment" of a norm to the "carrying out" of life itself. Important to all of these is that one does not simply act within reality as something apart from it; rather one's actions create, or recreate, reality. In a letter to Max Wertheimer a year later (Mannheim [1931c] 2001), Mannheim wrote that the act of interpretation was a constitutive element of existence.

Like Heidegger, Freyer and Schmitt, not to mention Lukács, Mannheim attempted to overcome the dualism of the contemplative subject and objective reality through practice. For the radical conservatives, the action of the subject (especially the collective subject), be it spiritual or physical, was not simply a means by which reality transformed itself but itself the determiner of reality—Nietzsche over Hegel. While Mannheim wanted to do away with the purely contemplative subject, he refused to conflate reality and purely voluntaristic action crystallized in a concept of decision. In modern societies, enactment was rendered uniquely problematical by distantiation, the loss of vital engagement in the traditional context of meanings that constitutes an enactment, with the result that a person "becomes detached" (*herausfallen*) from the conventional enactments which he continues to make, to some degree a paradoxical devitalization of a vital act. This is Mannheim's present formulation of the "alienation" that plays so important a part in Lukács, although the conception is already present in Simmel's original theories of "distance" and pervades neo-Romantic critiques of modern inauthenticity.

It may have been distracting for his auditors, but it is of the utmost importance that Mannheim then talks of executing an act of distantiation. Such a paradox is resolved by noting the dialectical relationship of the two terms. The ideal subject enacts a world, which changes both him and the world within which he acts. But at the same time, he perceives both himself and that world as an object, thus creating a distance. This leads to yet more enactments. The claim that distantiation can be turned from being a (malign) destiny into being an enactment that leaves the agent capable of further enactments at a higher level of self-control is the central argument of the sociological project. Sociology is practice, not contemplation. The proto-fascist thinkers attempt to undo distantiation instead of enacting it.

To distance is to objectify, but not to the degree that one becomes a neutral observer removed from the situation. Another term Mannheim uses in this context is "expansion" (*Erweiterung*). One expands oneself through the enactment of distantiation. Expansion does not mean abandonment of a specific historical location. In moving beyond the confines of a specific community (group), one does not become the purely communicative subject of positivistic social science. Distantiation means self-reflexivity, that is, making facts out of one's norms, not simply accepting their validity as given, but placing them in "brackets" (*Klammern*) to transcend them ([1930a] 2001: 75). Despite Mannheim's use of this Husserlian concept, "to transcend" did not mean for him what it did for many Idealist phenomenologists or for Max Scheler—to place something in brackets in order to determine its universal essence. Mannheim's version of "transcendence" can be seen in a second usage of the root word, as "fastening together" (*Verklammerung*), which he defined as "being interwoven" (*Verflochtenheit*) (54).[25] One placed something in brackets by fastening it to other things. Self-reflexivity meant placing oneself as a subject into a context so that one was object as well as subject. In the language of his earlier sociological theory of culture (Mannheim [1922–24] 1982), neither the purely conjunctive subject, in his concrete subjectivity, nor the purely communicative subject, in his abstract universality, is self-reflexive.

In this light, Mannheim significantly counterposed the sociological attitude to the religious attitude, which, he believed, is characteristic of primitive societies with unambiguous meanings. The "binding" of members to the primitive religious community is very strong, so that they are not able to achieve any distantiation, to extend themselves beyond the limitations of the closed community. As with his Zurich paper on competition, one sees here a combination of concepts from "A Sociological Theory of Culture" and *Ideology and Utopia*. The distinction between binding and distantiation runs parallel to the earlier one between the communal culture and the cultivated culture. Members of the communal culture are not able to lead an experimental life, because to experiment is to distance oneself, and they do not need to do so and are incapable of it. Conversely, distantiation characterizes both the cultivated culture and the free-floating intelligentsia. Mannheim believed that the latter was not bound (*gebunden*) to certain political positions, because its members' interaction with one another provided a degree of distantiation from any of the positions with which they were connected (*verbunden*). It was precisely this distantiation, this refusal to be bound, that Schmitt would attack in 1933. Accordingly, Mannheim labeled the Schmitt's position "reprimitivization," because it was an attempt to return to a confinement akin to that of the primitive religious community.

As he had done in his earlier works, Mannheim assigned social differentiation as the underlying cause for the dissolution of "unambiguous alignment of meaning" *(eindeutige Bedeutungsrichtung, Sinnausrichtung)*. But not all social differentiation creates this breakdown.[26] Only at the point where differentiation results in mutually antithetical life spheres, is unambiguity shattered. But differentiation itself does not necessarily result in self-reflexivity; the existence of the "heretic" does not make the orthodox believer self-reflexive.[27] Only when the other stands in a truly antithetical relationship to oneself—Mannheim here uses Kant's concept of antinomy, rather than Hegel's concept of contradiction to characterize the seemingly unbridgeable divide—only when one realizes that one is an object to the other, when one begins to entertain the notion that "I" am also an "it," does self-reflexivity begin. One regards oneself ironically as something that could be something else. One becomes open to the idea of one's own transformation. One can then adopt a sociological attitude, which entails an experimental life.

Mannheim termed the antinomic world aspirations that first dissolved the unambiguous meaningful community "utopias." A utopia successfully presents an alternative future to that of the original life sphere. However, it is unable to make that alternative future hegemonic. Thus, while this utopian element marks the beginning of life distancing, of separating its holders from their unambiguous life sphere, it does not complete this process into true self-reflexivity. The utopian world aspiration remains an absolute, or rather a counter-absolute. This is where he ended *Ideology and Utopia*, with utopian thought seemingly displaced by irreconcilable ideologies or a fatalistic realism. Mannheim announces in his lecture that he is himself moving beyond the treatment of utopia in *Ideology and Utopia*. It now appears as a preliminary phase. When the utopia's upholders try to implement it in the concrete world they must adopt an empirical attitude to the ambiguous concrete realities of social life. They must become self-reflexive to some degree or fail, but this self-reflexivity moves them beyond utopian faith.

Reflexivity still has its own dangers, for it means the recognition of pluralism and thus could lead to a relativistic fatalism and loss of will. The 1930 lectures make it clear that he did not mean to advocate some kind of defeatist relativism, as critics of his book charged. The sociological type that emerges out of utopian thought remains politically engaged, if only by virtue of a decision to do so, as in Max Weber. He cites Carl Schmitt's contention that "a bad decision [is] still more valuable than no decision at all" (34). At the same time, however, Mannheim rejects Schmitt's brand of political engagement—reprimitivization. Reprimitivization represented a conscious denial of the pluralism of modernity, a "decision" to regress to the unambiguous meaning of an unproblematic and unified culture on command, to become "primitive" in the face of the modern world. Mannheim uses two terms to describe this kind of enactment—the Freudian term "regression" and his own "turning back."[28] Mannheim identified Schmitt's (and implicitly Freyer's) position with Mussolini's fascism with its emphasis on the political myth, but he did not mention National Socialism, whose distinct characteristics he never discerned.[29] He saw quite clearly in 1930, however, that the complex reasons that led a Schmitt or a Freyer to align with fascism would not be controlling for the political consequences of their choice, since the social forces with which they converge have quite different reasons for action.

It is noteworthy that in these lectures Mannheim treated orthodox Marxism as a type of reprimitivization. Like fascism it is a form of regression; it too rejects the pluralism of alternatives in modern society for the sake of unconditional action. It is clearly superior to fascism, however, in that the system of thought that it closes off from new insights and questions is a highly advanced sociological view. Orthodoxy leads Mannheim to an examination of defensiveness, and thus to a lively response to many of his own critics, where the dogma being defended is scholarly—and schoolmasterly— rather than political. On the question of orthodox Marxism itself, Mannheim shows understanding. "If I were a miner and very badly off," he writes, "I would certainly be an orthodox revolutionary."

There is more than sympathy from a distance in the immediate sequel. He turns to the "affiliated intellectuals." They are in a dire predicament. As an intellectual, such a person is constantly undergoing sublimation and distantiation, since that is the condition of the intelligentsia "ever since it defected from its original group, at which point the intellectual abandoned the earliest unambiguous possibility of seeing the world and entered upon a level of consciousness with multiple possibilities. . . . There is present a tendency to see multidimensionally, but at the same time, a great uncertainty." The affiliated intellectual, however, "identifies himself with a position that is not altogether his own, but that is in some measure consonant with the dissatisfaction of the intelligentsia with the world as it is," yielding both identification and dualism. Speaking in words that cannot be separated from his history of profound admiration for Georg Lukács and friendship with him, Mannheim sketches a troubled portrait:

> He is under a compulsion, especially if he affiliates himself with the most extreme group. He finds himself in a situation where he is constantly binding his conscious-

ness to the sanctioned decision that he receives and experiences with the others.... He understands that this dogmatizing, this nailing fast of certain things, is very fruitful from the standpoint of action. Collective action is possible only when the direction of action is unequivocally laid down. He also understands that this orthodoxy is prescribed on the basis of a situation that is not actually a complete fit with his own. It means the presupposition of axiomatic propositions.... Insofar as this latter is particularistic, certain things can simply not be successfully mastered. ([1930a] 2001: 50–51)

As it happened, Lukács spent 1929 underground in Budapest, publishing a party-line broadsheet and serving as the anonymous contact. In May of that year, he "admitted the 'eclectic opportunism' and 'contradictory propositions'" of the Blum theses, the program for the Hungarian Party he had helped to draft, against the wishes of Béla Kun and Lajos Révai—the latter, one the most junior protégés of the Sunday Circle—and which fell afoul of the new Stalinist majority in the Comintern. Lukács' biographer, Kadarkay, continues:

> But this recantation proved futile. In October, the Comintern delivered its verdict. Branded as an "incorrigible factionalist," Lukács was expelled from the party leadership in Vienna and sternly "summoned to Moscow." (Kadarkay 295)

Lukács' closest friend and original comrade in the move to communism, Bela Balázs, wrote a play that year in which the Lukács character, portrayed as an unsparing "seeker-of-truth" "is executed for 'practical' political reasons, having supported his own death sentence, convinced as he was that a revolutionary lives or dies for an idea" (Kadarkay 292). Mannheim was in constant contact with Hungary and he would have known the details of Lukács' fate.

We believe that in the fatalism of misused reflexivity and the spasms of reprimitivization, one can hear the echo of the two ethics also rejected by Max Weber in "Politics as a Vocation," those of fatalism and conviction. And further, that the alternative Mannheim proposed in the experimental sociological attitude is ultimately modeled on Weber's ethic of responsibility, notwithstanding differences about the uses of scientific knowledge in its constitution. The first of these ethics is characterized by an abandonment of an ideal in an accommodation with the world, either by removing oneself from politics completely or adopting a pure instrumentality in political activity. This apolitical approach is akin to the position of von Wiese. The second ethic is characterized by a refusal to make any adjustment to the concrete world, to retreat back to an unambiguous ideal. This is akin to the reprimitivization of Schmitt and Freyer. The third ethic allows for the engagement for an ideal but with a sense of proportion, the ability to distance oneself enough from the ideal to allow for contextualization but without falling into fatalism. To put it in Mannheim's terms, the sociological attitude should combine decision (*Entscheidung*) and expansion (*Erweiterung*), so that they exist in a dialectical relationship to one another. Expansion without political engagement can lead to a sterile fatalism. Decision in defiance of sociological clarification assumes the form of self-denial and botched subservience to social forces actuated by social dynamics unrelated to the pained reasoning that brought intellectuals to their sacrifice of thought. In contrast to the two extremes of the first two Weberian ethics, the sociological person "feels his way through the mesh (*Verflechtungen*) of the actual situation" (48), using sociology as the instrument for a new "reformation of life" (35). Weber looked for the decisive personality and regretted that the bourgeoisie had not bred up the type. Mannheim, like Becker, expanded his focus to include the masses and believed that instilling the proper attitude, that is, some form of education, could bolster political experience.

As the lectures make plain, our outline of themes understates the extent to which Mannheim is concerned to frame the disciplined sociological inquiry to which the course is meant as an introduction. The first responsibility is to science in this expanded sense. But scientific cultivation is inseparable from political education. A short passage near the end of the manuscript indicates the direction in which Mannheim would travel: "Sociological method consists in seeing spiritual contents in a certain way. It experiences the contents quite differently from the man of everyday, insofar as his attitude is not sociological" (75). We believe that ultimately Mannheim sought to eliminate that distinction as much as possible by instilling the sociological attitude into ordinary people. This was a continuation of his efforts to preserve and transcend the humanistic ideal of cultivation by putting sociology at its center.

Mannheim's immediate design was, of course, doomed as he spoke. The cultivation that would prevail for twelve years in the place where he was teaching would be quite remote from the hopes of Carl Heinrich Becker. Symbolic of this fate is the career of the *völkisch* thinker Ernst Krieck, whose path crossed Mannheim's several times. Krieck was a schoolteacher who by 1922 had become a *völkisch* spokesman against the educational reforms of Haenisch and Becker. In 1923 he was awarded an honorary doctorate by Heidelberg University, when Mannheim was there. Such an award to an academic outsider was exceptional and was not well-received by most of the faculty. In 1928 he was put up for a new chair in education at Frankfurt University. Despite significant political pressure, the faculty rejected him on the basis of "scholarly standing." This was the year before Mannheim received his call to Frankfurt. Instead, Krieck took up a position in a pedagogical academy in the city. He joined the Nazi Party in 1932 at the time Mannheim was rejecting political partisanship. In May, 1933, a month after Mannheim was dismissed from his position by the new Hitler-led government, the same month that Carl Schmitt joined the Nazi Party, Krieck, now as rector of Frankfurt University, addressed the gathered faculty who had earlier rejected him as "national comrades!" (*Volksgenossen*) (Zneimer 1978: 147–148).

Mannheim's response to the catastrophe was in the spirit of the letter he wrote at the end of April, 1933 to his fond student, Nina Rubinstein, whose dissertation on the French emigrés he had been patiently nurturing since the last Heidelberg years:

> As a sociologist, you are called upon to understand what is happening and to allow events to run their course. Relinquish the habit of thinking about the long run. That no longer suits these days. One merely feels aggrieved and neglects the most urgent things. These are the reasons why I myself cannot answer your question about what I am planning to do. For the moment, I remain at my post as a Prussian official. No running away, certainly not yet. After one has worked so long on emigration, one is duty-bound to a certain sense of proportion. Noblesse oblige. (Kettler/Meja 1994; Rubinstein 2000).

The resolution to do his duty as a Prussian official is easily mocked, but his Prussia was the Prussia of Becker not Göring. He chose exile, after all, within days of the letter, but he did not abandon his duty as a sociologist. From his exile, first in Amsterdam and Paris and then in his final home in London, he asked the Rockefeller Foundation to finance a research project that would put him at the head of a team of prominent exiled social scientists, assisted by his best Frankfurt students. Mannheim requested $50,000 to fund an interdisciplinary collaborative study of "The Sociological Causes of the Cultural Crisis in the Era of Mass-Democracies and Autarchies" (RF/RG1.1/401S/73/969).

A prominent and characteristic feature of the proposal was Mannheim's hope of keeping his students together and at work. One of the Foundation's officials was impressed. The strongest argument in favor of the project, he reports, is that Mannheim's staffing scheme "would provide an excellent type of training for younger [refugee] scholars and help to salvage some of the exceptionally able younger German scholars who have not yet been taken care of." For the interdisciplinary senior staff, Mannheim proposed the psychologist Theodor Reik, the social historian Alfred von Martin, the political scientist Sigmund Neumann, and the legal sociologist, Franz L. Neumann. Mannheim also asked for five "young social scientists," as well as two "observers" in Germany and Russia. Another source adds Ernest K. Bramstead, Norbert Elias, W. Falk, Hans Gerth, Svend Riemer, and Albert Salomon—all but one former Mannheim students—presumably to fill the junior roles (Woldring 1987: 40).

The urgent occasion for study, he writes to the Rockefeller Foundation, is the conjunction between an "era of the most highly perfected technical rationalization and planning" and social-political forces that will, if unchecked, "lead to the dissolution of all forms of culture and a universal reversion to barbarism." His "sociological investigation into the social conditions for the growth and existence of 'culture'" is designed to uncover "the clue to the remedial measures needed" to direct the unavertable shift to the planning of culture not "according to the preconceived patterns of the various political groups" but according to knowledge capable of halting the abandonment of the "common Christian-humanitarian basis of Western society." The central analytical figures are the distinctions between unplanned and planned sectors of society and the correlate conceptions of elite and mass; and Mannheim's leading idea, as in his subsequent published writings, is that developments in the unplanned sector have led to destructive changes in function of liberal non-intervention, undermining the structured reproduction of cultural elites and their publics in favor of a vicious symbiosis of leaders and masses. What emerges perhaps more clearly here than in some of Mannheim's later writings is that his distinctive contribution to the widespread confident advocacy of planning was intended to be the planned reconstitution of an intellectual elite dedicated to high culture, albeit democratic in recruitment. This engagement with the central problem in John Stuart Mill's *On Liberty*, subjecting Mill's response to new tests of "time and place," (Cumming

1969), but sharing his determination to work within the reality of democracy, helps to explain Mannheim's subsequent relations with continuators of the culturally conservative strand in English liberalism. With Mill, it brings a reminder also of Humboldt, whom Mill so greatly admired. Mannheim's research proposal undertakes to integrate historical, comparative, and empirical studies of social mechanisms of elite (de)formation, with the sociologist functioning as coordinator of an interdisciplinary team.

This plan misfired, in part because the funds sought were astronomical and in part because the Rockefeller Foundation's advisors were not satisfied with Mannheim's credentials as an empirical researcher, by the emerging standards of American social science. Mannheim made the diagnostic effort by himself during the years of exile, finding support among Christian thinkers assembled by Joseph H. Oldham, the missionary whose initiatives had led to the Frankfurt Discussions in 1931. Much of his work is disfigured by the emergency, and none of it retains the freshness of his Weimar writings. But the energy and focus of his search transmitted itself to two authors whose separate ways did much to shape the next generation of American sociology, Edward Shils and C. Wright Mills. Shils was the actual translator of Mannheim's *Ideology and Utopia* and he guided Louis Wirth in his defense of the work. He also translated *Man and Society in an Age of Reconstruction*. Critical of Mannheim's planning doctrine and uncomfortable with his philosophy, he never fully acknowledged his debt (Shils 1941; Shils 1947; Shils 1968; Shils 1973; Shils 1980). But that is what Mannheim had learned to expect from his students. Mills never met Mannheim, but he wrote one of the first long critical appreciations of *Ideology and Utopia* and wrote his most ambitious books in collaboration with Mannheim's most devoted student, Hans Gerth (Mills 1940; Mills 1959; Mills 1963). Between Shils and Mills, the question of sociology and cultivation entered deeply into the institutional memory of American sociology, although Mannheim would have pointed out, wearing the black silk shirt that awed his students and twirling his customary unlit cigarette, that the memory is largely repressed and erupts all too often only in bouts of hysteria.

Mannheim's continuing importance is not least because of his deep respect for the achievements of the human spirit. That is after all what is behind all the talk of life and relationism. Humanity is not waiting for the sociologist to bring it revelations. Groups in society generate their own visions to guide their conduct, and these deserve recognition as valid acts of practical reason, always partial and always limited. The problem is the management of conflict among these visions, the danger of desperate lunges, the attractions of unreality. Sociologists are to be the voice of realism, skill and civility. In the end, Mannheim points the way beyond the fateful disjunction of culture and civilization (Elias 1978: 3–34). But it is a way of enactments, not a process.

In the first of his introductory lectures, Mannheim lays down the principle of limitation (*Beschränktheit*) for sociology. Written in his typical gnarled and technical language, this sober formula of enlightenment is perhaps still his most important legacy:

> The essence of limitation, in its deepest sense, consists less of limits on the wealth of what can be and is in fact known than of limits within the apparatus of conceptualization, of categorization. We try to grasp the whole of life through paradigms—models—appropriate to a specific narrow sphere of life. In this sense, everyone is limited. This limitation can only be overcome by means of a constant movement. This entails an attunement [*Einstellen*] to what is coming into being, using the apparatus of thought and everything that a person can bring to bear on things, a process of self-expansion, situating oneself in the center of what is happening. The present is marked by conflict through particularistic political tensions and disputes among countries, it is a time when particularistic attitudes are forced to take one another's measure. If it is impossible to overcome [*aufhebbar*] these tensions, we will see more clearly in such a situation if we undertake a self-audit [*Selbstrevision*] at every confrontation and conduct ourselves in the spirit of Goethe's words, that every well-observed new object calls forth a new organ in us. That is a decisive statement. If you want to know what essential learning is, note the following: to let such new organs take shape within ourselves and, never to rest until one has, in a new contexture of life, generated such a new organ. This is the self-expansion whose agent is above all sociology. (Mannheim [1930a] 2001: 4)

Notes

1. The parliamentary Social Democratic Party voted to leave the coalition against the pleadings of most socialist ministers, not least because irresistible pressure from the communist left made it seem impossible to accept further cuts in the swamped unemployment scheme (Mommsen 1989: 286–292).
2. As at Heidelberg, of course, both poles represented minorities, with the majority of professors pursuing their specialties and resisting the drama of "crisis" and conflict in the university (Schivelbusch 15–17).
3. Hammerstein (1989: 17) writes: "Frankfurt was from the beginning thought of as an institution receptive to experimentation, liberal and proceeding along new paths, an institution that, in addition to the traditional sciences, was also to examine those areas that received little attention at the established universities but that increasingly determined and alarmed the modern world."
4. Only Hamburg had a lower percentage of students in corporations. In contrast, the

percentage was 3.5 times as great at Marburg and twice as great at Heidelberg (Steinberg 1977: 46). Fraternity membership was a good predictor for Nazi student activity. For women students in social sciences at Frankfurt, see Honegger 1990, Kettler/Meja, 1993.

5. Neither Leo Lowenthal, Toni Oelsner nor Hans Gerth detected a strong antisemitic presence at the university before the Nazi seizure of power (Greffrath 1979: 63, 211, 227).
6. In the July, 1932 Reichstag elections, the Nazis garnered 38.7 percent of the vote, a little more than one percent above the national average. Of the largest fifteen cities in Germany, only in Breslau and Hannover did the Nazis get a higher percentage (Hamilton 1982: 201, 485).
7. The decisive event in guaranteeing this support was the Kapp Putsch of March, 1920, which underlined the need to educate a new generation of leaders in democratic ideals (Kluke 1972: 245).
8. In his introductory course of 1930, in fact, he had clearly relegated the religious outlook in a more conventional sense to the "primitive" stage of social development and had taken it as a mark of Schmitt's dubious "reprimitivization" that he mixes religious with sociological categories. See below. On the last point, see McCormick 1997. Mannheim's friendly association with Tillich's circle—and a possible encounter with William James' book— may have loosened his use of the term religious experience to include the special mode of "self-distantiation" that he had derived from his youthful enthusiasm of the mystics and retained life-long as a most personal topic.
9. Heimann took his degree under Alfred Weber. His role as theoretical interlocutor of Karl Mannheim is clear from Mannheim's letter to him (Mannheim 2001).
10. Kelsen was an avid Republican, it should be said, arguably unique among constitutional lawyers in his understanding of the democratic constitution (Luthardt 1987), and his presence at the head of the faculty's list also speaks against understanding the opposition to Mannheim as another antisemitic manifestation. Despite his profound differences with Marxist social democrats, Kelsen was himself a member of that party and gained effective leadership of the legal defense of the republican side as the crisis deepened, including the legal struggle over the suspension of the Prussian state government in 1932, where his opponent was Carl Schmitt (see Kettler 1984: and cp. Dyzenhaus 1997). Mannheim, for his part, took great offense at suggestions that political considerations entered into his appointment. In a letter of March 15, 1930, asking that his pensionable service be backdated to the beginning of his work as editorial assistant to Alfred Weber in 1921, Mannheim bitterly protested the rumor that his appointment was "political." The German Sociological Association, he said, had been asked to provide a "collective evaluation" of the candidates and they had listed him as the best qualified. He demanded that the Dean make public the excerpt from the Faculty minutes in which they chose him after the failure of the "jurists' list." There is no record of such action in the files made available, although there is a memo signed by Riezler about a meeting of the university board at which it was decided to make no objection to him if Kelsen declined. Mannheim's pension request was denied. The eventual effect of this decision was to exclude Mannheim from any compensation after his mandatory "retirement" in 1933, since the regulation offered compensation only after ten years' service (UF).
11. Schivelbusch does note that the Georgians were nowhere as prominent in Frankfurt as they were in Heidelberg (1982: 15). In any case, the effects of these battle

lines can be easily misjudged. A leading Georgian, Gundolf was Dean of the Philosophy Faculty in Heidelberg at the time of Mannheim's departure. There is a handwritten endorsement by Gundolf on Mannheim's letter notifying the Baden ministry of the Frankfurt call (10.12.29). He asks the minister to do his best to make a counter-offer to retain Mannheim in Heidelberg (UH).

12. See Mannheim's notes for his Frankfurt lectures in 1932 (KMP). A contemporary published essay by Mannheim is "On the Nature of Economic Ambition and Its Significance for the Social Education of Man" (Mannheim [1930b] 1952: 230–75).
13. Kettler/Meja 1995 argues that this dimension of Mannheim's work should be understood in the context of the late history of Liberalism since Mill, especially as this history has been structurally interpreted by R.D. Cumming 1969. cp. Loader 1985.
14. Scheler died in 1928 and did not address Nazism specifically. Rather he predicted the deterioration of democracy into irrational movements.
15, Mannheim is reprocessing materials developed in his more nuanced study of conservative thought [1925] 1986. The generalizations in our account stereotype the historical variations recognized by his treatment, even as he attempts, in the present context, to state an ideal type.
16. Loader and Kettler have published separate essays on Mannheim's 1930 lectures, marked by sharply contrasting emphases (Endreβ/Sruba 2000). While Loader traces changes in Mannheim's argument before and after those writings, as political conditions worsen, a trajectory of political disillusionment, Kettler emphasizes the extent to which the lectures comprehend and ground major themes in his overall project. Present purposes do not require the authors to resolve these contrasting preferences in their choice of perspective, especially since Mannheim so often urges the value of experimenting with more than one, while indicating that the preferences may not be a matter of choice anyway, in any simple sense.
17. This article appeared at the end of December in the *Stuttgarter Neues Tagblatt*. A week later (January 7, 1933) the same piece in a somewhat shortened form appeared in the *Hamburger Fremdenblatt*. Our translation is of the longer Stuttgart version. We wish to thank Reinhard Laube for bringing the Hamburg version to our attention.
18. This argument is very much in keeping with recent research on the Republic (Fritzsche 1996).
19. This is a theme he would repeat in the first of his major exile works, *Man and Society in an Age of Reconstruction*.
20. This theme was prominent in other lectures of the Frankfurt period. See below.
21. Concern about these limitations in the discipline's competition for students helped to bring about the meeting of sociology teachers in 1932. See above.
22. The essay form was a matter of special interest to Lukács, and it became the genre of choice for Mannheim. See Kettler/Meja 1995 and Loader 1985. In making his point that new sciences arise out of life before they are subjected to academic systematization, Mannheim oddly cited Max Weber's studies of the rationalization of the law through professional guilds. Weber did not privilege the earlier state of the law, and he expressly warned Lukács against essayistic proceedings in academic study (see above). One of Mannheim's early precursors, Adam Ferguson, also made his name with a famous extended essay, *An Essay on the History of Civil Society*, but meticulously organized his courses to conform with Baconian standards of systematization. His more prominent contemporary, David Hume,

followed Bacon himself in writing an essay on essays to point out the difference. See Kettler 1977. Mannheim, like Lukács, knew what he was doing when he resisted the Baconian demand for order in science. In *Ideology and Utopia*, he speaks of sociology of knowledge as a new "organon" of political knowledge.

23. In the absence of detailed records, the reasons for the Faculty's opposition to Mannheim must be a matter of conjecture. Yet the question is important for understanding his professional standing. Moreover, a long standard American survey of sociological theory misleadingly maintains, "Mannheim . . . is said to have owed his appointment at the University of Frankfort not to his Jewish ancestry but to the fact that he had done much to make Marxism *salonfähig*, i.e., socially and intellectually respectable" (Becker/Barnes 1938: III, 924). Mannheim's personnel file at the Johann-Wolfgang-Goethe University (UF) has only been made available to us in small part, but from the available correspondence it seems clear that the Prussian ministry, initially on the urging of Emil Lederer, vigorously pushed the case for offering the professorship to Mannheim over the strong and repeated objections of the Faculty. On September 7, 1929, the head of the Faculty writes to Professor Windelband, the competent official at the Ministry, to say that the Faculty had agreed that they would want a legal sociologist if the economic historian Lederer is unavailable, and reaffirmed their earlier decision about rejecting Mannheim and Adolf Löwe, whom Lederer had nominated as his associates, in the event of his acceptance. The reply from Windelband says that Lederer has indeed declined, and that the head of the division in the Ministry wants to discuss the situation with Arndt in person (September 28, 1929). Before the date set for the meeting, however, the ministry official peremptorily asks the Faculty "to express itself" as soon as possible on the question of calling Mannheim to the professorship. A letter from the Faculty's representative on November 27, 1929, alludes to a verbal conversation and to an enclosed copy of a formal reply to the letter concerning Mannheim. The latter text was not released to us by the university archivist, but its point can be inferred from the closing remarks in the covering letter: "I will only add, if I may, that we have in the meantime heard from a South-German colleague, who was recently present at a lecture by Professor (sic) Mannheim, that this lecture was simply incomprehensible to him. That is also what would happen to our students." It is known that the Faculty was then allowed to offer the position to Hans Kelsen before finally making the offer to Mannheim. There is also reliable evidence that Mannheim found professional support other than that Lederer and the Ministry. There is nothing discreditable to Mannheim in having earned the confidence of officials in the two state government(s) most consistently faithful to the democratic constitution. On the evidence available, however, we cannot question the good faith of the Frankfurt Faculty's initial opposition to Mannheim, especially since their eagerness to appoint either Lederer or Kelsen shows that they did not object to him on political or ethnic grounds.

24. For testimony by Nina Rubinstein and Kurt H. Wolff, see Kettler/Meja 1993. For angry criticism by the noted English sociologist, Morris Ginsberg, see Kettler/Meja 1995.

25. In the joint seminar with Alfred Weber, Mannheim spoke of a "mesh." Later, in *The Contemporary Tasks of Sociology*, Mannheim would again use "fastening together," which he defined as "the interweaving of the events of human happening with one another" (1932a: 27). In fact, several pages would be dedicated to

the problem set of fastening together (*Verklammerungsproblematik*) in that work (1932a: 23–27).
26. For example, in the monopoly stage described above, there is no dissolution despite differentiation.
27. In fact, one could argue that the "other" as seen by Schmitt in *The Concept of the Political* ([1928] 1976) discourages self-reflexivity.
28. Our rendering does not quite capture the German "*zurückschrauben*," which could be literally translated "screw back" or "ratchet back" and implies an element of force and resistance.
29. Mannheim was not unique among ethnically Jewish social scientists in downplaying anti-Semitism as a motif in German fascism, either in Germany or in exile. Cp. Neumann (1944). Mannheim did take the pattern quite far. In Mannheim 1940, his prime analysis of the German disaster, for example, there are merely two passing references to anti-Semitism. One notes that it was already prevalent in the eighteenth century, linking it with nationalism (89n1), and the other mentions it together with paganism as ideas of the groups in power (366). Jews also occur only twice, once as illustrating the scapegoating mechanism, following Harold Lasswell, and the second time as lowest outcast, to explain the psychological rewards of the willing followers. Mannheim's elderly Jewish parents, to whom he was close, survived the war in Budapest; and Mannheim's home was known as the headquarters for news from there (MP). But there is no trace of these concerns in his writings. Notions of self-hatred and denial are clearly insufficient. Mannheim lived in the best-known middle-class Jewish neighborhood in London, and the west end in Frankfurt had a similar reputation. It may be that Mannheim and the others were reluctant to be classed as special pleaders in their opposition to fascism, and to be relegated to "parochial" Jewish issues.

Bibliography

Archival Sources

Albert Salomon Collection, Leo Baeck Institute, New York City. [cited as SLB]
Archives of Nina Rubinstein, New York City. [cited as NR]
Correspondence between Eduard Heimann and Karl Mannheim, Tillich Papers, Box 601, #999–1010, Andover Theological Library, Harvard University, Cambridge/ MA. [cited as EHKM]
Heidelberg University Archives. UAH-IV–102/149, Bl. 49–60 (= Universitätsarchiv Heidelberg, Akten der Philosophischen Fakultät, 1919–1932). [cited as UAH]
Institut für Zeitungswesen an der Universität Heidelberg, Bericht über Lehrtätigkeit und Aufbau der Sammlungen im Sommersemester 1928, Generallandesarchiv Karlsruhe 235/3277. [cited as GLA]
July 25, 1938, letter from Karl Mannheim to Alfred Weber, Bundesarchiv, Koblenz, Germany. [cited as BK]
Interviews with Nina Rubinstein in New York City on October 31, 1987, and December 17, 1987. [cited as NRI]
Karl Mannheim Papers, University of Keele Library, Keele, Staffordshire. [cited as KMP]
Karl Mannheim's Personalakten, Johann-Wolfgang-Goethe-Universität, Frankfurt/Main. [cited as UF]
Max Horkheimer Archive, Frankfurt Municipal Library IX, 210. [cited as MHA]
Michael Polanyi Papers, Regenstein Library, University of Chicago. [cited as MP]
Louis Wirth Papers, Regenstein Library, University of Chicago. [cited as LWP]
Oscar Jászi Papers, Columbia University Library, Rare Books and Manuscript Library, New York City. [cited as CUL]
Read Bain, "Remarks on Mannheim's Ideology and Utopia." In LWP/ 67:2. [cited as RB]
Rockefeller Foundation Archive Center. [cited as RF]

Printed Sources

Adler, Max. 1922. *Staatsauffassung des Marxismus*. Vienna: Wiener Volksbuchhandlung (=Marx-Studien. Vol IV, 2nd Half).
Adler, Max. [1924] 1982. "Wissenschaft und soziale Struktur." in Meja/Stehr 1982, pp. 128–157.

Alemann, Heine von. 1981. "Leopold von Wiese und das Forschungsinstitut für Sozialwissenschaften in Köln 1919 bis 1934." In Wolf Lepenies, ed., *Geschichte der Soziologie*, vol. 2, pp. 349–389. Frankfurt/Main: Suhrkamp.
Alexander, Thomas/Parker, Beryl. 1930. *The New Education in the German Republic*. London: Williams & Norgate.
Antrick, Otto. 1966. *Die Akademie der Arbeit in der Universität Frankfurt/Main*. Darmstadt: Eduard Roether.
Aschheim, Steven E. 1992. *The Nietzschean Legacy in Germany, 1890–1990*. Berkeley: University of California Press.
Bambach, Charles R. 1995. *Heidegger, Dilthey and the Crisis of Historicism*. Ithaca: Cornell University Press.
Becker, Carl H. 1919a. *Gedanken zur Hochschulreform*. Leipzig: Quelle & Meyer.
Becker, Carl H. 1919b. *Kulturpolitische Aufgaben des Reiches*. Leipzig: Quelle & Meyer.
Becker, Carl H. 1925. *Vom Wesen der deutschen Universität*. Leipzig.
Becker, Carl H. 1930. *Die Pädagogische Akademie im Aufbau Unseres Nationalen Bildungswesens*. Leipzig: Quelle & Meyer.
Becker, Hellmut. 1976. "Portrait eines Kultusministers: Zum 100. Geburtstag von Carl Heinrich Becker (12. April 1976)," *Merkur*, 30: 365–376.
Becker, Howard/Barnes, Harry Elmer. 1938. *Social Thought from Lore to Science*. New York: D.C. Heath.
Below, Georg von. 1916. *Die deutsche Geschichtschreibung von den Befreiungskriegen bis zu unseren Tagen*. Leipzig: R. Oldenbourg.
Below, Georg von. 1919a. "Soziologie als Lehrfach; Ein kritischer Beitrag zur Hochschulreform," [*Schmollers*] *Jahrbuch für Gesetzgebung, Verwaltung und Volkswirtschaft im Deutschen Reich*, 43: 59–110.
Below, Georg von. 1919b. "Was ist 'Soziologie'? Eine Frage des Universitätsunterrichts," *Hochland*, 16: 550–555.
Below, Georg von. 1920–1921. "Soziologie und Hochschulreform; Eine Entgegnung," *Weltwirtschaftliches Archiv*, 16: 512–527.
Below, Georg von. 1926. "Zum Streit um des Wesen der Soziologie," *Jahrbücher für Nationalökonomie und Statistik*, 124: 218–242.
Below, Georg von. 1928. *Die Enstehung der Soziologie*. Jena.
Berlau, A. Joseph. 1949. *The German Social Democratic Party, 1914–1921*. New York: Columbia University Press.
Berlin, Isaiah. 1969. *Four Essays on Liberty*. London: Oxford University Press.
Bialas, Wolfgang. 1998. "Zwischen geschichtsphilosophischer Distanzierung und poltischer Nähe: Philosophische Diagnosen der Zeit um 1930." In Ehrlich/John 1998, pp. 47–72.
Bledstein, Burton J. 1976. *The Culture of Professionalism: The Middle Class and the Development of Higher Education in America*. New York: W.W. Norton.
Blomert, Reinhard. 1995. "Wandlungen im Wissenschaftsverständnis in der Weimarer Republik. Die Kultursoziologie von Alfred Weber und Karl Mannheim." In Hans G. Nutzinger, ed., *Zwischen Nationalökonomie und Universalgeschichte. Alfred Webers Entwurf einer umfassenden Sozialwissenschaft in heutiger Sicht*, pp. 161–195. Marburg: Metropolis.
Blomert, Reinhard. 1999. *Intellektuelle im Aufbruch: Karl Mannheim, Alfred Weber, Norbert Elias und die Heidelberger Sozialwissenschaften der Zwischenkriegszeit*. Munich: Hanser.
Böhme, Klaus. 1975, ed. *Aufrufe und Reden deutscher Professoren im Ersten Weltkrieg*. Stuttgart: Philipp Reclam.

Borinski, Fritz. 1984. "Hermann Heller: Lehrer der Jugend und Vorkämpfer der freien Erwachsenenbildung." In Müller/Staff 1984, pp. 89–110.
Botstein, Leon. 1991. *Judentum und Modernität: Essays zur Rolle der Juden in der deutschen und oesterreichischen Kultur, 1848 bis 1938.* Vienna & Köln: Böhlau.
Breuer, Stefan. 1995. "Das Syndicat der Seelen. Stefan George und sein Kreis." In Treiber/Sauerland 1995, pp. 328–375.
Brockhaus' Konversations-Lexicon [Der große Brockhaus]. 1928–1935. 20 vols. Leipzig: Brockhaus.
Bruch, Rüdiger vom. 1980. *Wissenschaft, Politik und öffentliche Meinung, Gelehrtenpolitik im Wilhelminischen Deutschland 1890–1914.* Husum: Matthiesen.
Bruch, Rüdiger vom. 1988. "Historiker und Nationalökonomen in wilhelminischen Deutschland." In Klaus Schwabe, ed., *Deutsche Hochschullehrer als Elite 1815–1945*, pp. 105–150. Boppard: Harald Boldt.
Bruch, Rüdiger vom/Graf, Friedrich Wilhelm/Hübinger, Gangolf. 1989, eds. *Kultur und Kulturwissenschaften um 1900.* Stuttgart: Franz Steiner.
Bruford, W.H. 1975. *The German Tradition of Self-Cultivation: "Bildung" from Humboldt to Thomas Mann.* Cambridge: Cambridge University Press.
Brunet, René. 1922. *The New German Constitution.* Trans. Joseph Gollomb. New York: Knopf.
Brunner, Otto/Conze, Werner/Koselleck, Rainer. 1972–84. *Geschichtliche Grundbegriffe.* 7 vols. Stuttgart: Klett-Cotta.
Buckmiller, Michael. 1980. "Praxis als soziale Pflicht. Korsch und die freistudentische Bewegung," In Karl Korsch, *Gesamtausgabe. Recht, Geist und Kultur*, pp. 13–47. Frankfurt/Main: Europäische Velagsanstalt.
Caldwell, Peter C. 1997. *Popular Sovereignty and the Crisis of German Constitutional Law; The Theory and Practice of Weimar Constitutionalism.* Durham: Duke University Press.
Cassirer, Ernst. 1951. *The Philosophy of the Enlightenment.* Trans. Fritz C. A. Koelln/James P. Pettegrove. Princeton: Princeton University Press.
Congdon, Lee. 1991. *Exile and Social Thought: Hungarian Intellectuals in Germany and Austria, 1919–1933.* Princeton: Princeton University Press.
Coser, Lewis A. 1965, ed. *Georg Simmel.* Englewood Cliffs/NJ: Prentice Hall.
Cumming, Robert Denoon. 1969. *Human Nature and History.* Chicago: University of Chicago Press.
Curtius, Ernst Robert. [1929] 1990. "Sociology—and its limits." In Meja/Stehr, 1990, pp. 113–120.
Curtius, Ernst Robert. 1932. *Deutscher Geist in Gefahr.* Stuttgart & Berlin: Deutsche Verlags-Anstalt.
Demm, Eberhard. 1990. *Ein Liberaler in Kaiserreich und Republik. Der politische Weg Alfred Webers bis 1920.* Boppard/Rhein: Harald Boldt.
Demm, Eberhard. 1999. *Von der Weimarer Republik zur Bundesrepublik. Der politische Weg Alfred Webers 1920–1958.* Düsseldorf: Droste.
Demm, Eberhard. 2000. *Geist und Politik. Gesammelte Aufsätze zu Alfred Weber.* Frankfurt/Main: Peter Lang.
Döring, Herbert. 1975. *Der Weimarer Kreis: Studien zum politischen Bewußtsein verfassungstreuer Hochschullehrer in der Weimarer Republik.* Meisenheim/Glan: Anton Hain.
Dunckmann, Karl. [1927] 1982. "Eine soziologische Begründung der Wissenschaft." In Meja/Stehr 1982, pp.192–212.

Düwell, Kurt. 1971. "Staat und Wissenschaft in der Weimarer Epoche; Zur Kulturpolitik des Ministers C.H. Becker." In Theodor Schieder, ed., *Beiträge zur Geschichte der Weimarer Republik*, pp. 31–74. Munich: R. Oldenbourg.
Dyzenhaus, David. 1997. *Truth's Revenge: Carl Schmitt, Hans Kelsen, and Hermann Heller in Weimar*. New York: Clarendon.
Elias, Norbert. 1994. *Reflections on a Life*. Trans. Edmund Jephcott. London: Polity.
Ehrlich, Luther/John, Jürgen. 1998, eds. *Weimar 1930. Politik und Kultur im Vorfeld der NS-Diktatur*. Vienna, Köln, & Weimar: Böhlau.
Endreß, Martin/Srubar, Ilya. 2000, eds. *Karl Mannheims Analyse der Moderne. Mannheims erste Frankfurter Vorlesung von 1930. Edition und Studien (Jahrbuch für Soziologiegeschichte 1996)*. Opladen: Leske und Budrich.
Fogarasi, Adalbert. 1930. "Die Soziologie der Intelligenz und die Intelligenz der Soziologie. Beiträge zur Theorie der Ideologie," *Unter dem Banner des Marxismus*, 4: 359–375.
Floud, Jean. 1966. "Karl Mannheim," *New Society*, 29 December: 96–98.
Foitzik, Jan. 1985. "Zwei Dokumente aus dem Untergrund," *Internationale Wissenschaftliche Korrespondenz zur Geschichte der deutschen Arbeiterbewegung*, 21, 2: 142–182.
Fraenkel, Ernst. [1930] 1968: *Zur Soziologie der Klassenjustiz*. Darmstadt: Wissenschaftliche Buchgesellschaft.
Frank, Josef Maria. 1932. *Fever Heat; A Drama of Divided Germany*. Trans. F.H. Lyon. London: Macmillan.
Freudenthal, Margarete. [1934] 1986. *Gestaltwandel der städtischen, bürgerlichen und proletarischen Hauswirtschaft*. Frankfurt/Main: Ullstein.
Freyer, Hans. 1920. "Das Problem der Utopie," *Deutsche Rundschau*, 183: 321–345.
Freyer, Hans. 1925. *Der Staat*. Leipzig: Fritz Rechfelden.
Freyer, Hans. 1926. "Soziologie als Geisteswissenschaft," *Archiv für Kulturgeschichte*, 16: 113–126.
Freyer, Hans. 1930a. "Ethische Normen und Politik," *Kantstudien*, 35: 99–114.
Freyer, Hans. 1930b. *Soziologie als Wirklichkeitswissenschaft: Logische Grundlegung des Systems der Soziologie*. Leipzig: B.G. Teubner.
Freyer, Hans. 1931a. *Einleitung in die Soziologie*. Leipzig.
Freyer, Hans. 1931b. *Revolution von Rechts*. Jena: Eugen Diederich.
Freyer, Hans. 1931c "Zur Bildungskrise der Gegenwart," *Die Erziehung*, 6: 597–626.
Freyer, Hans. 1932. "Die Universität als hohe Schule des Staates," *Die Erziehung*, 7: 520–537, 669–689.
Freyer, Hans. 1933. *Das politische Semester: Ein Vorschlag zur Universitätsreform*. Jena: Eugen Diederich.
Frisby, David. 1983. *The Alienated Mind: The Sociology of Knowledge in Germany, 1918–1933*. London: Heineman.
Frisby, David. 1988. *Fragments of Modernity*. Cambridge/MA: The MIT Press.
Frisby, David. 1990. "Introduction to the Translation." In Georg Simmel, *The Philosophy of Money*, Second Enlarged Edition, pp. 1–49. London: Routledge.
Fritzsche, Peter. 1996. "Did Weimar Fail?," *Journal of Modern History*, 68: 629–656.
Gábor, Éva. 1983. "Mannheim in Hungary and in Weimar Germany," *Newsletter of the International Society for the Sociology of Knowledge*, 9, 1/2: 7–14.
Gadamer, Hans-Georg. 1975. *Truth and Method*. New York: Crossroad.
Geiger, Theodor. 1930. "Panik im Mittelstand," *Die Arbeit*, 7: 637–653.
Gluck, Mary. 1985. *Georg Lukács and his Generation, 1900–1918*. Cambridge/MA: Harvard University Press.

Goldman, Harvey. 1992. *Politics, Death and the Devil*. Berkeley & Los Angeles: University of California Press.
Greffrath, Mathias. 1979. *Die Zerstörung einer Zukunft: Gespräche mit emigrierten Sozialwissenschaftlern*. Hamburg: Rowohlt.
Gunnell, John. 1993. *The Descent of Political Theory*. Chicago: University of Chicago Press.
Habermas, Jürgen.1989. *The Structural Transformation of the Public Sphere*. Trans. Thomas Burger. Cambridge/MA: MIT Press.
Haenisch, Konrad. 1918. "Sozialdemokratische Kulturpolitik," *Die Glocke*, 4: 335–352.
Haenisch, Konrad. 1919. "Aus dem neuen Kultusministerium: Ein offener Brief an Professor Saenger," *Die neue Rundschau*, 30: 17–27.
Hamilton, Richard F. 1982. *Who Voted for Hitler?* Princeton: Princeton University Press.
Hammerstein, Notker. 1989. *Die Johann Wolfgang Goethe-Universität Frankfurt am Main; Von der Stiftungsuniversität zur staatlichen Hochschule, 1914–1950*. Neuwied & Frankfurt/Main: Alfred Metzner.
Hammerstein, Notker. 1995. *Antisemitismus und deutsche Universitäten 1871–1933*. Frankfurt/Main: Campus.
Hansert, Andreas. 1992. *Bürgerkultur und Kulturpolitik in Frankfurt am Main*. Frankfurt/Main: Waldemar Kramer.
Haselbach, Dieter. 1990. "Franz Oppenheimer." In Steinert 1990, pp. 55–71.
Hegel, G.W.F. 1981. *Hegel's Phenomenology of Spirit*. Trans. A.V. Miller. Oxford: Oxford University Press.
Hegel, G.W.F. 1991. *Elements of the Philosophy of Right*. Trans. H.B. Nisbet. Cambridge: Cambridge University Press.
Hennis, Wilhelm. 1994. "Die volle Nüchternheit des Urteils. Max Weber zwischen Carl Menger und Gustav von Schmoller. Zum hochschulpolitischen Hintergrund des Wertfreiheitspostulat." In Gerhard Wagner/Heinz Zipprian, eds., *Max Webers Wissenschaftslehre*, pp. 105–145. Frankfurt/Main: Suhrkamp.
Herf, Jeffrey. 1986. *Reactionary Modernism: Technology, culture, and politics in Weimar and the Third Reich*. Cambridge: Cambridge University Press.
Heuss, Theodor. [1946] 1994. *Robert Bosch. His Life and Achievements*. New York: Henry Holt.
Hoeges, Dirk. 1994. *Kontroverse am Abgrund: Ernst Robert Curtius und Karl Mannheim. Intellektuelle und "freischwebende Intelligenz" in der Weimarer Republik*. Frankfurt/Main: Fischer.
Honigsheim, Paul. 1926. "Der Max-Weber-Kreis in Heidelberg," *Kölner Vierteljahrshefte für Soziologie*, 5: 270–287.
Honegger, Claudia. 1990. "Die ersten Soziologinnen in Frankfurt." In Steinert 1990, pp. 88–89.
Humboldt, Wilhelm von. 1956. *Schriften zur Anthropologie und Bildungslehre*. Ed. Andreas Flitner. Düsseldorf & Munich: Helmut Küpper.
Humboldt, Wilhelm von. 1967. "On the Historian's Task," *History and Theory*, 6: 57–71.
Humboldt, Wilhelm von. 1969. *The Limits of State Action*. Ed. J.W. Burrow. Cambridge: Cambridge University Press.
Husserl, Edmund. [1911] 1962. *Ideas: General Introduction to Pure Phenomenology*. Trans. W.R. Boyce Gibson. New York: Collier.
Iggers, Georg G. 1962. "The Image of Ranke in American and German Historical Thought," *History and Theory*, 2: 17–40.

Iggers, Georg G. 1968. *The German Conception of History*. Wesleyan/CT: Wesleyan University Press.
Jäckh, Ernst. 1931, ed. *Politik als Wissenschaft. Zehn Jahre Deutsche Hochschule für Politik*. Berlin: Hermann Reckendorf.
Jäckh, Ernst/Suhr, Otto. 1952. *Geschichte der Deutschen Hochschule für Politik*. Berlin: Gebrüder Weiss.
Jaspers, Karl. 1919. *Psychologie der Weltanschauungen*. Berlin: Springer.
Jay, Martin. 1970. "The Frankfurt School's Critique of Karl Mannheim and the Sociology of Knowledge," *Telos*, 20: 72–89.
Kant, Immanuel. [1803] 1964. "Über Pedagogik," In *Werke*, vol. XII, pp. 695–761. Frankfurt/Main: Suhrkamp.
Kant, Immanuel. 1992. *The Conflict of the Faculties*. Trans. Mary J. Gregor. Lincoln: University of Nebraska Press. Karádi, Éva/Vezér, Erzsébet. 1985, eds. *Georg Lukács, Karl Mannheim und der Sonntagskreis*. Frankfurt/Main: Sendler.
Kadarkay, Arpad. 1991. *Georg Lukács. Life, Thought, and Politics*. Oxford: Basil Blackwell.
Käsler, Dirk. 1983. "In Search of Respectability: The Controversy over the Destination of Sociology during the Conventions of the German Sociological Society, 1910–1930." In Robert A. Jones/Henrika Kuklick, eds., *Knowledge and Society: Studies in the Sociology of Culture*, vol. 4, pp. 227–272. Greenwich/CT: JAI Press.
Käsler, Dirk. 1984. *Die frühe deutsche Soziologie und ihre Entstehungs-Milieus 1909 bis 1934*. Opladen:Westdeutscher Verlag.
Kaufmann, Walter. 1965. *Hegel: A Reinterpretation*. Garden City/NY: Doubleday.
Kelsen, Hans. 1920. *Sozialismus und Staat. Eine Untersuchung der politische Theorie des Marxismus*. Leipzig: Hirschfeld.
Kettler, David. 1967. "Sociology of Knowledge and Moral Philosophy: The Place of Traditional Problems in the Formation of Mannheim's Thought," *Political Science Quarterly* 82, 3: 399–426.
Kettler, David. 1971. "Marxism and Culture. Lukács in the Hungarian Revolutions of 1918/19." *Telos*, 10: 35–92.
Kettler, David. 1977. "History and Theory in Ferguson's *Essay on the History of Civil Society*: A Reconsideration," *Political Theory*, 5: 437–460 Kettler, David. 1984. "Works Community and Worker' Organization: A Central Problem in Weimar Labour Law," *Economy and Society*, 13: 278–303.
Kettler, David. 2000. "'Can we master the global tensions or must we suffer shipwreck on our own history?'" In Endreß/Srubar 2000, pp. 293–309.
Kettler, David/Meja, Volker. 1993. "Their 'Own Peculiar Way': Karl Mannheim and the Rise of Women," *International Sociology*, 8: 5–55.
Kettler, David/Meja, Volker. 1994. "'That typically German kind of sociology which verges towards philosophy': The Dispute about *Ideology and Utopia* in the United States," *Sociological Theory*, 12: 279–303.
Kettler, David/Meja, Volker. 1995. *Karl Mannheim and the Crisis of Liberalism. The Secret of the New Times*. New Brunswick & London: Transaction.
Kettler, David/Meja, Volker/Stehr, Nico. 1982. "Introduction: Karl Mannheim's early writings on cultural sociology." In Mannheim 1982, pp. 11–29.
Kettler, David/Meja, Volker/Stehr, Nico. 1986. "The Design of Conservatism." In Mannheim 1986, pp. 1–26.
Killy, Walther/Vierhaus, Rudolf. 1998, eds. *Deutsche Biographische Enzyklopädie*. Munich.

Kirchheimer, Otto. [1932] 1967. "Legalität und Legitimität." In Otto Kirchheimer, *Politische Herrschaft*. Frankfurt/Main: Suhrkamp.
Kirchheimer, Otto. [1933] 1976. "Bemerkungen zu Carl Schmitts 'Legalität und Legitimität." In Wolfgang Luthardt, ed. *Von der Weimarer Republik zum Faschismus*. Frankfurt: Suhrkamp.
Klingemann, Carsten. 1985. "Soziologie im NS-Staat. Vom Unbehagen an der Soziologiegeschichtsschreibung." *Soziale Welt* 36, 3: 366–388 Klingemann, Carsten. 1986. "Soziologen vor dem Nationalsozialismus. Szenen aus der Selbstgleichschaltung der Deutschen Gesellschaft für Soziologie." In Josef Hülsdunker/Rolf Schellhase, eds., *Sozialgeschichte. Identität und Krisen einer 'engagierten' Disziplin*, pp. 59–84. Berlin: Duncker & Humblot.
Klingemann, Carsten. 1992. "Social-Scientific Experts — No Ideologues. Sociology and Social Research in the Third Reich." In Stephen P. Turner and Dirk Käsler, eds., *Sociology Responds to Fascism*, pp, 127–154. London: Routledge.
Kluke, Paul. 1972. *Die Stiftungsuniversität Frankfurt am Main 1914-1932*. Frankfurt/Main: Waldemar Kramer.
Kolk, Rainer. 1995. "Das schöne Leben. Stefan George und sein Kreis in Heidelberg." In Treiber/Sauerland 1995, pp. 310–327.
König, René. 1987. *Soziologie in Deutschland*. Munich: Carl Hanser.
Kracauer, Siegfried. 1995. *The Mass Ornament: Weimar Essays*. Trans. Thomas Y. Levin. Cambridge/MA: Harvard University Press.
Kramme, Rüdiger. 1995. "Philosophische Kultur als Programm. Die Konstituierungsphase des *Logos*." In Treiber/Sauerland 1995, pp. 119–149.
Krieger, Leonard. 1957. *The German Idea of Freedom*. Chicago: University of Chicago Press. [Langbehn, Julius]. 1922. *Rembrandt als Erzieher*. Leipzig: C.L. Hirschfeld.
Lassman, Peter/Velody, Irving/Martins, Herminio. 1989. *Max Weber's 'Science as a Vocation'*. London: Unwin Hyman.
Laube, Reinhard. 2000. "Mannheims 'Kategorie der Bürgerlichkeit:' Bürgerlichkeit und Antibürgerlichkeit im Spiegel der Suche nach der 'wirklichen Wirklichkeit.'" In Endreß/Srubar 2000, pp. 263–291..
Lederer, Emil. 1911. "Das ökonomische Element und die politische Idee im modernen Parteiwesen," *Zeitschrift für Politik*, 5: 535–557.
Lederer, Emil. 1923. "Aufgaben einer Kultursoziologie." In Melchior Palyi, ed., *Hauptprobleme der Soziologie. Erinnerungsgabe ffir Max Weber*, v. 2, pp. 149–17 1. Munich & Leipzig: Duncker & Humblot.
Lederer, Emil. 1931. "Die Klassenschichtung, ihr soziologischer Ort und ihre Wandlungen," *Archivftir Sozialwissenschaft und Sozialpolitik*, 65: 539ff.
Lepenies, Wolf. 1988. *Between Literature and Science: the Rise of Sociology*. Trans. R.J. Hollingdale. Cambridge: Cambridge University Press.
Lepsius, M. Rainer. 1987. "Sociology in the Interwar Period: Trends in Development and Criteria for Evaluation." In Meja/Misgeld/Stehr, *Modem German Sociology*, pp. 37–56. New York: Columbia University Press.
Lichtblau, Klaus. 1996. *Kulturkrise und Soziologie um die Jahrhundertwende: Zur Genealogie der Kultursoziologie in Deutschland*. Frankfurt/Main: Suhrkamp.
Liebersohn, Harry. 1982. "Leopold von Wiese and the ambivalence of functionalist sociology," *Archives europiennes de sociologie*, 23: 123–149.
Lieberman, Ben. 1994. "Testing Peukert's Paradigm: The 'Crisis of Classical Modernity' in the 'New Frankfurt,' 1925–1930," *German Studies Review*, 17: 287–303.
Lindenlaub, Dieter. 1967. *Richtungskdmpfe im VereinfUr Sozialpolitik*. Wiesbaden: Franz Steiner.

Loader, Colin. 1976. "German Historicism and Its Crisis," *Journal of Modem History,* 48, on-demand supplement: 85–119.
Loader, Colin. 1985. *The Intellectual Development of Karl Mannheim: Culture, Politics and Planning.* Cambridge: Cambridge University Press.
Loader, Colin. 1997. "Free Floating: The Intelligentsia in the Work of Alfred Weber and Karl Mannheim," *German Studies Review,* 20: 217–234
Loader, Colin. 2000. "Kann ein experimentelles Leben geplant werden? Mannheims zweite Übergangsperiode." In Endreß/Srubar 2000, pp. 171–196.
Lüwith, Karl. 1986. *Mein Leben in Deutschland vor und nach 1933: Ein Bericht.* Stuttgart: Metzler.
Lukács, Georg. [1911] 1971. *Soul and Form.* Trans. Anna Bostock. Cambridge/MA: The MIT Press.
Lukács, Georg. 1915. "Zum Wesen und zur Methode der Kultursoziologie," *Archiv für Sozialwissenschaft und Sozialpolitik,* 39: 216–222.
Lukács, Georg. [1920a] 1973. "The Old Culture and the New Culture." In Bart Grahl/Paul Piccone, eds., *Towards a New Marxism: Proceedings of the First International Telos Conference, October 8–11, 1970, Waterloo, Ontario,* pp. 21–30. St. Louis: Telos.
Lukács, Georg. 1920b. "On the Question of Organizing Intellectuals," *Kommunismus* (February 8, 1920).
Lukács, Georg. [1923] 1968. *History and Class Consciousness.* Cambridge/MA: The MIT Press.
Lukács, Georg. [1924] 1971. *Lenin: A study on the Unity of His Thought.* Cambridge/MA: The MIT Press.
Lukács, Georg. [1933] 1982. *Wie ist die faschistische Philosophie in Deutschland entstanden?* Budapest: Akadémia Kiadó.
Luthardt, Wolfgang. 1986. *Sozialdemokratische Verfassungstheorie in der Weimarer Republik.* Opladen: Westdeutscher Verlag.
Mann, Thomas. 1983. *Reflections of a Nonpolitical Man.* Trans. Walter D. Morris. New York: Frederick Ungar.
Mann, Thomas/Mann, Heinrich. 1969. *Briefwechsel, 1900–1949.* Oldenburg: S. Fischer.
Mannheim, Karl. [1918a] 1970. "Seele und Kultur." In Mannheim 1970, pp. 66–84.
Mannheim, Karl. [1918b] 1985. "Georg Simmel als Philosoph." In Karádi/Vezér 1985, pp. 150–153.
Mannheim, Karl. [1919a] 1985. "Die Grundprobleme der Kulturphilosophie." In Karádi/Vezér 1985, pp. 206–231.
Mannheim, Karl. [1919b] 1985. "Ernst Bloch, Geist der Utopie." In Karádi/Vezér pp. 254–259.
Mannheim, Karl. [1919b] 1985. "Ernst Bloch, Geist der Utopie." In Karádi/Vezér, pp. 254–259.
Mannheim, Karl. [1920] 1993. "A Review of Georg Lukács' Theory of the Novel." In Mannheim 1993, pp. 131–135.
Mannheim, Karl. [1921–1922] 2001. "Heidelberg Letters: Soul and Culture in Germany." In Mannheim 2001, pp. 79–97.
Mannheim, Karl. [1921] 1993. "On the Interpretation of Weltanschauung," In Mannheim 1993, pp. 136–187.
Mannheim, Karl. [1922] 2001. "Science and Youth." In Mannheim 2001, pp. 99–104.
Mannheim, Karl. [1922a] 1953. "Structural Analysis of Epistemology." In Mannheim 1953, pp.15–73.
Mannheim, Karl. [1922b] 1970. "Zum Problem einer Klassifikation der Wissenschaften." In Mannheim 1970, pp. 155–165.

Mannheim, Karl. [1922–24] 1982. *Structures of Thinking*. Ed. David Kettler/Volker Meja/Nico Stehr. Trans. Jeremy J. Shapiro/Shierry Weber Nicholson. London: Routledge & Kegan Paul.
Mannheim, Karl. [1924] 1952. "Historicism," in Mannheim 1952, pp. 33–83.
Mannheim, Karl. [1925a] 1952. "The Problem of a Sociology of Knowledge." In Mannheim 1952, pp. 134–190.
Mannheim, Karl. [1925b] 1986. *Conservatism. A Contribution to the Sociology of Knowledge*. Ed. David Kettler/Volker Meja/Nico Stehr. Trans. David Kettler/Volker Meja. London & New York: Routledge & Kegan Paul.
Mannheim, Karl. [1926] 1993. "The Ideological and the Sociological Interpretation of Intellectual Phenomena." In Mannheim 1993, pp. 244–259.
Mannheim, Karl. [1927] 1953. "Conservative Thought." In Mannheim 1953, pp. 74–164.
Mannheim, Karl. 1928. "Der Sechste deutsche Soziologentag in Zürich." *Frankfurter Zeitung* (October 5): 1–2.
Mannheim, Karl. [1928] 1952. "The Problem of Generations." In Mannheim 1952, pp. 276–322.
Mannheim, Karl. 1929a. "Die Bedeutung der Konkurrenz im Gebiete des Geistigen." In *Verhandlungen des sechsten deutschen Soziologentages vom 17. bis 19. September 1928 in Zürich*, pp. 35–83. Tübingen: J.C.B. Mohr (Paul Siebeck).
Mannheim, Karl. 1929b. *Ideologie und Utopie*. Bonn: Cohen.
Mannheim, Karl. [1929a] 1993. "Competition as a Cultural Phenomenon." In Mannheim 1993, pp. 399–437. [Trans. Of 1929a]
Mannheim, Karl. [1929b] 1993. "Problems of Sociology in Germany." In Mannheim 1993, pp. 438–446.
Mannheim, Karl. [1929c] 2001. "The Intellectualism Dispute: Protocols of the Joint Meetings of the Seminars of Professor Alfred Weber and Dr. Karl Mannheim. Heidelberg, February 21 and 27, 1929. In Mannheim 2001, pp. 109–129.
Mannheim, Karl. [1929d] 2001. "On the Incorporation of Research in the Journalistic Medium (Zeitungswesen) into University Science." In Mannheim 2001, pp. 105–108.
Mannheim, Karl. [1930a] 2001. "An Introduction to Sociology." In Mannheim 2001, pp. 1–78.
Mannheim, Karl. [1930b] 1952. "On the Nature of Economic Ambition and Its Significance for the Social Education of Man." In Mannheim 1952, pp. 230–275.
Mannheim, Karl. [1931a] 1969. "Wissensoziologie," In Mannheim 1969, pp. 227–267.
Mannheim, Karl. [1931b] 1936. "The Sociology of Knowledge." In Mannheim 1936, pp. 237–280. [Trans. of 1931a]
Mannheim, Karl [1931c] 2001. "On the Historical Character of Concepts: Letter of Karl Mannheim to Max Wertheimer." In Mannheim 2001, pp. 141–144.
Mannheim, Karl. [1931d] 2001. On Religious Experience and Rationalization: Interventions in the 'Frankfurt Discussions' with Paul Tillich, Max Horkheimer, Theodor Wiesengrund [Adorno] and others. June, 1931." In Mannheim 2001, pp. 133–139. [Trans. Of sections of Tillich [1931] 1983]
Mannheim, Karl. [1931–1932] 2001. "Lectures on Method." In Mannheim 2001, pp. 158–168.
Mannheim, Karl. 1932a. *Die Gegenwartsaufgaben der Soziologie*. Tübingen: J.C.B. Mohr (Paul Siebeck).

Mannheim, Karl. [1932a] 2001. "The Contemporary Tasks of Sociology: Cultivation and the Curriculum." In Mannheim 2001, pp. 145–158. [Trans. of sections of Mannheim 1932a]
Mannheim, Karl. [1932b] 2001. "The Spiritual Crisis in the Light of Sociology." In Mannheim 2001, pp. 169–173.
Mannheim, Karl. [1932]. 1993. "The Sociology of Intellectuals," in *Theory, Culture & Society* 10: 69–80.
Mannheim, Karl. [1933] 1956. "The Democratization of Culture," In Mannheim 1956, pp. 171–246.
Mannheim, Karl. [1934] 1953. "German Sociology (1918–1933)." In Mannheim 1953, pp. 209–228.
Mannheim, Karl. 1935. *Mensch und Gesellschaft im Zeitalter des Umbaus*. Leiden: Sijthoff.
Mannheim, Karl. [1935] 2001. "In Defense of Functional Reason: Correspondence between Eduard Heimann and Karl Mannheim about Mannheim's *Mensch und Gesellschaft im Zeitalter des Umbaus*." In Mannheim 2001, pp. 175–194.
Mannheim, Karl. 1936. *Ideology and Utopia*. London: Routledge & Kegan Paul.
Mannheim, Karl. [1938] 2001. Letter to Alfred Weber (July 25, 1938). In Mannheim 2001, pp. 130–131.
Mannheim, Karl. 1940. *Man and Society in an Age of Reconstruction*. London: Routledge & Kegan Paul .
Mannheim, Karl. 1946. "Die Rolle der Universitäten." In *Neue Auslese: Aus den Schriften der Gegenwart*, ed., The Allied Information Service, I, 4: 49–53.
Mannheim, Karl. 1952. *Essays in the Sociology of Knowledge*. Ed. Paul Kecskemeti. London: Routledge & Kegan Paul.
Mannheim, Karl. 1953. *Essays on Sociology and Social Psychology*. Ed. and trans. Paul Kecskemeti. London: Routledge & Kegan Paul.
Mannheim, Karl. 1956. *Essays on the Sociology of Culture*. Ed. and trans. Ernest Manheim/Paul Kecskemeti. London: Routledge & Kegan Paul.
Mannheim, Karl/Stewart, W.A.C. 1962. *An Introduction to the Sociology of Education*. London: Routledge & Kegan Paul.
Mannheim, Karl. 1969. *Ideologie und Utopie*, 5th ed. Frankfurt/Main: Schulte-Bulmke.
Mannheim, Karl. 1970. *Wissenssoziologie*. Ed. Kurt H. Wolff. Neuwied: Luchterhand.
Mannheim, Karl. 1971. "Karl Mannheim's Letters to Lukács, 1910–1916," *The New Hungarian Quarterly*, XVI, 57: 93–105.
Mannheim, Karl. 1993. *From Karl Mannheim*. Ed. Kurt H. Wolff. New Brunswick & London: Transaction.
Mannheim, Karl. 1996. *Mannheim Károly levelezése 1911–1946*. Ed. Éva Gábor. Budapest: Argumentum Kiadó, Lukács Archívum.
Mannheim, Karl. 2001. *Sociology as Political Education*. Ed. David Kettler/Colin Loader. Trans. David Kettler/Colin Loader. New Brunswick: Transaction.
Manuel, Frank. 1956. *The New World of Henri Saint-Simon*. Cambridge/MA: Harvard University Press.
Matthiesen, Ulf. 1988. "'Im Schatten einer endlosen großen Zeit.' Etappen der intellektuellen Biographie Albert Salomons," In Ilja Srubar, ed, *Exil. Wissenschaft. Identität. Die Emigration deutscher Wissenschaftler, 1933–1945*, pp. 299–350. Frankfurt/Main: Suhrkamp
Matthiesen, Ulf. 1990. "Kontrastierungen/Kooperationen: Karl Mannheim in Frankfurt (1930–1933)." In Steinert 1990, pp. 72–87.
McClelland, Charles E. 1980. *State, Society, and University in Germany 1700–1914*. Cambridge: Cambridge University Press.

McCormick, John. 1997. *Against Politics as Technology: Carl Schmitt's Critique of Liberalism*. New York & Cambridge: Cambridge University Press.
McCormick, John. 2001. "From Constitutional Technique to Caesarist Ploy: Carl Schmitt's Theory of Dictatorship." In Peter Baehr, ed. *From Bonapartism to National Socialism: Essays in the Theory of Dictatorship*. Cambridge: Cambridge University Press.
Meinecke, Friedrich. [1907] 1970. *Cosmopolitanism and the Nation State*. Trans. Robert B. Kimber. Princeton: Princeton University Press.
Meinecke, Friedrich. 1922. "Drei Generationen deutscher Gelehrtenpolitik," *Historische Zeitschrift*, 125: 248–283.
Meinecke, Friedrich. [1936] 1965. *Die Entstehung des Historismus*. Munich: Oldenbourg.
Meja, Volker/Stehr, Nico. 1982, eds. *Der Streit um die Wissenssoziologie*, 2 vols. Frankfurt/Main: Suhrkamp.
Meja, Volker/Stehr, Nico. 1990, eds. *Knowledge and Politics. The Sociology of Knowledge Dispute*. London & New York: Routledge.
Milchman, Alan/Rosenberg, Alan. 1993. "Resoluteness and Ambiguity: Martin Heidegger's Ontological Politics, 1933-1935," *Philosophical Forum*, 25: 72–93.
Milchman, Alan/Rosenberg, Alan. 1997. "Martin Heidegger and the University as a Site for the Transformation of Human Existence," *Review of Politics*, 59: 75–95.
Mill, John Stuart. [1859] 1977. "On Liberty." *Essays on Politics and Society*. Toronto: University of Toronto Press.
Mill, John Stuart. 1963. "The Spirit of the Age." In *Essays on Politics and Culture*, ed. Gertrude Himmelfarb, pp. 1–44. Garden City/NY: Anchor.
Miller, Susanne. 1978. *Die Bürde der Macht*. Düsseldorf: Droste.
Mills, C. Wright. 1940. "Methological Consequences of the Sociology of Knowledge," *American Journal of Sociology*, 46: 316–330.
Mills, C. Wright. 1959. The Sociological Imagination. Oxford: Oxford University Press.
Mills, C. Wright. 1963. *Power, Politics and People: The Collected Essays of C. Wright Mills*. Ed. Irving Louis Horowitz. New York: Ballantine.
Mommsen, Hans. 1989. *The Rise and Fall of Weimar Democracy*. Chapel Hill: University of North Carolina Press.
Mosse, George L. 1964. *The Crisis of German Ideology*. New York: Grosset & Dunlap.
Müller, Christoph/Staff, Ilse. 1984, eds. *Der Soziale Rechtsstaat*. Baden-Baden: Nomos.
Muller, Jerry Z. 1987. *The Other God that Failed: Hans Freyer and the Deradicalization of German Conservatism*. Princeton: Princeton University Press.
Muller, Jerry Z. 1991. "Carl Schmitt, Hans Freyer and the Radical Conservative Critique of Liberal Democracy in the Weimar Republic," *History of Political Thought*, 12: 695–715.
Nettl, Peter. 1970. "Ideas, Intellectuals and Structures of Dissent." In Philip Rief, ed., *On Intellectuals*, pp. 57–134. Garden City/NY: Anchor.
Neumann, Franz L. 1932. *Koalitionsfreiheit und Reichsverfassung. Die Stellung der Gewerkschaften im Verfassungssystem*. Berlin: Heymanns.
Neumann, Franz. 1944. *Behemoth: The Structure and Practice of National Socialism, 1933-1944*. New York: Oxford University Press.
Oelkers, Jürgen. 1998. "Deutsche Klassik in deutscher Reformpädagogik. Übergänge um 1930." In Ehrlich/John 1998, pp. 73–97.

Oexle, Otto Gerhard. 1988. "Eine politischer Historiker: Georg von Below." In Notker Hammerstein, ed., *Deutsche Geschichtswissenschaft um 1900*, pp. 283-312. Stuttgart: Franz Steiner.
Pauck, Wilhelm/Pauck, Marion. 1976. *Paul Tillich: His Life and Thought*, vol. 1. New York: Harper & Row.
Paulsen, Friedrich. 1899. "Ueber Parteien und Parteipolitik," *Preussische Jahrbücher*, 95: 393–411.
Pels, Dick. 1993. "Missionary Sociology between Left and Right. A Critical Intoduction to Mannheim," *Theory, Culture & Society*, 10: 45–68.
Peukert, Detlev J. K. 1993. *The Weimar Republic; The Crisis of Classical Modernity*. New York: Hill & Wang.
Raith, Dirk. 1999. "Lebenserfahrung und historische Distanz. Nina Rubinstein (1908–1996) und ihr Beitrag zur Soziologie der politischen Emigration,"*Archiv für die Geschichte der Soziologie in Österreich. Newsletter Nr. 19*: 32–41.
Ratz, Ursula. 1980. *Sozialreform und Arbeiterschaft*. Berlin: Colloquium Verlag.
Reill, Peter Hanns. 1994. "Science and the Construction of the Cultural Sciences in Late Enlightenment Germany: The Case of Wilhelm von Humboldt," *History and Theory*, 33: 345–366.
Riedel, Manfred. 1963. "Der Staatsbegriff der deutschen Geschichtsschreibung des 19. Jahrhunderts in seiner Verhältnis zur klassisch-politischen Philosophie," *Der Staat*, 2: 41–63.
Ringer, Fritz K. 1969. *The Decline of the German Mandarins; the German Academic Community, 1890–1933*. Cambridge/MA: Harvard University Press.
Rosen, Stanley. 1974. *G.W.F. Hegel. An Introduction to the Science of Wisdom*. New Haven & London: Yale University Press.
Rosenberg, Arthur. 1965. *A History of the Weimar Republic*. New York: Russell & Russell.
Rosenberg, Hans. 1966. *Bureaucracy, Aristocracy and Autocracy: The Prussian Experience 1660–1815*. Boston: Beacon.
Rubinstein, Nina [1930] 1999. "Die französische Emigration, insbesondere die Transformation ihrer Ideologie (1930). Mit Anmerkungen von Karl Mannheim," *Archiv für die Geschichte der Soziologie in Österreich. Newsletter Nr. 19*: 42–47.
Rubinstein, Nina [1933] 2000. *Die französische Emigration nach 1789. Ein Beitrag zur Soziologie der politischen Emigration*. Graz: Nausner & Nausner.
Russell, James E. 1899. *German Higher Schools: The History, Organization and Methods of Secondary Education in Germany*. London: Longmans, Green.
Ryder, A.J. 1967. *The German Revolution of 1918*. Cambridge: Cambridge University Press.
Sallis-Freudenthal, Margarete. 1977. *Ich habe mein Land gefunden*. Frankfurt/Main: Knecht.
Salomon, Albert. 1926a. "Max Weber," *Die Gesellschaft*, 1: 130–153.
Salomon, Albert. 1926b. "Zur Soziologie des Geniebegriffs," *Die Gesellschaft*, 1: 504ff.
Salomon, Albert. 1926c. "[Review of] Karl Jaspers, *Max Weber. Eine Gedenkrede* and Marianne Weber, *Max Weber. Ein Lebensbild*," *Die Gesellschaft*, 1.
Salomon, Albert. 1928. "[Review of] Alfred Weber, *Ideen zur Staats—und Kultursoziologie* 1927." Typescript in Salomon Collection, Leo Baeck Institute, New York.
Salomon, Albert. 1930. "[Review of] Friedrich Glum, *Das geheime Deutschland. Die Aristokratie der demokratischen Gesinnung*," *Die Gesellschaft*, 5: 571–574.
Salomon, Albert. 1931. "Innenpolitische Bildung." In Jäckh 1931, pp. 94–110.

Salomon, Albert. 1934. "Max Weber's Methodology," *Social Research*, 1: 147–168.
Salomon, Albert. 1935a. "Max Weber's Sociology," *Social Research*, 2: 60–73.
Salomon, Albert. 1935b. "Max Weber's Political Ideas." *Social Research*, 2: 368–383.
Salomon, Albert. 1936. "[Review of] Karl Mannheim, Mensch und Gesellschaft im Zeitalter des Umbaus," *Social Research* 3: 113–117.
Salomon, Albert. 1947. "Karl Mannheim. 1893–1947," *Social Research* 14: 350–364.
Sárközi, Mátyás. 1986. "The Influence of Georg Lukács on the Young Karl Mannheim in the Light of a Newly Discovered Diary." *Slavic and Eastern European Review*, 64: 436–7.
Scaff, Lawrence A. 1990. "Modernity and the tasks of a sociology of culture," *History of the Human Sciences*, 3: 85–100.
Scheler, Max. 1924, ed. *Versuche zu einer Soziologie des Wissens*. Munich: Duncker & Humblot.
Scheler, Max. 1961. *On the Eternal in Man*. Trans. Bernard Noble. New York: Harper & Row.
Scheuerman, William E. 1997. *Between the Norm and the Exception*. Cambridge/MA: The MIT Press.
Schivelbusch, Wolfgang. 1982. *Intellektuellendämmerung. Zur Lage der Frankfurter Intelligenz in den zwanziger Jahren*. Frankfurt/Main: Insel.
Schluchter, Wolfgang. 1980. *Rationalismus der Weltbeherrschung*. Frankfurt/Main: Suhrkamp.
Schmitt, Carl. [1922] 1985. *Political Theology: Four Chapters on the Concept of Sovereignty*. Trans. George Schwab. Cambridge/MA: The MIT Press.
Schmitt, Carl. 1924. "Die Diktatur des Reichspräsident nach Art. 48 der Reichsverfassung," In *Veröffentlichungen der Vereinigung der deutschen Staatsrechtslehrer*,v. i, pp. 63–104. Berlin: Walter de Gruyter.
Schmitt, Carl. 1926. *Die geistesgeschichtliche Lage des heutigen Parlamentarismus*, 2nd ed. Munich & Leipzig: Duncker & Humblot.
Schmitt, Carl. [1928] 1976. *The Concept of the Political*. Trans. George Schwab. New Brunswick/NJ: Rutgers University Press.
Schmitt, Carl. 1928. *Verfassungslehre*. Munich & Leipzig: Duncker & Humblot.
Schmitt, Carl. 1930. "Staatsethik und pluralischer Staat," *Kantstudien*, 35: 28–42.
Schmitt, Carl. 1931. *Der Hüter der Verfassung*. Tübingen: J.C.B. Mohr (Paul Siebeck).
Schmitt, Carl. 1932. *Legalität und Legitimität*. Munich: Duncker & Humblot.
Schmitt, Carl. 1933. "Die deutschen Intellektuellen," *Westdeutscher Beobachter: Amtliches Organ der NSDAP*, 9, 126 (May 31): 1–2.
Schmitt, Carl. 1950. *Ex captivitate salus. Erfahrungen der Zeit 1945/47*. Cologne: Greven.
Schmitt, Carl. 1988. *The Crisis of Parliamentary Democracy*. Trans. Ellen Kennedy. Cambridge/MA: The MIT Press. [Trans. of Schmitt, 1926]
Schmoller, Gustav. 1913. "Fürst Bülow und die preußisch-deutsche Politik im Frühjahr 1907." In Schmoller, *Characterbilder*, pp. 95–111. Munich & Leipzig.
Scholtz, Gunter. 1991. *Zwischen Wissenschaftsanspruch und Orientierungsbedürfnis: Zu Grundlage und Wandel der Geisteswissenschaften*. Frankfurt/Main: Suhrkamp.
Schorske, Carl. 1955. *German Social Democracy. 1905–1917*. Cambridge/MA: Harvard University Press.
Schwabe, Klaus. 1969. *Wissenschaft und Kriegsmoral: Die deutschen Hochschullehrer und die politischen Grundfragen des Ersten Weltkrieges*. Göttingen: Musterschmidt.
Shils, Edward A. 1941. "Irrationality and Planning: A note on Mannheim's *Man and Society in an Age of Transformation*," *Journal of Liberal Religion*, 2: 148–153.

Shils, Edward A. 1947. "In Memorium: Karl Mannheim 1893–1947," *Erasmus*, 1, 4 (Feb. 15): 195–196.
Shils, Edward A. 1968. "Karl Mannheim." In *International Encyclopedia of the Social Sciences*, v. 9, pp. 557–562. New York: The Free Press.
Shils, Edward. 1973. "*Ideology and Utopia* by Karl Mannheim." Twentieth Century Classics Revisited. *Daedalus*, 103, 1: 83–89.
Shils, Edward. 1980. *The Calling of Sociology*. Chicago: University of Chicago Press.
Shklar, Judith. 1976. *Freedom & Independence. A Study of the Political Ideas of Hegel's 'Phenomenology of Mind'*. Cambridge: Cambridge University Press.
Simon, Christian. 1988. *Staat und Geschichtswissenschaft in Deutschland und Frankreich, 1871–1914*. 2 vols. Bern: Peter Lang.
Sinzheimer, Hugo. 1938. *Jüdische Klassiker der deutschen Rechtswissenschaft*. Amsterdam: Hertzberger.
Smend, Rudolf. 1928. *Verfassung und Verfassungsrecht*. Munich & Leipzig: Duncker & Humblot.
Sorkin, David. 1983. "Wilhelm von Humboldt: The Theory and Practice of Self-Formation (*Bildung*), 1791–1810," *Journal of the History of Ideas*, 44: 55–73.
Speier, Hans. 1989. "Karl Mannheim as Sociologist of Knowledge." In *The Truth in Hell and Other Essays on Politics and Culture, 1935–1987*, pp. 35–49. Oxford: Oxford University Press.
Spranger, Eduard. [1910] 1960. *Wilhelm von Humboldt und die Reform des Bildungswesens*. Tübingen: Max Niemeyer.
Spranger, Eduard. 1923. "Die drei Motive der Schulreform." In Spranger, *Kultur und Erziehung*, pp. 115–137. Leipzig: Quelle & Meyer.
Spranger, Eduard. 1925. "Die Soziologie in der Erinnerungsgabe für Max Weber," *Schmollers Jahrbuch*, 49: 1379–1395.
Spranger, Eduard. 1928. *Das deutsche Bildungsideal der Gegenwart in geschichtsphilosophischer Beleuchtung*. Leipzig: Quelle & Meyer.
Spranger, Eduard. [1930] 1990. "Ideology and Science." In Meja/Stehr 1990, pp. 239–240.
Spranger, Eduard. 1932. "Gegenwart (September 1932)." In *Volk, Staat, Erziehung: Gesammelte Reden und Aufsätze*, pp. 176–211. Leipzig: Quelle & Meyer.
Steinberg, Michael Stephen. 1977. *Saber and Brownshirts: The German Students' Path to National Socialism, 1918–1935*. Chicago: University of Chicago Press.
Steinert, Heinz. 1990, ed. *Die (mindestens) zwei Sozialwissenschaften in Frankfurt und ihre Geschichte*. Frankfurt/Main: Studientexte zur Sozialwissenschaft 3, Johann-Wolfgang-Goethe Universität.
Stern, Fritz. 1960. "The Political Consequences of the Unpolitical German." In *History 3*, pp. 104–134. New York: Meridian.
Stölting, Erhard. 1986. *Akademische Soziologie in der Weimarer Republik*. Berlin: Duncker & Humblot.
Stoltenberg, Hans Lorenz. 1926. *Soziologie als Lehrfach an deutschen Hochschulen*. Karlsruhe: G. Braun.
Tenbruck, Friedrich. 1959. "Formal Sociology." In Wolff 1959, pp. 61–99.
Tillich, Paul. [1931] 1983. "Das Frankfurter Gespräch." In Tillich, *Briefwechsel und Streitschriften*, pp. 314–369. Frankfurt/Main: Evangelisches Verlagswerk.
Tompert, Helene. 1969. *Lebensformen und Denkweisen der akademischen Welt Heidelbergs im Wilhelminischen Zeitalter, vornehmlich im Spiegel zeitgenössischer Selbstzeugnisse*. Lübeck & Hamburg: Matthiesen.
Treiber, Hubert/ Sauerland, Karol. 1995, eds. *Heidelberg im Schnittpunkt intellektueller Kreise*. Opladen: Westdeutscher Verlag.

Bibliography 223

Troeltsch, Ernst. 1922. *Der Historismus und seine Probleme*, vol. I: *Das logische Problem der Geschichtsphilosophie*. Tübingen: J.C.B. Mohr (Paul Siebeck).
Vondung, Klaus. 1976. "Zur Lage der Gebildeten in der wilhelmischen Zeit." In Vondung, ed., *Das wilheminische Bildungsbürgertum: Zur Sozialgeschichte seiner Ideen*, pp. 20–33. Göttingen: Vandenhoeck & Ruprecht.
Wagner, Peter. 1990. *Sozialwissenschaften und Staat: Frankreich, Italien, Deutschland 1870–1980*. Frankfurt/Main: Campus.
Weber, Alfred. 1918. "Die Bedeutung der geistigen Führer in Deutschland," *Die neue Rundschau*, 29: 1249–1268.
Weber, Alfred. 1920. "Prinzipelles zur Kultursoziologie (Gesellschaftsprozeß, Zivilisationsprozeß und Kulturbewegung)," *Archiv für Sozialwissenschaft und Sozialpolitik*, 47: 1–49.
Weber, Alfred. 1925. *Die Krise des modernen Staatsgedankens in Europa*. Stuttgart, Berlin & Leipzig: Deutsche Verlags-Anstalt.
Weber, Alfred. 1931. *Das Ende der Demokratie? Ein Vortrag*. Berlin: Junker & Dünnhaupt.
Weber, Marianne. 1977. "Academic Conviviality," *Minerva*, 15: 214–246
Weber, Max. 1922. *Gesammelte Aufsätze zur Religionssoziologie*. Tübingen: J.C.B. Mohr (Paul Siebeck).
Weber, Max. 1946. *From Max Weber: Essays in Sociology*. Ed. and trans. H.H. Gerth/ C. Wright Mills. New York: Oxford University Press.
Weber, Max. 1949. *The Methodology of the Social Sciences*. Glencoe/IL: The Free Press.
Weber, Max. 1958. *The Protestant Ethic and the Spirit of Capitalism*. Trans. Talcott Parsons. New York: Scribner.
Weber, Max. 1973. "The Power of the State and the Dignity of the Academic Calling in Imperial Germany: The Writings of Max Weber on University Problems." Ed. E.S. Shils. *Minerva*, 11, 4: 1–62.
Weil, Hans. [1930] 1967. *Die Entstehung des deutschen Bildungsprinzips*, 2nd ed. Bonn: H. Bouvier.
Wende, Erich. 1959. *C. H. Becker: Mensch und Politiker*. Stuttgart: Deutsche Verlags-Anstalt.
Wiese, Leopold von. 1920. "Die Soziologie als Einzelwissenschaft," *Schmollers Jahrbuch*, 44: 31–51.
Wiese, Leopold von. 1921. "Zur Methodologie der Beziehungslehre," *Kölner Vierteljahrshefte für Sozialwissenschaften*, 1: 47–55.
Wiese, Leopold von. 1924. *Allgemeine Soziologie als Lehre von der Beziehungen und den Beziehungsgebilden der Menschen, Teil I: Beziehungslehre*. Munich & Leipzig: Duncker & Humblot.
Wiese, Leopold von. 1928. *Allgemeine Soziologie, Teil II: Gebildelehre*. Munich & Leipzig: Duncker & Humblot.
Wiese, Leopold von. 1929a. "Vorbemerkungen." In *Verhandlungen des Sechsten deutschen Soziologentages vom 17. bis 19. September 1928 in Zürich*, pp. vii–ix. Tübingen: J.C.B. Mohr (Paul Siebeck).
Wiese, Leopold von. 1929b. "Die Konkurrenz, vorwiegend in soziologisch-systematischer Betrachtung." In *Verhandlungen des Sechsten Deutschen Soziologentages vom 17. bis 19. September 1928 in Zürich*, pp. 15–35. Tübingen: J.C.B. Mohr (Paul Siebeck).
Wiese, Leopold von. 1931. *Soziologie. Geschichte und Hauptprobleme*. Berlin: G.J. Göschen.

Wiese, Leopold von. 1931/32. "Die Frankfurter Dozententagung," *Kölner Vierteljahrhefte für Soziologie*, 10: 439–449.
Wiese, Leopold von. 1933. *System der allgemeinen Soziologie als Lehre von den sozialen Prozessen und den sozialen Gebilden der Menschen (Beziehungslehre)*, 2nd ed. Munich & Leipzig: Duncker & Humblot.
Wiese, Leopold von. 1936. "Der gegenwärtige Entwicklungszustand der allgemeinen Soziologie," in Ernst Jurkat, ed., *Reine und Angewandte Soziologie. Eine Festgabe für Ferdinand Tönnies zu seinem achzigsten Geburtstage am 26. Juli 1935*. Leipzig: Hans Buske.
Will, Wilfried van der/Burns, Rob. 1982, eds. *Arbeiterkulturbewegung in der Weimarer Republik*. Frankfurt/Main: Ullstein.
Winnig, August. 1930. *Das Reich als Republik*. Stuttgart & Berlin: Cotta.
Winnig, August. 1935. *Heimkehr*. Hamburg: Hanseatische Verlag.
Witt, Peter-Christian. 1985. "The Prussian Landrat as Tax Official, 1891–1918; Observations on the Political and Social Function of the German Civil Service." In Georg G. Iggers, ed., *The Social History of Politics: Critical Perspectives in West German Historical Writing since 1945*, pp. 137–154. Leamington Spa: Berg.
Woldring, Henk E.S. 1986. *Karl Mannheim: The Development of His Thought*. Assen & Maastricht: Van Gorcum.
Wolff, Kurt H. 1959, ed. *Georg Simmel, 1858–1918*. Columbus: The Ohio State University Press.
Wolin, Richard. 1992. "Carl Schmitt: The Conservative Revolutionary Habitus and the Aesthetics of Horror," *Political Theory*, 20: 424–447.
Zinn, Alexander. 1992. "Gehaßt oder Instrumentalisiert? Soziologie im Dritten Reich aus der Perspektive des Reichsministeriums für Wissenschaft," *Zeitschrift für Soziologie*, 21: 347–365.
Zneimer, Richard. 1978. "The Nazis and the Professors: Social Origin, Professional Mobility, and Political Involvement of the Frankfurt University Faculty, 1933–1939," *Journal of Social History*, 12: 147–158.

Index

Academic freedom (*Lehrfreiheit*), 2, 16, 35, 37
Academy of Labor, Frankfurt, 65, 67, 181
Adenauer, Konrad, 81
Adler, Max, 87, 104, 110, 154–157, 160, 170, 174, 182
Adorno, Theodor Wiesengrund, 6, 55, 163–165, 167, 170, 176
Alemann, Heine von, 82–84
Alembert, Jean d', 28
Alexander, Thomas, 67
Alliance of German Craftsmen, 102
Althoff, Friedrich, 35
Antrick, Otto, 65, 67
"Appeal to the World of Culture," 65
Aristophanes, 94
Aschheim, Steven, 43
Association for Social Policy, 44, 82
Attitude, sociological, 15, 161, 182, 189–191, 193, 195, 196, 198, 199

Bacon, Francis, 28, 192, 205, 206
Balázs, Bela, 198
Bambach, Charles, 48, 116
Barnes, Harry Elmer, 206
Bauhaus, 92
Baumgarten, Eduard, 174
Becker, Carl Heinrich, 14, 15, 18, 41, 52–58, 61, 64, 66, 67, 73, 80, 83, 99, 110, 114, 135, 157, 178, 179, 182, 192, 193, 199, 200
Becker, Hellmut, 52, 66
Becker, Howard, 206
Beckmann, Max, 179
Below, Georg von, 15, 55–59, 67, 68, 83, 124, 190, 191
Benda, Julien, 68
Bentley, Arthur, 175
Bergson, Henri, 67, 149
Berlau, A. Joseph, 66
Berlepsch, Hans Freiherr von, 44
Berlin, University of, 21, 42, 67, 74
Berlin, Isaiah, 20
Bernstein, Eduard, 158
Bialas, Wolfgang, 48
Bismarck, Otto von, 10, 11, 34, 35, 53, 136
Bledstein, Burton, 2
Bloch, Ernst, 133, 140
Blomert, Reinhard, 90, 93, 152, 157, 158, 162, 173
Blumenbach, Friedrich, 41
Bluntschli, J.C., 53
Böhme, Klaus, 47, 65
Borinski, Fritz, 18
Bosch, Robert, 102, 103
Botstein, Leon, 41 Bramstead, Ernest K., 201
Breuer, Stefan, 63
Brockhaus' *Konversations-Lexicon, 8, 22, 30, 31*
Bruch, Rüdiger vom, 33, 34, 38
Bruford, W.H., 19, 64, 65
Brunet, René, 67, 78
Brunner, Otto, 71 Buckmiller, Michael,

225

71, 101 Budapest, 41, 42, 66, 134, 135, 140, 146, 173, 198, 207
Buffon, Georges Comte de, 41
Bureaucracy, *see* officials
Burns, Rob, 65
Burrow, J.W., 20, 40

Caldwell, Peter, 18, 45, 136
Calling, vocation (*Beruf*), 16, 71–73, 76, 77, 90, 101, 169, 187, 198
Capitalism, 127, 134, 144–146, 152, 153, 160, 167
Cassirer, Ernst, 40
Cézanne, Paul, 158
Class, 145, 158, 190, 191
   Aristocratic, 36, 45, 75, 85, 118, 185
   Bourgeois, 36, 75, 104, 118, 124, 136, 137, 143, 144, 146, 149, 150, 151, 154, 155, 160, 199
   Proletarian, 60, 75, 77, 87, 104, 125, 143–145, 149, 151, 153–155, 165, 167, 174, 192
Class consciousness, 139, 142–145, 148, 151, 192
"Clouds, The," 94
Competition, 84–90, 129
Comte, Auguste, 29, 127
Congdon, Lee, 41
Conservatism, 34, 39, 40, 58, 62, 90, 111, 129, 132, 134, 137, 192, 194, 205
Cortés, Donoso, 136
Crisis, 1, 2, 10, 15, 16, 61, 75, 86, 110, 115, 119, 120, 127, 142–144, 167, 170, 187, 188, 190, 200, 203
   in education, 2, 4, 8, 48, 49
   of classical modernity, 11, 12, 47–50, 178
   of cultivation, 8, 12, 31, 34, 47, 49, 52, 111, 117
   of mass culture, 170, 200, 201
   of rationality, 165
Croce, Benedetto, 160
Cultural politics, 52, 59
Culture, 9, 12, 20, 28, 34, 43, 52, 59, 61, 68, 75, 117, 140, 142, 145–147, 149, 164, 165, 167, 183, 195, 197, 201, 202
   Tragedy of, 9, 140
   vs. civilization, 104, 142, 145, 146, 150, 151, 181, 203
Cultivated bourgeoisie (*Bildungs-bürgertum*), 11, 33, 34, 37, 43, 49, 118, 155
Cultivation (*Bildung*)2, 6, 7–46, 52, 54, 58–61, 72, 75, 76, 91, 92, 96, 99–103, 109, 110, 117–121, 143, 151, 160, 168, 169, 171, 183–185, 187, 199, 262
   Democratic, 7, 15, 77, 170, 183, 185, 188
   Humanistic ideal of, 7, 10, 12, 28, 33, 39, 55, 59, 61, 64, 70, 114, 117–119, 122–124, 132, 148, 151, 152, 170, 183–189, 199
   Political, 78, 79, 122, 136
   See also education, pedagogy
Cumming, Robert Denoon, 33, 40, 202
Curtius, Ernst Robert, 15, 16, 58–64, 68, 128, 146, 152, 190

Decisionism, 90, 113, 115–117, 120, 122–125, 189, 194, 196, 197, 199
   See also will
Demm, Eberhard, 68, 69, 93, 95, 104, 152, 153, 157, 159, 162, 172–174
Democracy, democratization, 12, 17, 18, 44, 50, 51, 56, 59, 62, 65, 99, 183–186, 188, 205
Derrida, Jacques, 16
Descartes, René, 149
Dialectics, 114, 129, 144, 150, 153, 154, 191, 193, 194, 199
Differentiation, 195, 196, 206
Dilthey, Wilhelm, 31, 34, 89, 135, 137, 162
Discursive coalition, 10, 11, 15, 19, 35, 36, 38, 39, 45, 49, 54
Disjunction, 115
Distantiation, 114, 130, 170, 185, 186, 190, 193–195, 197, 199, 204
Döring, Herbert, 177

Index 227

Dostoevsky, Fyodor, 42, 133, 140, 173
Droysen, Johann, 73
Dunckmann, Karl, 88
Durkheim, Emile, 81
Düwell, Kurt, 55
Dyzenhaus, David, 18, 136, 204

Ebert, Friedrich, 136
Ecstasy, 133, 168–170
Education, 5, 93, 100, 119, 133, 143, 145, 151, 188
    Political, 4, 16, 51, 71–80, 91, 92, 95, 96, 99, 100, 110, 122, 136, 143, 170, 187, 199
    Sociological, 5, 96, 99, 171
    See also cultivation, pedagogy
Elias, Norbert, 94, 95, 147, 153, 173, 182, 200, 203
Elite, 12, 36, 44, 49, 61, 62, 100, 102, 168, 169, 174, 184–186, 188, 201
Enactment (*Vollzug*), 115–117, 120, 187, 193, 194, 203
Endreß, Martin, ix, 94, 205
Engels, Friedrich, 139, 144, 155
Enlightenment, 19, 28, 37, 40, 56, 171
Ernst, Paul, 48
Existentialism, 114, 115, 154, 190
Expansion (*Erweiterung*), 194, 199, 203
Experimental life, 127, 192, 195, 196, 199, 203

Falk, W., 201
Fascism, 109–138, 143, 178, 184, 190, 197
    See also National Socialism
Ferguson, Adam, 205
Fichte, Johann Gottlieb, 16, 34, 142
Floud, Jean, 136
Fogarasi, Adalbert, 172, 173
Fraenkel, Ernst, 175
Francke, Ernst, 44
Frank, Josef Maria, 67
Frankfurt, 96, 97, 177–179, 203, 204
    Johann-Wolfgang-Goethe University of, 4, 55, 177–182, 200, 203, 206
Freyer, Hans, 98, 101, 110–115, 117, 139, 144, 154, 162–174, 182, 188, 192, 193, 197, 199
Frick, Heinrich, 176
Frisby, David, 17, 49 Fritzsche, Peter, 205

Gábor, Éva, 42, 140
Gadamer, Hans-Georg, 42
Geiger, Theodor, 97, 106
George, Stefan, 63, 67, 73, 75, 178, 182, 204, 205
Gerber, Carl Friedrich von, 45
German Sociological Association, 82–84, 87, 97, 106, 154, 156, 160, 173, 204
Gerth, Hans, ix, 201, 202, 204
    Die Gesellschaft, 103, 104, 156, 157
Gierke, Otto von, 47
Ginsberg, Morris, 206
Gluck, Mary, 41, 140 Glum, Friedrich, 103
Goebbels, Josef, 102
Goethe, Johann Wolfgang von, 8, 19, 76
Goldenberg, Boris, 95
Goldman, Harvey, 42, 43
Göring, Hermann, 200
Gothein, Eberhard, 157
Greffrath, Mathias, 179, 204
Guardini, Romano, 171
Gundolf, Friedrich, 63, 67, 205
Gunnell, John, 44

Habermas, Jürgen, 37, 175, 176
Haenisch, Konrad, 50–52, 54, 56, 66, 179, 200
Hamilton, Richard, 177, 179, 204
    Hammerstein, Notker, 32, 179, 182, 203
Hansert, Andreas, 179
Hardenburg, Karl August von, 20
Hegel, G.W.F., 8, 14, 22, 26, 32, 34, 37, 42, 89, 90, 112, 126, 135, 140, 142, 169, 194, 196
Heidegger, Martin, 69, 89, 110, 112, 114–117, 125, 126, 135, 176, 182, 193

Heidelberg, 63, 64, 68, 69, 75, 94, 106, 140, 148, 157, 177, 178, 182, 200, 203
Heimann, Eduard, 6, 133, 137, 138, 170, 171, 204
Heller, Hermann, 18, 55, 67, 111, 134, 137, 182
Hennis, Wilhelm, 16
Heraclitus, 8
Herder, Johann Gottfried, 19
Heuss, Theodor, 74, 102, 103
Hilferding, Rudolf, 155, 156
Hindenburg, Paul von, 102
Historical School of National Economy, 45
Historicism, 7, 19, 28, 30, 32, 33, 35, 45, 53, 56, 58, 142, 185
Hitler, Adolf, 95, 102, 110, 111, 136, 137, 182, 200
Hochschule für Politik, 66, 73–78, 80, 102
Hoeges, Dirk, 4, 60, 63, 64, 68
Hoffmann, Adolf, 57, 66
Honegger, Claudia, 204
Honigsheim, Paul, 12, 13, 17, 40, 63
Horkheimer, Max, 6, 55, 163, 165, 167, 170, 176, 182
Hugenberg, Alfred, 183
Humboldt, Wilhelm von, 19–27, 31–37, 40–43, 45, 47, 54, 56, 59, 71, 72, 74, 76, 101, 117, 183, 202
Hume, David, 205, 206
Husserl, Edmund, 195

Idealism, 8, 28, 33–35, 43, 44, 63, 65, 70, 73, 140, 142, 143
Ideas, 23, 149   of 1914, 11, 47, 48, 51, 56, 66, 72
     of 1789, 51, 66
Ideology, 58, 61, 67, 79, 88, 91, 106, 113, 115, 125, 129, 151, 172, 175, 189, 196
Iggers, Georg, 19, 32, 43 Individuality, 8–10, 12, 21–24, 56, 68, 117, 118, 120, 184
   See also personality

Institute: for Social Research, Frankfurt, 6, 164, 182
   for the Sciences of the State and Society, Heidelberg, 93, 104, 105
   of Education, London, 6
   of Pedagogy, Budapest, 6, 9
   of Social Science, Cologne, 81, 101
Intellectualism, 92, 109, 147–150
Intellectuals, intelligentsia, 37, 42, 62, 65, 68, 90–92, 94, 95, 96, 100, 102, 103, 112, 115, 120, 122, 130, 134. 135, 137, 143, 157, 168, 171, 178, 190, 195, 197
Irrational, rational, 90, 150–152, 162, 169–171, 188

Jäckh, Ernst, 73, 74, 102, 103
Jaffé, Edgar, 157
Jaffé, Else, 69, 148, 172
James, William, 176, 204
Jaspers, Karl, 69
Jay, Martin, 6
Jászi, Oscar, 95, 140, 176
Jews:
   in academia, 40, 41, 45, 46, 104, 179, 207
   in Frankfurt, 65, 178, 179, 207
John, Jürgen, 104

Kahler, Erich, 73, 102
Kant, Immanuel, 27–30, 37, 42, 142, 154, 196
Karádi, Éva, 140
Kadarkay, Arpad, 198
Kapp Putsch, 66, 204
Käsler, Dirk, 48, 81, 86, 174
Kaufmann, Walter, 42
Kautsky, Karl, 104
Kelsen, Hans, 55, 105, 134, 156, 174, 182, 204, 206
Kettler, David, 10, 16, 17, 16, 42, 55, 63, 65, 66, 87, 105, 109, 140, 151, 153, 157, 172–176, 181, 182 ,200, 204–206
Kierkegaard, Soren
Kirchheimer, Otto, 18, 111, 137

Index

Klingemann, Carsten, 105
Kluke, Paul, 178, 179, 182, 204
Kolk, Rainer, 63
Kölner Vierteljahrshefte für Soziologie, 82, *101*
König, René, 82, 88, 105, 106, 135
Kracauer, Siegfried, 4, 48, 49
Kramme, Rüdiger, 8
Krieck, Ernst, 199, 200
Krieger, Leonard, 20
Kun, Béla, 141, 198

Labande, Paul, 45
Lagarde, Paul, 43
Landmann, Ludwig, 178
Langbehn, Julius, 43
Laski, Harold J., 175
Lassman, Peter, 102
Lasswell, Harold, 207
Laube, Reinhard, 114, 135, 150, 205
Lederer, Emil, 18, 55, 74–76, 103, 133, 140, 148, 154, 157–161, 172, 174, 175, 181–183, 206
Leibniz, Gottfried Wilhelm, 21
Lenin, Vladimir, 142, 145, 173
Lepenies, Wolf, 67
Lepsius, M. Rainer, 81
Liberalism, 13, 19, 20, 40, 41, 56, 90, 92, 121, 123, 124, 129, 134, 137, 202, 205
Lichtblau, Klaus, 40
Lieberman, Ben, 179
Liebersohn, Harry, 82, 85
Life, three forms of, 9, 10
Life-based method, 96, 106, 115
Loader, Colin, 17, 63, 109, 132, 134, 152, 174–176, 205
Locarno Treaties, 73, 74
Logos, *8, 141*
Löwe, Adolf, 157, 182, 206
Lowenthal, Leo, 204
Löwenthal, Richard, 95
Löwith, Karl, 114, 135
Ludendorff, Erich, 48, 55, 65, 103
Lukács, Georg, 8, 9, 17, 42, 63, 66, 74–76, 87, 103, 104, 106, 127, 133, 134, 138–151, 153, 154, 157, 160, 170–175, 180, 192–194, 196, 197, 205, 206
Luthardt, Wolfgang, 175, 204

Machiavelli, Niccolo, 100, 173
Macpherson, C.B., 20
Maistre, Joseph de, 136
Man, Heinrich de, 182
Manheim, Ernest, 135
Mann, Heinrich, 64, 65
Mann, Thomas, 64, 65
Mannheim, Julia, 103, 134, 164, 173
Mannheim, Karl, writings of:
  "A Review of Georg Lukács' Theory of the Novel," 7, 8, 141
  "Competition as a Cultural Phenomenon," 84, 88–90, 115, 187, 195
  Conservatism. A Contribution to the Sociology of Knowledge, 19, 34, 67, 205
  "Conservative Thought," 87, 159
  The Contemporary Tasks of Sociology, 92, 97–101, 114, 183, 187, 206
  Correspondence with Eduard Heimann, 204
  "The Democratization of Culture," 16, 44, 50, 169, 184–187, 189
  "Georg Simmel als Philosoph," 45
  "German Sociology (1918–1933)," 15
  "Die Grundprobleme der Kulturphilosophie," 40
  "Heidelberg Letters," 63
  "The Ideological and the Sociological Interpretation of Intellectual Phenomena," 103
  Ideology and Utopia, 4, 6, 34, 58, 61, 62, 67, 79, 92–94, 109, 111, 113, 114, 123, 130–132, 165, 172, 175, 176, 186, 195, 202, 206
  "An Introduction to Sociology" (1930 lectures), 5, 6, 75, 94, 114, 119, 123, 130, 132, 134, 135, 161, 169, 171, 189–207
  Lectures, 1931–1932, 5, 50, 96, 106, 115, 183, 205

Letter to Alfred Weber, 69, 95, 204
Letter to Max Wertheimer, 119, 181, 193
Man and Society in an Age of Reconstruction, 137, 138, 170, 202, 205
"On the Incorporation of Research in the Journalistic Medium into University Science," 162, 163, 175, 176, 180
"On the Nature of Economic Ambition and Its Significance for the Social Education of Man," 205
"The Problem of Generations," 87
"Problems of Sociology in Germany," 62
Protocols of Joint Meetings of the Seminars of Mannheim and Alfred Weber, 94, 104, 146–153, 159
"Science and Youth," 3, 4, 162
"Der Sechste deutsche Soziologentag in Zürich," 88
"Seele und Kultur," 9, 23
"The Sociology of Intellectuals," 5, 68
"The Sociology of Knowledge," 5
"The Spiritual Crisis in the Light of Sociology," 137, 187, 188, 205
"Structural Analysis of Epistemology,"
Structures of Thinking, 20, 27, 40, 43, 156, 172, 195
"Zum Problem einer Klassifikation der Wissenschaften," 43
Manuel, Frank, 133
Martin, Alfred von, 106, 113, 201
Marx, Karl, 76, 104, 127, 139, 144, 145, 157, 160, 163, 172, 174
Marxism, 6, 86, 87, 105, 118, 119, 126, 132, 133, 139–176, 178, 183, 189, 190, 192, 197
Massification, 184, 188
Matthiesen, Ulf, 63, 68, 74–76, 182
Maurras, Charles, 68
McClelland, Charles, 21, 24, 26, 27, 36, 42

McCormick, John, 18, 136, 137, 174, 204
Meinecke, Friedrich, 32, 35, 41, 42, 44, 65, 73
Meja, Volker, 10, 16–18, 42, 55, 63, 65, 68, 87, 105, 109, 147, 153, 157, 174–176, 182, 200, 204, 206
Merton, Robert, 159
Milchman, Alan, 115, 116, 135
Mill, John Stuart, 19, 40, 75, 101, 119, 133, 201, 202
Miller, Susann, 52, 66
Mills, C. Wright, 202
Mission, 5, 9, 15, 26, 30, 51, 68, 89, 90, 106, 128, 164, 165, 192
Mommsen, Hans, 203
Moot, the, 166, 167, 176, 202
Morality, 126
Mosse, George, 42, 43
Müller, Adam, 56, 58
Müller, Christoph, 67, 111, 134
Muller, Jerry, 110, 113, 125, 129, 137
Mussolini, Benito, 109, 111, 134, 197
Myth, 126, 127, 182, 189, 197

Napoleon, 25
National Socialism, 79, 102, 105, 110, 114–117, 135–137, 169, 170, 177, 179, 180, 183, 197, 200, 204, 205
See also fascism
Naumann, Friedrich, 52, 74, 103
Nettl, Peter, 42
Neue Sachlichkeit, 179
Neumann, Franz, 68, 111, 137, 201, 207
New Frankfurt, 179
Nietzsche, Friedrich, 7, 29, 30, 39, 40, 43, 67, 103, 112, 114, 116, 194

Oelkers, Jürgen, 59
Oelsner, Toni, 204
Oexle, Otto Gerhard, 57
Officials (*Beamten*), 12, 24, 34–36, 38, 39, 44, 49, 73
Oldham, Joseph H., 176, 202
Oppenheimer, Franz, 55, 81

Index

Papen, Franz von, 102, 136
Parker, Beryl, 67
Parliamentarism, 14, 39, 59, 60, 111, 123, 124, 145, 159, 177, 178, 189
Parties, 12, 16, 38, 39, 45, 47, 50, 52, 55, 57, 59, 59, 60, 67, 76, 78–80, 91, 115, 124, 125, 158, 177, 181
Pascal, Blaise, 171
Pauck, Wilhelm, Marion, 180, 182
Paulsen, Friedrich, 45
Pedagogy, 4, 7, 51, 93, 96, 151, 152, 182, 188, 189, 192
  See also cultivation, education
Peguy, Charles, 68
Pels, Dick, 5
Personality, 33, 42, 43, 53, 54, 56, 58, 64, 72, 91, 117, 122, 186
  See also individuality
Peukert, Detlev, 11, 48
Phenomenology, 154, 195
Philosophy, *see* science, philosophical
Planning, 73, 138, 201
Plato, 149
Plenge, Johann, 47
Politics, political, 55, 57, 64, 65, 68, 72, 73, 75, 76, 79, 80, 90–93, 121–128, 145, 153, 175, 186, 192, 197–199, 206
Pollock, Frederick, 163, 165, 167, 170
Positivism, 28–30, 32, 33, 35, 45, 56, 139
Preuss, Hugo, 103
Professors, 13, 26, 27, 35, 37–39, 44, 47–49, 53, 62, 65, 177, 182
  See also university, students
Prussia, 24, 25, 37, 41, 49, 51, 85, 87, 135, 136, 180, 200
Psychoanalysis, 152
Public, 28, 34–39, 50, 53, 68, 88, 89, 91, 93, 96, 115, 118, 123, 124, 162, 163, 189

Radbruch, Gustav, 18, 67, 103, 133, 157
Raith, Dirk, 174
Ranke, Leopold von, 32, 33, 43, 56, 116
Ratz, Ursula, 44

Realdialektik, *129*
Reflexivity, 151, 172, 185–188, 194–196, 198, 206
Reik, Theodor, 201
Reill, Peter Hanns, 40, 41
Relativism, 8, 15, 30, 33, 48, 58, 61, 142, 196
Religion, 77, 133, 163–166, 168–171, 176, 180, 181, 195, 202, 204
Reprimitivization, 132, 143, 171, 190, 192, 195–197, 199
Révai, Lajos, 198
Revolution, 1, 9, 28, 89, 104, 134, 137, 139, 142, 143, 145, 151, 181, 198
  from the Right, 125–128, 134, 189
Rickert, Heinrich, 31, 43, 63, 69, 172
Riemer, Svend, 201
Riezler, Kurt, 55, 164, 165, 176, 180–182
Ringer, Fritz, 9, 48, 61, 68 Ritook, Emma, 134
Rockefeller Foundation, 102, 104, 200, 201
Romanticism, 8, 28–30, 35, 42, 56, 92, 99, 134, 142, 149, 190, 194
Rosen, Stanley, 42
Rosenberg, Alan, 115, 116, 135
Rosenberg, Arthur, 49
Rosenberg, Hans, 36
Rubinstein, Nina, 94, 106, 174, 200, 206
Russell, James, 33, 43
Ryder, A.J., 66

Saint-Simon, Henri, 119, 127, 133, 192
Sallis-Freudenthal, Margarete, 94, 175
Salomon, Albert, 16, 71–80, 91, 103, 104, 111, 117, 122, 133, 157, 160, 163, 201
Salomon-Delatour, Gottfried, 103
Salz, Arthur, 45
Savigny, Friedrich von, 56, 58
Scaff, Lawrence, 160, 161
Schäfer, Dietrich, 45
Scheler, Max, 12, 13, 17, 40, 64, 82, 154, 174, 184, 194, 205
Schelting, Alexander von, 103

Scheuerman, William, 18, 111, 136
Schiller, Friedrich, 10
Schivelbusch, Wolfgang, 18, 111, 136
Schlegel, Friedrich, 42, 117
Schleicher, Kurt von, 136
Schleiermacher, Friedrich, 42, 71
Schluchter, Wolfgang, 101
Schmitt, Carl, 18, 55, 67, 75, 78, 89, 90, 103, 104, 110–115, 122–127, 130, 132, 134–138, 174, 182, 183, 189, 192, 193, 195–197, 199, 200, 206
Schmoller, Gustav, 34, 44, 45, 72
School: for Citizens, 74
  for Humanistic Studies, Budapest, 9
  Secondary (*Gymnasium*), 21, 26, 36, 41–43, 51, 61, 66, 67
Scholtz, Gunter, 33
Schorske, Carl, 65
Schumpeter, Joseph, 157, 159
Schwabe, Klaus. 65
Science (*Wissenschaft*), 2–4, 11, 17, 19–21, 25, 26, 29–33, 43, 44, 52, 60, 72, 75, 115, 121, 122, 130, 131, 135, 142, 199
  Ethical (*Ethoswissenschaft*), 128
  Human sciences (*Geisteswissenschaften*), 31–33, 37–40, 64, 83, 86, 191
  Natural sciences (*Naturwissenschaften*), 23, 31, 83, 149
  Philosophical sciences, 8, 21 27–31, 37, 40, 54, 60, 75, 80, 83, 89, 105, 142, 162, 172, 191
  Politics as, 16, 53, 58, 73, 90, 93–96, 131
Shils, Edward, 176, 202
Shklar, Judith, 42
Simmel, Georg, 9, 23, 39, 40, 45–47, 83, 137, 140, 193, 194
Simon, Christian, 38
Sinzheimer, Hugo, 137, 181
Smend, Rudolf, 16, 41, 67, 124
Socialism, Social Democratic Party, 33, 38, 44, 47, 51, 55, 57, 59, 64–67, 90, 129, 134, 137, 141, 157, 192, 203, 204

Society, fragmentation of, 13, 188
Society for Social Reform, 44
"Sociologism," 58, 61, 89, 128
Sociology, 14, 15, 25, 50–64, 75, 80–89, 92, 96–102, 105, 106, 113, 114, 117, 118, 122, 128–132, 139–176, 141, 143, 152, 162, 163, 165, 169, 178,182–184, 187, 187–194, 199, 202, 203, 206
  Applied, 87, 88
  as a science grounded in actuality (*Wirklichkeitswissenschaft*), 110, 127, 128
  Chairs of, 54, 57, 67, 80, 81
  Cultural, 43, 75, 86, 135, 152, 160–162, 172–174, 191
  Functional, 166
  Marxistic, 75, 104, 133, 160
  of Knowledge, 4–6, 61, 90, 91, 100, 112, 129, 154, 191
  of the Spirit, 17, 169, 191
  Political, 16, 75, 76, 78, 79, 90, 91, 117
  Teaching of, 97, 99–101, 106, 107, 193
Socrates, 94, 95
Sombart, Werner, 81, 147
Sorkin, David, 24
Soul (*Seele*), psychic, 9, 14, 22, 23, 41, 59, 61, 75, 76, 85, 117, 128, 130, 133, 141, 142, 147, 149–152, 168, 170, 174, 187
Spann, Othmar, 67
Specialization, 3, 4, 10, 11, 29, 31–33, 40, 52–54. 57, 59, 72, 77, 83, 86, 87, 97, 100, 121, 146, 170, 187, 190, 191
Speier, Hans, 95, 157
Spengler, Oswald, 17, 48
Spirit (*Geist*), spiritual, 8, 9, 15, 22, 23, 42, 58, 59, 61, 64, 65, 68, 75, 85, 89, 116, 117, 120, 130, 147, 151, 156, 170, 174, 187
Spranger, Eduard, 13–15, 17, 21, 23–25, 32, 58–62, 68, 117, 124, 128, 135, 146, 152
Srubar, Ilya, 94, 205

Index

Staff, Ilse, 67, 111, 134
State, 10, 12, 19–21, 24–26, 34, 35–38, 40, 42, 45, 49, 52, 64, 68, 73, 85, 121–126, 132, 136, 137, 145, 189
Staudinger, Hans, 173
Stehr, Nico, 147
Stein, Karl Freiherr vom, 20, 25
Stein, Lorenz von, 127
Steinberg, Michael Stephen, 179, 203, 204
Stern, Fritz, 43, 44, 65
Stoltenberg, Hans Lorenz, 104
Stölting, Erhard, 55, 56, 81, 82, 178
Students, 3, 4, 13, 24, 26, 35, 36, 52, 53, 62, 71, 72, 94–96, 101, 122, 179, 189, 193, 201, 203–205
 See also youth, university, professors
Suhr, Otto, 102
Sunday Circle, Budapest, 140, 166, 198

Tenbruck, Friedrich, 105
Tillich, Hannah, 164
Tillich, Paul, 18, 55, 121, 138, 163–165, 170, 176, 180–182
 Frankfurt Conversations of, 138, 163–170, 176, 180, 181
Tolstoy, Leo, 72
Tompert, Helene, 63
Tönnies, Ferdinand, 81, 82
Transcendence, 195
Treitschke, Heinrich von, 34, 42, 44, 72
Troeltsch, Ernst, 17, 21, 22, 41, 44, 72

University, 2–4, 11, 13, 16, 17, 25–36, 39, 40, 49, 52, 62, 63, 66, 67, 70, 76, 77, 80, 116, 121, 135, 178, 183
 Reform of, 9, 20, 21, 24, 27, 28, 50–64, 135
 See also professors, students
Utopia, 61, 79, 113, 128, 130–136, 140, 145, 166, 170, 172, 181, 190, 192, 196

Value-freedom, 84, 86–90, 99, 119, 155
Versailles Treaty, 66, 74, 136, 137
Vezér, Erzsébet, 140
Vitalism (*Lebensphilosophie*), 3, 41, 43, 54, 67, 149, 161, 162, 193

Volk, *13, 37, 117, 118, 120, 123–126, 130, 132, 137, 189*
Vondung, Klaus, 36, 37

Wagner, Peter, 11, 38, 45
Weber, Alfred, 6, 63–65, 68, 69, 81, 87, 92–95, 104, 135, 140, 142, 146, 155, 157, 159–163, 170 172–175, 177, 180, 181, 204, 206
Weber, Marianne, 63, 64, 76
Weber, Max, 5, 16, 17, 34, 35, 44, 45, 63, 64, 66, 71–78, 81, 89–91, 93, 100, 101, 112, 119, 133, 140, 144, 145, 152, 160, 163, 172, 174, 178, 180, 186, 192, 196, 198, 199, 203
Weil, Hans, 19, 36, 37, 41
Weimar Republic, 4, 11, 12, 16, 18, 29, 47–69, 122, 139, 171, 173
 Constitution of, 14, 16, 18, 67, 74, 78, 109, 123, 129, 136, 137, 204
Wende, Erich, 55
Wertheimer, Max, 119, 181
Wiese, Leopold von, 15, 81–86, 96–101, 105–107, 112, 113, 128, 139, 154, 155, 174, 178, 182, 190, 191, 198
Will, volition, 51, 60, 100, 109, 113, 114, 117–126, 128–132, 148, 151, 189, 193, 194, 196
Will, Wilfried van der, 65
Windelband, Wilhelm, 206
Winnig, August, 66
Wirth, Louis, 176
Witt, Peter-Christian, 45
Woldring, Henk, 157, 159, 176, 201
Wolfers, Arnold, 102
Wolff, Kurt H., 43, 45, 94, 191, 206
Wolin, Richard, 110
World view (*Weltanschauung*), 34, 192

Young Plan, 177
Youth, 3, 4, 17, 39, 40, 45, 61, 63, 96, 134, 192
 See also students

Zinn, Alexander, 105
Zilsel, Edgar, 103
Zneimer, Richard, 200